OXFORD MEDICAL PUBLICATIONS

Clinical Dermatology
An Illustrated Textbook

PHILIP L. HILLSMAN, M.D.

CLINICAL DERMATOLOGY

An Illustrated Textbook

RONA M. MacKIE, MD, FRCP, FRCPath, FRSE
Professor of Dermatology, University of Glasgow

Second Edition

Oxford New York Tokyo
OXFORD UNIVERSITY PRESS
1986

Oxford University Press, Walton Street, Oxford OX2 6DP

Oxford New York Toronto
Delhi Bombay Calcutta Madras Karachi
Petaling Jaya Singapore Hong Kong Tokyo
Nairobi Dar es Salaam Cape Town
Melbourne Auckland

and associated companies in
Beirut Berlin Ibadan Nicosia

Oxford is a trade mark of Oxford University Press

Published in the United States
by Oxford University Press, New York

© *Rona M. MacKie, 1981, 1986*

First edition 1981
Second edition 1986

British Library Cataloguing in Publication Data
Mackie, Rona M.
Clinical dermatology: an illustrated
textbook.—2nd ed
1. Dermatology
I. Title
616.5   RL71
ISBN 0–19–261582–3

Library of Congress Cataloging in Publication Data
Mackie, Rona M.
Clinical dermatology.
(Oxford medical publications)
Includes bibliographies and index.
1. Skin—Diseases.   2. Dermatology.   I. Title.
II. Series.   [DNLM: 1. Skin Diseases.   WR 140 M158c]
RL71.M254   1986   616.5   85–32010
ISBN 0–19–261582–3 (pbk.)

Set by Latimer Trend & Company Ltd, Plymouth
Printed in Hong Kong

Preface to the second edition

Since the first edition of this book in 1981 there have, happily, been several advances in the management of the commoner skin diseases. Because of this, the treatment sections of the chapters on psoriasis, acne, and dermatitis have been extensively revised and rewritten. The rest of the text has been updated and Chapter 15 has been extensively revised.

From a personal point of view, one of the most interesting areas to update has been the 'growth point' sections at the end of each chapter. A genuine growth area of 1980 should now be more appropriately included in the body of the relevant chapter. In most instances this has been the case.

A few selected references are now included at the end of every chapter to encourage further reading at a time when interest and enthusiasm should, I hope, be greatest.

My colleagues in the University Department and at the Western Infirmary have, as always, offered helpful suggestions. Without their friendly and constructive discussions which are a natural part of our professional daily life, my own working life would be much less enjoyable.

Miss Una Syme has once again performed the steadily more difficult task of converting handwritten notes to pristine typescript, for which I am extremely grateful. My husband, Dr Euan MacKie, has offered total support and invaluable advice over word processing. Both have been most welcome.

Glasgow   R. M. M.
May 1986

Contents

molluscum contagiosum; orf; herpes simplex; herpes zoster. *Fungal infections:* candida infections; dermatophyte infections; pityriasis versicolor. *Cutaneous infestations:* scabies; pediculosis capitis; pediculosis corporis; pediculosis pubis. *Sexually transmitted diseases:* syphilis; gonorrhoea; Reiter's syndrome. Growth points. Further reading. Notes.

1

Introduction:
The scope and language of dermatology;
history taking, examination, and ancillary tests

The skin is the largest single organ in the body. Its multiple functions include temperature control, fluid balance, sensation, immunological function, protection from ultraviolet damage, and the expression of racial and sexual characteristics.

The ease with which the skin can be examined clinically and histologically has in the past had drawbacks as well as advantages. Thus, although this facility has led to an extensive morphological and histological classification of the many varieties of skin disease, it has, at the same time, diverted attention from studies of the underlying mechanisms. In consequence, the art of diagnosis and, up to a point, treatment, has until recently outstripped the science of pathophysiology.

In the past decade, however, investigative dermatology has made considerable strides and is catching up on clinical aspects. Many research groups, in Europe, North America, and other parts of the world, are engaged in biochemical, pharmacological, physiological, and immunological studies designed to increase understanding both of the normal function of the skin and its many cell types, and of abnormalities of structure and function in pathological conditions. Comparative dermatology is also an expanding and fascinating subject of great importance, both economically and in the search for naturally occurring animal models of human disease states such as malignant melanoma and atopic dermatitis.

All family doctors must have a thorough grounding in dermatology as 10–12 per cent of their patients present with cutaneous lesions. It is therefore highly desirable for general practitioner training schemes to include rotation through a dermatology unit, thus allowing trainees to gain experience of both in-patient and out-patient clinical dermatology, and the practical use of topical therapy. This is particularly important as, unless some time is spent learning the use of traditional and useful topical remedies, it will not be possible for the family doctor to treat patients with chronic disorders without frequent and unnecessary hospital visits. It is easy to learn the appropriate remedy from a textbook, but the mode and frequency of application are best learnt by taking part in in-patient or out-patient dermatological dressing sessions. In no other branch of medicine is the actual method of application as important as the actual medicament prescribed.

HISTORY-TAKING

The majority of dermatological patients referred to hospital require to be seen only as out-patients. It is therefore important that skin out-patient departments are well equipped, and provide privacy and resonably attractive surroundings. Most dermatologists prefer to work in daylight, although some of the newer 'natural' fluorescent lights are reasonable alternatives and essential for mid-afternoon onwards in Scotland in the winter months. Patients visited in poorly-lit wards in other parts of the hospital should be taken to an adequate source of daylight if transient and mild skin eruptions, such as that of rubella, are to be accurately identified. The use of a pen-torch is not adequate.

In a proportion of dermatological out-patients presenting with obvious and localized disorders, such as hand warts or athlete's foot, history-taking can be relatively brief, but in many other conditions, such as generalized pruritus or a suspected drug eruption, a careful framework of questions will ensure that no vital point is missed. In some departments a printed sheet either in the hospital notes or handed to the patient for completion while waiting to be seen helps to expedite this process.

Obvious points in the history are:

1 *Duration of signs and symptoms.* Is the condition of recent onset or long-standing? Has it tended to improve, deteriorate, or otherwise vary in severity?

2 *Present and previously affected body sites.* Patients tend to ignore lesions habitually covered by clothing and, in contrast, to express apparently inappropriate concern over minor lesions on the face or hands. For example, chronic severe fungal infection of the feet may give rise to severe secondary sensitization on the hands, but the patient may forget the lesions on the feet or even deny the existence of such lesions on direct questioning.

3 *The nature of the symptoms.* Is the condition itchy, painful, or burning? Is it aggravated or even initiated by sunlight?

4 *Drug history.* Enquire about topical treatment to the lesion— not only prescriptions from the family doctor, but also domestic remedies and those bought over the counter. The latter may contain sensitizing agents such as local anaesthetics or antihistamines. Enquire also about systemic drug therapy used for this or any other condition. To some elderly patients the word 'drug' implies abuse, whereas 'medicines', 'bottles', and 'tablets' do not have this association. If a drug eruption is suspected a relative may often be of value in bringing for inspection the current battery of medicaments. Many elderly patients rapidly come to regard digoxin and diuretics as part of their diet, and forget to include them in the list. Do not forget to ask about laxatives, hypnotics, and simple analgesics. Very few people regard aspirin as a drug, but it could, for example, be causing or perpetuating chronic urticaria. Ask specifically about aspirin-containing products in such cases. An accurate drug history is particularly important in hospital in-patients who develop a skin rash. The majority of all dermatological consultations requested by other consultants for their patients relate to suspected drug eruptions. An accurate history of all drugs taken orally over the preceding month is essential. Patients can suddenly develop a reaction to drugs they have taken for many years, so do not ignore long-standing prescriptions.

5 *General medical history.* This may give valuable clues to an otherwise puzzling diagnosis. For example, red, glazed, atrophic lesions on the shin may be associated with diabetes mellitus (necrobiosis lipoidica) or more raised, tumid lesions on the same site to previous thyrotoxicosis (pretibial myxoedema).

6 *Occupational history.* Sometimes a single word is adequate description—typist or architect—but frequently very much more detail is needed. If industrial dermatitis is high on the list of likely diagnosis, and particularly if the patient appears to have legal action in mind, it is important that the details of his occupation and exposure to sensitizing agents is written down in detail. It can be difficult for the doctor to be questioned months or even years later on inadequate notes in these circumstances. Terms such as shipyard worker or factory employee are not helpful, and a reasonable description of the average working day's activities should be obtained, including details of protective clothing issued and washing facilities. Factory visits and discussion with the factory medical officer may be extremely valuable and give insight into an otherwise obscure condition.

7 *Recreational history.* This becomes increasingly important with the growth of leisure time. Gardening (sensitization to plants such as primulae) or household repair work (sensitization to epoxy resin adhesives) are obvious examples.

8 *Travel history.* Tropical diseases, such as leprosy or leishmaniasis, may spring up in unexpected places as air travel brings tropical and subtropical areas within the budget of holiday-makers. A history of recent occupational and recreational travel including brief refuelling stops may be necessary before puzzling presentations are diagnosed.

9 *Family history.* This should include both blood relatives (e.g. in atopic dermatitis) and also household contacts (e.g. in scabies).

10 *The patient's views on the cause of his condition can be valuable.* He may correctly incriminate sunlight (photosensitivity), exposure to cold (physical urticaria), or animal contact (eruptions due to infestation of household pets).

EXAMINATION

Ideally all patients should be asked to undress and to wear only a hospital gown for examination. To examine only the readily access-ible areas of a cutaneous eruption on an elderly patient clad in numerous layers of underclothes can lead to unfortunate diagnostic errors, and time taken persuading him or her to undress is usually well spent and occasionally reveals treatable cutaneous malignancy. Obviously, a less rigid approach is permissible when children or adults are referred with simple hand warts, but in general the rule is sound. A simple diagram of the sites affected is often more informa-tive at the return visit weeks later than several sentences written describing the condition on the first attendance, particularly if the patient is likely to see a different doctor on this occasion. A photographic record is valuable in cases likely to need long-term follow-up.

Distribution of lesions can be helpful in selecting more likely diagnoses and some commoner patterns are shown in Fig. 1.1. The lesions themselves may be either primary manifestations of the

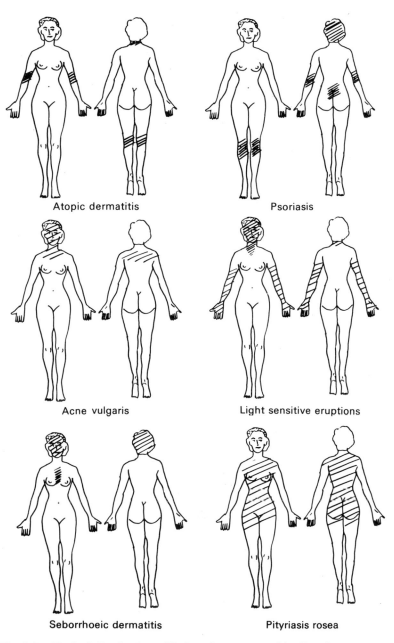

Atopic dermatitis

Psoriasis

Acne vulgaris

Light sensitive eruptions

Seborrhoeic dermatitis

Pityriasis rosea

Fig. 1.1. Typical distribution of lesions in common skin disorders

disease process or secondary to modifying influences, such as scratching or infection. Primary and secondary lesions are defined in Table 1.1. In chronic conditions, primary and secondary lesions often co-exist; for example, in chronic atopic dermatitis secondary lichenification due to rubbing may be superimposed on primary erythema and papules.

Lesions should be palpated to determine the extent of infiltration which in the case of skin tumours may be considerable and in any potentially malignant lesion the local draining lymph nodes should be examined. Many dermatological patients mistakenly believe that

Table 1.1.   Primary and secondary lesions of the skin

Primary	
Macule	a flat, circumscribed area of altered skin colour
Papule	a small, circumscrimed elevation of the skin
Nodule	a solid, circumscribed elevation whose greater part lies beneath the skin surface
Weal	a transient, slightly raised, and usually flat lesion, characteristically with a pale centre and a pink margin
Vesicle (blister)	a small (less than 5 mm in diameter), circumscribed, fluid-containing elevation
Bulla (blister)	similar to a vesicle but larger
Pustule	a collection of pus
Plaque	a flat-topped palpable lesion
Purpura	visible collection of free red blood cells within the skin
Telangiectasia	dilated capillaries permanently visible on the skin surface
Secondary	
Scale	thickened, loose, readily detached fragments of stratum corneum
Crust	dried exudate
Excoriation	a shallow abrasion often caused by scratching
Ulcer	an excavation due to loss of tissue including the epidermal surface
Scar	a permanent lesion that results from the process of repair by replacement with connective tissue
Lichenification	areas of increased epidermal thickness with accentuation of skin markings which develop in response to chronic rubbing

their disease is infectious, a misconception shared by employers, who are reluctant to engage employees with visible skin disease, and by some hairdressers who are reluctant to accept customers with scalp psoriasis. By handling lesions freely during examination and by discussing the relevance of transmissibility, it is possible to reassure patients and restore their confidence. Time may need to be spent in explaining briefly the difference between inherited disease and contagious conditions as lay people tend to confuse the two. It may also be important to discuss the nature of cutaneous malignancy as for many people the word 'cancer' is a death sentence, whereas skin cancer covers a wide range of variants of which the commonest is basal cell carcinoma. As this lesion has nearly 100 per cent 5-year cure and survival rate after local excision, vigorous reassurance and explanation is justified.

SPECIAL TESTS

A variety of simple techniques are available to confirm or substantiate a positive clinical diagnosis.

Mycological examination

In suspected fungal infections, such as athlete's foot and scalp ringworm, scrapings of superficial scales from skin lesions, particularly the advancing edges, should be both examined microscopically and set up for culture. For immediate microscopy (the direct test), they should be mounted in potassium hydroxide and gently warmed. Culture and identification of the fungi (the indirect test) should also be performed, but this takes several weeks.

With the skin held taut, fine superficial scales are removed from the surface by gentle scraping with a scalpel blade at an angle of about 30° to the skin surface. The skin should not bleed. The resulting fine powdery scale is either placed directly on a slide for immediate microscopy or wrapped dry in a piece of dark paper (for ease of identification of the scale), and sent to the laboratory for culture.

Wood's lamp

This emits long-wave ultraviolet radiation in the 320–365 nm range of the spectrum. In certain fungal infections the lesions or the affected hairs fluoresce under the lamp. Lesions due to *Microsporum canis* and *M. audouini* will show a brilliant green fluorescence, while in those due to *Trichophyton schoenleinii* a dull green fluorescence is present. The lamp should be switched on 10 minutes before use, and the patient should be examined in a darkened room to allow any positive fluorescence to be identified easily.

Wood's light also dramatically illuminates areas of altered melanin pigmentation, and an area of vitiligo which looks small on daylight examination may appear much more extensive if viewed under Wood's light.

Extraction of the acarus in scabies

Many dermatologists will not make a diagnosis of scabies unless they can extract the scabies mite from the superficial epidermal layers. The technique requires only patience, good eyesight, and a needle. A putative scabies burrow, usually on the wrist or between the fingers, is gently explored with the needle and the female mite may be found clinging near the tip. Many patients find it difficult to accept that even they can be infected by scabies, but this demonstration will be more convincing than any conversation, and also ensures excellent patient co-operation in therapy.

If it is not clear in which direction the burrow is running in the epidermis, another simple technique is to paint the area with Indian ink and then wash off the superficial excess. The ink will run into the burrow and outline it clearly.

Skin biopsy

Diagnostic biopsy is often necessary when cutaneous lesions are atypical, and excision biopsy of a small and possibly malignant nodule can be both a diagnostic and a therapeutic measure. When biopsying a *rash*, it is best to include an area of normal skin at the edge for comparison. When excising a small nodule, remove also an elliptical area of normal skin with its long axis along Langer's lines to ensure optimal healing and minimal scarring (Fig. 1.2). If a blister is to be biopsied it is better to remove a small lesion in its entirety on a base of normal skin, rather than to take a wedge out of a larger lesion. It is also important that the blister be fresh, i.e. not more than 24 hours old, otherwise secondary changes and attempts at healing may confuse the picture.

Small skin biopsies carried out for clinical diagnostic purposes may be needed:

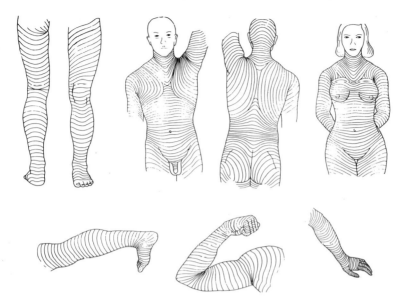

Fig. 1.2. Lange's lines. The long axis of a biopsy scar should be oriented along these lines.

1 for routine pathological examination—much the commonest;
2 for immunopathological testing—an increasingly important supplement to 1;
3 for electron microscopy—particularly important if biopsying an infant with a blistering skin disease;
4 for tissue culture studies.

If there is any possibility of 2, 3, or 4 being required, consult with the laboratory *before* the biopsy is performed as special handling of the specimen is required. No patient enjoys a skin biopsy, and repeating the test 2 or 3 days later because the first sample was not properly handled is unacceptable.

Biopsies may be performed either by conventional scalpel excision or by the use of disposable punches 3–8 mm in diameter. In either case local anaesthesia should be achieved with 1–2 per cent xylocaine without adrenalin which may cause artefactual changes. The choice of method depends on availability of sterile biopsy packs and individual preference. In general, however, greater tissue preservation and more accurate histological interpretation can be obtained by an elliptical excision specimen as the circular twisting movement needed to loosen the base of the punch biopsy specimen may cause traction and distortion of cell nuclei at the lateral edge of the sample.

Whichever method is chosen, the sample should be handled with the minimum of trauma. Forceps must not be applied to the specimen as these will cause pressure artefacts. Instead, the use of the Kilner or Gillies hook is recommended (Fig. 1.3). This should be inserted at one end of the biopsy and the specimen can then be dissected out (Fig. 1.4). The specimen should be orientated on a small piece of blotting paper before being placed in fixative to prevent the sample curling and becoming distorted during fixation.

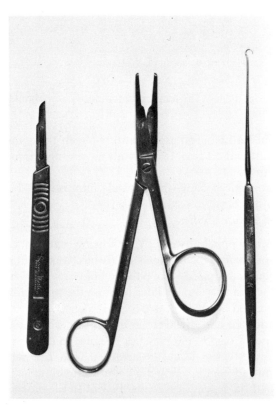

Fig. 1.3. Instruments required for elliptical skin biopsy. A fine-bladed (no. 15 blade), combined scissors/needle holder, and the Gillies or Kilner hook.

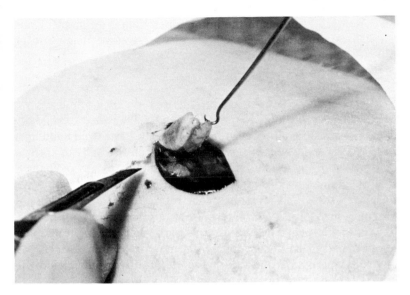

Fig. 1.4. The Kilner or Gillies hook in position during the removal of an ellipse of skin. If inserted at one end of the biopsy, trauma to the specimen is minimal. Forceps should not be used for this purpose as they may distort the specimen.

Immunopathology

In certain skin diseases, particularly blistering disorders and connective tissue diseases, cutaneous immunopathology is a valuable adjunct to conventional histology in confirming a diagnosis. Both immunofluorescence and immunoperoxidase techniques may yield useful information, but the former are far more commonly used. Lesions biopsied for immunofluorescence study should be 'snap frozen' and rapidly transported to the laboratory without being allowed to thaw. The identification of circulating antibodies directed against epidermal components may also be of diagnostic value in pemphigus (p. 211), pemphigoid (p. 216) and systemic lupus erythematosus (p. 144). In suspected cases of these conditions a blood sample should also be submitted but this should *not* be frozen. If the laboratory dealing with this material is some distance away, the serum from the sample can be separated and sent, without freezing, by regular mail. There is currently a great deal of research interest in the use of monoclonal antibodies against tissue components, such as the lymphocyte subsets in the immunoperoxidase technique. Time will tell how useful these methods are for routine diagnostic or prognostic purposes in dermatology.

Clinical photography

In dermatology, one good colour photograph of a lesion can be worth considerably more than several descriptive paragraphs. Many dermatologists therefore take their own photographs and build up a collection of slides for teaching. Sequential photography of chronic or slowly growing lesions can give an invaluable record of changes in, for example, morphoea (p. 154) or a congenital pigmented naevus (p. 188), and of spontaneous resolution of certain types of vascular naevi (p. 271). If access to a department of medical illustration is available, prior discussion with the photographer about the exact site to be recorded, the magnification necessary, and any subsequent need of black-and-white prints for publication will ensure the best possible end-product.

Patch testing

This is a routine procedure in all cases of suspected allergic contact dermatitis. Although it looks deceptively simple, it should not be undertaken by inexperienced clinicians as both false negative and false positive results may be obtained.

The basic procedure involves applying the suspected allergen in *an appropriate concentration in an appropriate base* to the patient's skin and examining the area for a delayed hypersensitivity response after 48 and 96 hours. In practice, the patient usually has a battery of 20 substances applied. These are known as the European Standard Patch Test Battery because they are the 20 substances most likely to cause allergic dermatitis in Europe. Additional small test sets are commercially available for hairdressers, for those with footwear problems, etc. The material is applied in an occlusive cup with a micropore or similar backing (Fig. 1.5).

The results of patch tests may have long-term implications for future employment prospects and great care should be taken both to apply the material and read the test properly. Patients and factory doctors frequently wish to carry out their own patch tests with a particular suspected allergen, but this is not usually the best way to obtain optimal information.

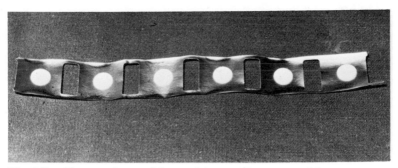

Fig. 1.5. Al-test strips used for applying patch test materials.

Situations in which patch testing is of value are further discussed in Chapter 5.

'Allergy tests'

Many parents of children with chronic skin problems, particularly atopic dermatitis, will request 'allergy tests' for their child. These are the prick tests used by both dermatologists and respiratory physicians to confirm a diagnosis of type I allergy. A battery of allergens is available. A drop of an extract of each (commonly used ones include pollens and house dust mite) is laid on the skin and gentle pressure with a needle applied to the skin surface. A positive result is a weal or flare developing within 20 minutes. Although these tests are of value for hay fever patients in identifying allergens most likely to be responsible and against which desensitization may be of value, desensitization is not at present helpful in treating atopic dermatitis. This should be explained to parents as multiple needle pricks can be very distressing to a young child and the information gained will not help in treating the child. Every year dermatologists see hopeful patients or parents who have been led to believe that 'allergy tests' carried out in the hospital will lead to new treatment and cure of their eczema. This false promise of cure is at present misleading.

NOTES

2

Basic skin biology

Some knowledge of normal skin anatomy and physiology is obviously essential for the proper understanding of pathological states. Skin biology is also a topic of interest in its own right, as many current studies in this field are likely to throw some light on important events in other areas, such as the reason for the loss of adhesion between cells in certain malignancies. Many important basic discoveries have yet to be made on the interrelationship between the different cell types in the skin. It is of interest to remember that, although the Langerhans cell was first identified over 100 years ago by Paul Langerhans while a medical student, it is only in the past decade that steps towards biological understanding of the function of the Langerhans cell have been made.

Normal anatomy

The skin can be divided into three main components, the epidermis, the dermis, and the skin appendages which comprise the pilosebaceous follicle (hair follicle and sebaceous gland), the eccrine sweat glands, and the apocrine glands. In a few disease states the subcutis also may become involved in a pathological process affecting the overlying skin.

THE EPIDERMIS

The epidermis is traditionally divided into four layers, the basal or germinative layer, composed of small keratinocytes some of which undergo cell division, the 'prickle cell' or Malphigian layer, the stratum granulosum or granular layer identified by densely staining granules of keratohyalin, and the stratum corneum composed of flat, anucleated squames (Fig. 2.1). A fifth layer, the stratum

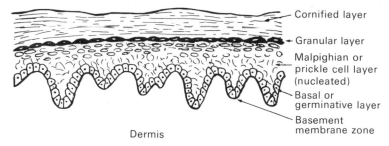

Fig. 2.1.   Diagrammatic view of the layers of the epidermis.

lucidum, is seen only in the thick skin of the palms and soles, and is thought by some workers to be an artefact of histological fixation. The thickness of the epidermis varies according to body site, age, and sex. The inner arm epidermis of an elderly female may have an epidermis only four or five cell layers thick, whereas the normal skin of the sole of an active male may be 20–30 or more layers thick (Figs 2.2–2.5).

The epidermal keratinocyte

In their transit from the germinative basal layer to the stratum corneum the epidermal keratinocytes progressively mature from nucleated cells capable of mitosis to flat, anucleated squames. In the deeper epidermal layers they are polygonal or elongated, and as they approach the surface they become flatter, until in the stratum corneum the uppermost layers are thin flakes. The forces controlling this conformational change are not yet understood.

The main function of keratinocytes is to provide an impermeable barrier and all layers of the epidermis are involved in this, as also are epidermal lipid secretions.

The major structural protein of the epidermis is a-keratin which is synthesized in the living cells and aggregates to form tonofilaments. At the periphery of the cells bundles of tonofilaments (tonofibrils) insert into desmosomes which are strong points of attachment between cells (Fig. 2.6). These attachments give rise to the 'prickles' seen histologically in the Malphigian layer. The tonofilament-desmosome system minimizes the effects of mechanical stress in the epidermis by distributing it between the cells.

During keratinization the keratinocytes flatten, and their nuclei and cytoplasmic organelles are lost, leaving the tonofilaments

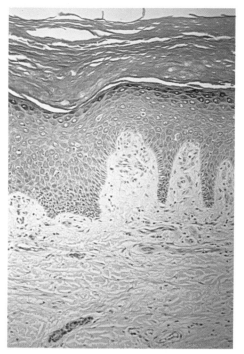

Fig. 2.2.   Skin from sole of foot stained with haematoxylin and eosin. Note thick cornified layer compared with Fig. 2.3.

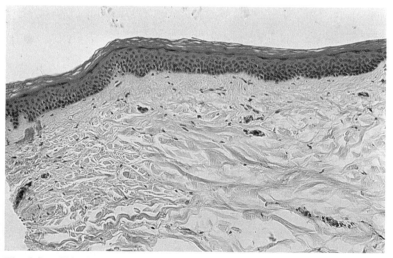

Fig. 2.3.   Skin from dorsum of foot. Note much thinner cornified layer.

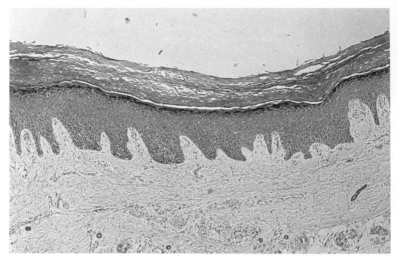

Fig. 2.4.   Skin of palm of hand. Note again relatively thick cornified layer.

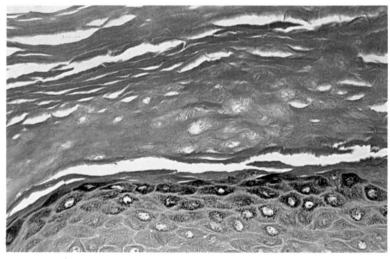

Fig. 2.5.   Detail of granular layer of skin from sole of foot.

embedded in a matrix which may be partly derived from the keratohyalin granules of the granular layer. The cell envelopes become thickened and toughened, and a lipid-containing material is deposited between the cells. The constant shedding of fully kera-

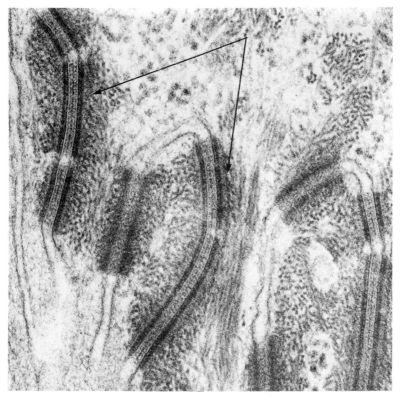

Fig. 2.6. Electron micrograph to show demosomes adhering between neighbouring epidermal cells (× 85 000).

tinized cells from the surface of the skin is normally balanced by the production of new cells in the basal layer.

The time taken for a cell to leave the basal layer, reach the skin surface, and to desquamate is normally about 4 weeks, of which half is spent in the living layers and half in the stratum corneum. These times can be considerably altered in disease states, and in psoriasis, for example, the whole process takes about 4 days.

Other cells within the epidermis

Although keratinocytes form the bulk of the epidermis, three other cell types are also present and are sometimes termed *epidermal symbionts*, implying a beneficial interrelationship between them and the adjacent keratinocytes. These cells are the melanocyte, the Langerhans cell, and the Merkel cell.

The *melanocyte* is of neuroectodermal origin and migrates in foetal life from the neural crest. Melanocytes are normally found in the human epidermis, the retina, the brain, and in small numbers in the mesentery. The recognized function of melanocytes is to produce the pigment melanin which has a photoprotective action. The chemical pathway for its synthesis is from tyrosine through dihydroxyphenylalanine (DOPA) and dihydroxyindole to melanin which is then complexed with protein. Melanin granules can be seen with the light microscope and the actual structure on which melanization takes place, the melanosome, can be seen on electron microscopy to have a very regular structure (Fig. 2.7). Melanocytes are dendritic

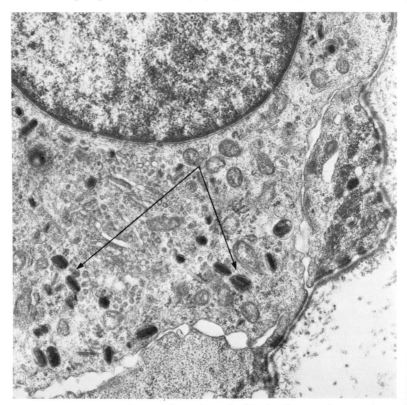

Fig. 2.7.   Electron micrograph to show the black, electron-dense melanosomes forming in the cytoplasm of the melanocyte (× 18 000).

cells with many processes extending out from the central body of the cell. As melanosome synthesis and melanization proceed, the mature melanin granules move out to the terminal portion of the dendrites where they are in close contact with neighbouring keratinocytes. Melanin is then transferred from the melanocyte to the keratinocyte by a dynamic process in which the keratinocyte actively ingests the terminal dendritic portion of the melanocyte. Subsequent absorption of the remnants of plasma membrane leaves the melanin granules lying free within the keratinocyte. They then form a protective cap over the upper part of the cell nucleus, and are thought to protect it from possible ultraviolet radiation and resultant damage to nuclear DNA.

Epidermal melanocytes normally are found only in the basal layer and the ratio of melanocytes to basal cells varies in different body areas, from 1 in 5 on the face to 1 in 20 on covered sites. Each melanocyte is in contact with many keratinocytes, as the dendrites may extend upwards for a considerable distance into the epidermis, and the combination of a melanocyte with the neighbouring keratinocytes which it supplies with melanin is termed the epidermal melanin unit (Fig. 2.8). Racial differences in pigmentation are due to different rates of melanogenesis and not to larger numbers of melanocytes in darker-skinned races. Melanocytes are seen on light microscopy, using the normal haematoxylin and eosin (H & E) stain, as slightly larger clear cells in the basal layer. For specialized studies of these cells the DOPA oxidase histochemical technique is used.

Abnormalities involving melanocytes may be due to:

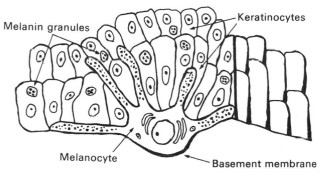

Melanin granules — Keratinocytes

Melanocyte — Basement membrane

Fig. 2.8. Diagram of the epidermal melanin unit. Note that the melanocyte is in close contact with 20–30 epidermal keratinocytes and supplies them with melanin.

1 faulty or incomplete migration of melanocytes to the epidermis in foetal life. In this situation collections of melanocytes are seen in the dermis and the lesion is termed a blue naevus (p. 188);
2 lack of enzymes necessary for melanin pigment production by the melanocytes, resulting in albinism (p. 181);
3 loss of melanocytes from the basal layer of the epidermis, e.g. in vitiligo (p. 183);
4 benign proliferation of melanocytes, as in lentigo;
5 malignant proliferation of melanocytes in malignant melanoma (p. 291).

The naevus cells which constitute pigmented naevi have many similarities to melanocytes, but ultrastructural studies suggest some justification for differentiating between the naevus cell and the melanocyte. The natural history of the pigmented naevi (p. 186) would strongly suggest that epidermal melanocytes are capable in some situations of differentiation into naevus cells.

The Langerhans cell. This is also a dendritic cell found in the epidermis, but in contrast to the melanocyte it is usually found in the suprabasal layers. This cell is not normally seen with normal H & E staining of the epidermis. On ultrastructural examination the characteristic granules—the Birbeck granules—are seen (Fig. 2.9). These are racquet-shaped structures whose function is unknown. The Langerhans cell is of mesenchymal origin and current evidence suggests that it is a modified macrophage. Until recently, the cell has been stained either by gold chloride or using the histochemical ATPase reaction. In the past 3 years, however, two monoclonal antibodies have become commercially available which react with antigenic components on the Langerhans cell plasma membrane. These two antibodies (OKT 6 and NA1 34) are increasingly used for studies of Langerhans cells. Figure 2.10 shows a skin sample stained by these antibodies using the immunoperoxidase technique. In this example the skin has been cut parallel to the skin surface rather than, as is more common, at right angles. The dense meshwork of Langerhans cells is well shown by this method. There are about 720 Langerhans cells/mm^2 on the skin surface and they therefore are a significant component of the epidermis. The Langerhans cells has surface receptors for the Fc component of IgG, for C$_3$ and for Ia (*I*mmune-*a*ssociated) or HLA-Dr related antigens, and is considered

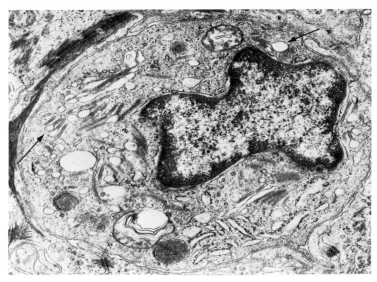

Fig. 2.9. Electron micrograph of Langerhans cells to show specific tennis racquet-shaped Langerhans granules in cytoplasm.

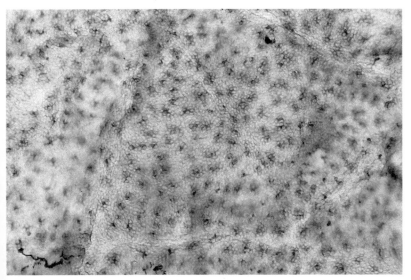

Fig. 2.10. Epidermal sheet preparation stained with monoclonal antibody NA 1/34, which recognizes Langerhans cells.

to be an important arm of the immune system involved in the presentation of epidermally absorbed antigen to lymphocytes.

The Merkel cell. These cells are found in the epidermis and in the dermis, and are currently thought to be of neural crest origin. As with Langerhans cells, they are not seen with conventional stains for light microscopy, but are identified ultrastructurally by the presence of large numbers of electron dense granules containing catecholamines seen in the cytoplasm. These cells are seen in greatest numbers adjacent to nerve terminals and in areas of maximum sensory function such as the finger pads. Recent ultrastructural studies have shown that they contain keratin-related filaments, suggesting that they may be modified epithelial cells.

THE BASEMENT MEMBRANE (Fig. 2.11)

Lying between the epidermis and dermis is the basement membrane, which plays the major role in adhesion of epidermis to dermis. It is a complex, layered structure and comprises a basal lamina of ectoder-

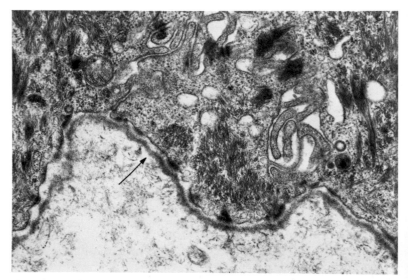

Fig. 2.11. Electron micrograph of basement membrane zone dividing the basal layer of the epidermis from the underlying dermis ($\times$ 20 500).

mal origin, a sub-basal lamina, anchoring fibrils, and micro fibrils reaching into the upper layers of the dermis. The basement membrane can be visualized on light microscopy by special stains such as periodic acid Schiff (PAS). It is abnormal in a variety of conditions, e.g. epidermolysis bullosa (p. 277). It would appear that the basement membrane is not a rigid impervious barrier between the epidermis and dermis, but that certain cell types, such as Langerhans cells and possibly lymphocytes, can 'traffic' easily through the membrane.

THE DERMIS

The epidermis is completely dependent on the underlying dermis for support and nutrition. *Collagen*, which forms the bulk of the dermis, provides the support, and two other proteins, *elastin* and *reticulin*, are present in smaller amounts, and contribute to extensibility and tensile strength. All three are set in an amorphous material termed *ground substance*.

Fibroblasts are the most numerous cells in the dermis and are responsible for synthesizing the three dermal proteins. Macrophages, mast cells, and lymphocytes are also normal dermal cellular components, but their numbers may be increased in certain pathological states. The cutaneous vasculature, nerve supply, and skin appendages are also embedded in the ground substance.

The upper part of the dermis, termed the papillary dermis, is in intimate contact through the basement membrane with the epidermis. Adhesion is strengthened by the interdigitation of the dermal rete pegs with the under surface of the epidermis, thus greatly increasing the surface area available for epidermal-dermal contact. These convolutions are clearly seen in the thick skin of the palms and soles where they are well developed.

The deeper layer of the dermis, the reticular dermis, is composed of coarser collagen bundles than the papillary dermis. The difference between the collagen component of the papillary and reticular dermis is highlighted either by the use of a special collagen stain, such as the Masson stain, or by the use of polarized light.

The dermal vasculature is responsible for nutrition and temperature control. Arterioles and venules are linked by a superficial and a deep capillary plexus (Fig. 2.12). In the resting state the vascular channels in the dermis are only functioning at 10–30 per cent of capacity. The reserve is utilized physiologically when strenuous exercise, such as marathon running, results in the need to rapidly lose body heat. In pathological states where the entire skin surface is inflamed the end result may be a very significant increase in blood flow through the skin, resulting in high output cardiac failure.

Congenital capillary abnormalities may present as vascular naevi (p. 269). The dermis is also rich in lymphatics, normally invisible on light microscopy, which provide an important drainage system for removing material such as mediators of inflammation from the dermis.

The cutaneous nerve supply has two components, the peripheral sensory nerves and the sympathetic autonomic nerves, supplying the vasculature and hair follicles. Both myelinated and unmyelinated fibres are present. Two encapsulated terminals, the Meissner corpuscle and the Pacinian corpuscle, are occasionally seen with the light microscope and act as mechanoreceptors (Fig. 2.13).

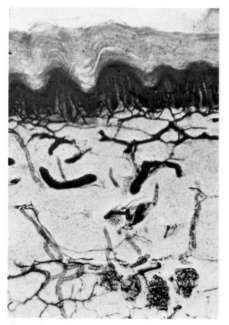

Fig. 2.12.　Alkaline phosphatase preparation to show the darkly stained blood vessels in the dermis. Note the rich supply to the superficial dermis.

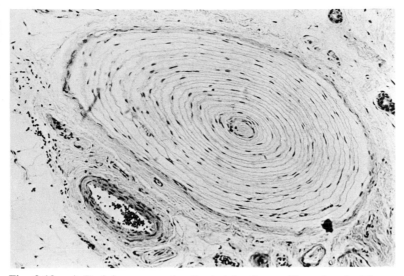

Fig. 2.13. A Pacinian corpuscle situated in the papillary dermis. These structures are mechanoreceptors.

THE SKIN APPENDAGES

Three main appendages traverse the epidermis and dermis. These are the pilosebaceous unit, the apocrine sweat glands, and the eccrine sweat glands.

The pilosebaceous unit is a complex structure comprising the hair follicle, one or more sebaceous glands, and the arrector pili muscle (Fig. 2.14). The hair follicle is an invagination of the epidermis into the dermis and it terminates around a richly vascular dermal papilla. The part of the follicle around the papilla actively divides and is the hair root (Fig. 2.15). The hair shaft growing within the pilosebaceous canal has an outer cuticle, an intermediately placed cortex and a central medulla. There are three main varieties of human hair—the terminal hair of the scalp and eyebrow; androgen-dependent terminal hair of the beard, axilla, and pubic area; and fine vellus hair present on other body sites.

Terminal hair follicles undergo a regular cycle of growth activity. The growing phase is termed anagen, the resting phase is catagen,

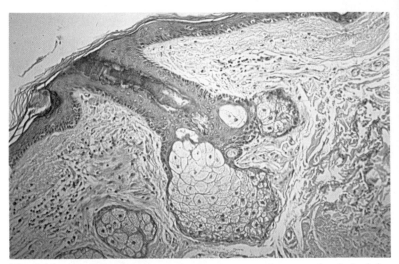

Fig. 2.14. The pilosebaceous unit, showing two sebaceous glands draining into a hair follicle which is in continuity with the epidermal surface.

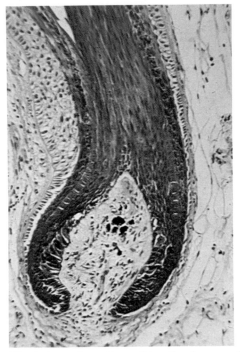

Fig. 2.15. The hair root portion of a pilosebaceous follicle. Note the vascular dermal pipilla and presence of some pigment (melanin granules).

and the phase of shedding of hair is telogen. Percentages of scalp follicles in these phases vary: usually around 86 per cent are in anagen, and 14 per cent in catagen and telogen. The hair fall which many women experience 3–9 months after parturition is due to a change in these percentages during pregnancy when a higher proportion of follicles are held in anagen and enter telogen synchronously after delivery.

Sebaceous glands secrete by a *holocrine* mechanism in that sebum is formed by disintegration of glandular cells (Fig. 2.16). In infancy and childhood sebaceous glands are small, almost vestigial structures, but at puberty they enlarge and become functionally active due to endocrine stimulation. Blockage of the free flow of sebum results in acne vulgaris (p. 59). The arrector pili muscle seen attached to the pilosebaceous complex is a vestigial structure in man.

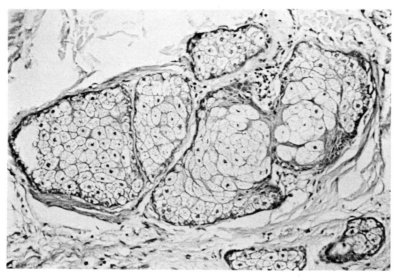

Fig. 2.16. Isolated sebaceous glands. Individual cells are destroyed to produce secretion from these structures.

Eccrine sweat glands are important in thermoregulation and are distributed over the entire body surface. The deepest secretory portion of the gland is a coiled structure situated in the reticular dermis, and the excretory portion spirals through the papillary dermis and epidermis to the surface. In the thick epidermis of the palms and soles this spiral duct may be cut transversely in several places and the keratinocytes surrounding these cross-sections will be seen to be smaller and paler than those of the surrounding Malphigian layer. The secretory portion of the eccrine gland is composed of two distinct types of cell, the one small and darkly-staining, the other larger, clear, and eosinophilic. This double population helps to distinguish eccrine gland structure from apocrine glands (Fig. 2.17).

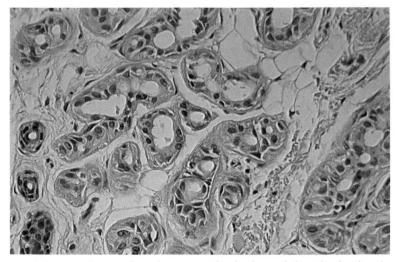

Fig. 2.17. A cluster of eccrine sweat glands situated deep in the dermis. The two distinct cell types comprising these glands can be seen.

The apocrine glands are found mainly in the axillary and pubic areas, and have no recognized function in man (Fig. 2.18). The secretory portion consists of acini with a single layer of high columnar eosinophilic cells around which there are occasional myoepithelial cells (Fig. 2.19). The duct leads into a pilosebaceous follicle above the level of the sebaceous gland duct opening within the dermis.

THE NAIL

The nail is formed from an epidermal invagination. The *nail plate* grows out from the *nail matrix*, and rests on the underlying nail bed. The proximal part of the nail is the lunula which is paler than the

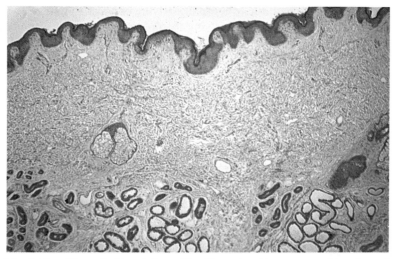

Fig. 2.18. Normal skin of the axilla. Note the thin rugose epidermis and the clusters of apocrine sweat glands in the dermis.

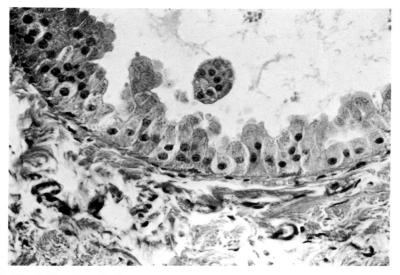

Fig. 2.19. Detail of apocrine sweat gland. The high columnar secretory cells with round nuclei can be easily distinguished from the myoepithelial cells lying with flattened nuclei at the periphery.

distal part of the nail due to loose underlying connective tissue. The protective thin membrane overlying the proximal part of the lunula is the cuticle, and loss of this can lead to chronic low-grade infection around the nail bed.

GROWTH POINTS

Epidermal cell culture

For many years the technique of fibroblast culture has been well established and allowed useful biochemical studies to be carried out on large numbers of cells. Until recently, research workers have found it much more difficult to grow any type of epidermal cell in culture. In the past few years, however, the methodology for keratinocyte culture has been established. This will allow a wide range of pharmacological, immunological, and biochemical studies to be carried out.

Very recently modifications of these methods have been applied to normal melanocytes so that these can now also be grown *in vitro*. As yet, it has not proved possible to isolate pure populations of either Langerhans cells or Merkel cells for culture and the establishment of cell lines. These would be very useful advances.

Skin-associated lymphoid tissue (SALT)?

It is now known that there are subsets of lymphocytes which have a 'special relationship' with the gastro-intestinal tract. This tissue is referred to as GALT—gastrointestinal-associated lymphoid tissue. It has been suggested that a similar type of tissue exists for skin— skin-associated lymphoid tissue, or SALT. The concept that skin could be involved in immunoregulation has been greatly strengthened by the recent work on photoimmunology showing that *in man* ultraviolet light in the natural sunlight range can both affect Langerhans cell function and also *in mice* induce a specific subset of T suppressor lymphocytes.

FURTHER READING

Baran, R. and Dawber, R. P. R. (eds): *Diseases of the nails and their management.* Blackwell, Oxford (1984).
    A comprehensive account of nail disorders.
Goldsmith, L.: *The biochemistry and physiology of the skin.* Oxford University Press, Oxford (1983).
    A two-volume, very well referenced, comprehensive text.

Montagna, W. and Parakkal, P. F.: *The structure and function of the skin* (3rd edn). Academic Press, New York and London (1974).
A very readable text.

Rook, A. J. and Dawber, R. P. R.: *Diseases of the hair and scalp.* Blackwell, Oxford (1982).
A comprehensive treatise on hair disease.

Rowden, G.: The Langerhans Cell. *CRC Critical Reviews in Immunology* **3**, 95 (1981).
An excellent review of all aspects of the Langerhans cell as understood in 1981.

NOTES

3

Psoriasis and other papulo-squamous diseases

PSORIASIS

Psoriasis is one of the commonest of all skin diseases. All doctors require to be familiar with the many different types of clinical presentation, and to know the currently available range of treatments with their advantages and disadvantages.

Definition. A chronic relapsing and remitting papulo-squamous skin disease which may appear at any age and affect any part of the skin surface.

Incidence

Reports from those parts of the world where figures are available indicate that among Caucasians the incidence of psoriasis is about 1–2 per cent. This is probably a significant underestimate, firstly because patients with mild psoriasis may not seek medical help, and secondly because incidence figures are often derived from hospital records and therefore those treated solely by family doctors or choosing to live with their disease will be excluded.

The sexes are affected equally and the onset may be at any age. The commonest age of onset, however, is in the second and third decade.

Aetiology

Numerous defects in psoriatic skin have been and continue to be reported. These have been observed in terms of altered gross pathology, ultrastructure, and biochemistry. It is important to establish whether these are essential to the basic psoriatic process or whether they are simply secondary phenomena. This can be difficult, but unless the abnormality can be demonstrated both in the clinically abnormal and in the apparently normal skin of psoriatic patients it is unlikely to be a feature primarily involved in the pathogenesis of the disease. Table 3.1 lists some of the observed abnormalities in the involved skin of patients with psoriasis.

The most important abnormality observed to date in psoriasis is an increased epidermal cell proliferation rate. Radiolabelling techniques have been used to measure the *turnover time* of epidermal cells maturing in their transit through the skin. In normal skin this is about 27 days, whereas in psoriatic skin it is only 4 days. With similar techniques, it has been shown that, while the germinative component of normal human epidermis is confined to the basal layer, in psoriatic skin it comprises the lower three layers of epidermal cells. It seems, therefore, that the rapid turnover of psoriatic cells is due not only to an increase in the number of actively dividing cells, but also to an acceleration in their rate of reproduction.

Genetic factors play a role in the pathogenesis of psoriasis and approximately one-third of patients have a positive family history. Twin studies suggest that the pattern of inheritance is multifactorial

Table 3.1.   A range of abnormalities found in psoriatic skin

Abnormalities	Comment
Accelerated transit time of keratinocytes through the epidermis	The most consistent observation in psoriatic skin
Increased mitotic activity Increased rate of DNA synthesis	Not only the basal layer keratinocytes, but also cells two or three layers above
Increased levels of phospholipase A_2 activity	Availability of free arachidonic acid
Presence of keratin proteins of molecular weights different from those in normal skin	Is this a primary abnormality or a consequence of the rapid turnover time?
Elevated levels of polyamine synthesis	May well be secondary to rapid cell proliferation
Increased levels of plasminogen activator	

and that environmental factors may be required for clinical expression of latent disease. Recent studies on the human leukocyte antigen (HLA) system have shown an association, in Caucasians, between psoriasis and both HLA-B13 and HLA-BW17. Patients with pustular psoriasis have a higher than normal incidence of the HLA B27 antigen. Currently, much research is devoted to the association between the HLA-D and HLA-Dr locus antigens, and expression of the disease.

Immunological aspects of psoriasis have also stimulated aetiological theories based on the concept that psoriatic keratinocytes have an abnormal surface antigen exposed to the immune system. As a result, an immune response is triggered off, antibodies against abnormal keratin are produced, and when immune complexes are formed damage ensues. It is theoretically possible partly to explain the *Koebner* or *isomorphic phenomenon* in immunological terms. The Koebner phenomenon describes the tendency for psoriatic lesions to develop at sites of skin trauma, such as mechanical friction, sunburn, or lesions of childhood illnesses such as varicella. Possibly, the abnormal or unstable keratinocyte surface antigens or the abnormal keratin formed in those who are genetically predisposed, are exposed, by trauma, to the immune system which then reacts, triggering a hyperproliferative response in the epidermis.

Some β-adrenergic blocking drugs may aggravate pre-existing psoriasis and a few patients treated with certain β-blockers develop a severe, persistent, psoriasiform eruption (p. 228).

Pathology

The important and diagnostic histological features in psoriatic lesions are parakeratosis, absence of the granular layer, and elongation and clubbing of the epidermal rete ridges. Large, thin-walled capillaries can be seen in the papillary dermis and in more active lesions there are clumps of polymorphonuclear leukocytes within the stratum corneum—so-called 'Munro microabscesses'.

Clinical features

Classically, psoriasis vulgaris presents as erythematous, scaly lesions, involving most commonly the extensor aspects of the knees and elbows, and the scalp (Fig. 3.1). Other common sites are the hands and the sacral area. The total area affected ranges from a few tiny lesions to almost all the body surface. Untreated, the individual

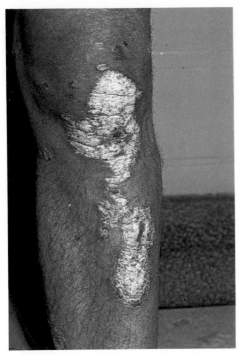

Fig. 3.1.   Classic untreated lesions of psoriasis vulgaris. These lesions are commonly seen on the knees, elbows, and sacrum, and present as plaques topped by white or silvery scales.

lesions are elevated, palpable, and topped by grayish-white or micaceous scale. Rubbing them after gently removing the scale reveals pin-point bleeding from the dilated superficial capillaries (Auspitz' sign).

Variants

Guttate or *'raindrop' psoriasis* is commoner in children than in adults, and presents as multiple small psoriatic lesions mainly on the trunk. This pattern is frequently preceded by a streptococcal throat infection.

Seborrhoeic psoriasis or *psoriasis inversus* are descriptive terms applicable when classical psoriatic lesions on the scalp are associated with less typical erythematous, finely scaling lesions in the body folds, especially the groins, axillae, and inframammary regions. It can be very resistant to therapy.

Erythrodermic psoriasis presents as an extensive erythema with, at times, very few classical scaling psoriatic lesions. Grossly increased blood flow through the skin may lead to loss of thermoregulation and to high output cardiac failure.

Pustular psoriasis refers to varieties of psoriasis in which sterile pustules are a feature (Fig. 3.2). When present they tend to occur at the advancing edge of psoriatic lesions. They may also be seen in erythrodermic psoriasis and the combination of erythroderma and sterile pustules is termed the *von Zumbusch* type of psoriasis, a serious and, at times, life-threatening variety. Pustular psoriasis may

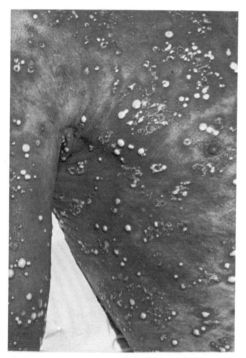

Fig. 3.2 Pustular psoriasis. Sheets of sterile pustules develop rapidly on a background of erythematous skin. The patient had been using large quantities of a potent topical steroid for his psoriasis.

also be seen as a less grave, but extremely chronic variant on the palms and soles. These lesions respond poorly to currently available therapy.

Although psoriasis has been said to be asymptomatic, many patients with actively developing lesions complain of pruritus. This is of no great significance unless scratching elicits fresh lesions due to the Koebner phenomenon. After the first attack of psoriasis, relapses and remissions are frequent. A few fortunate individuals, after a single episode of guttate psoriasis, enter an almost complete and prolonged remission. More commonly, however, mild involvement of the scalp, knees, and elbows persists with, at varying intervals, episodes of more widespread involvement. Some psoriatics find their lesions improve over the years, whilst in others the process becomes more widespread and troublesome. Childhood psoriasis, although less common than in adults, tends to be both persistent and difficult to treat. Some patients receiving β-blocker therapy find their pre-existing psoriasis deteriorates, while others develop psoriasis for the first time. Recent observations that patients with psoriasis and arthritis treated for the latter by benoxaprofen (now withdrawn) experienced clearing of their skin lesions have stimulated research 40 into the mechanism (p. 56). Lithium, used in the management of manic and hypomanic states, will aggravate pre-existing psoriasis.

Nail involvement

A proportion of patients with long-standing psoriasis develop nail changes, including small pits on the nail plate and separation of part of the nail from the nail bed (onycholysis) with subungual hyperkeratosis. Discoloration of the nail resembling grease spots is also seen (Fig. 3.3).

Psoriatic arthropathy

This is a distinctive seronegative arthropathy usually seen in patients with established cutaneous lesions of psoriasis. The sacro-iliac and distal interphalangeal joints are most commonly involved, but any joint may be affected by this mutilating variety of arthropathy. A higher incidence of arthropathy is seen in those with psoriatic nail changes. Occasionally, psoriatic arthropathy is diagnosed in the

Fig. 3.3. Typical psoriatic nail changes. Note the separation of the distal part of the nail from the underlying nail plate (oncholysis) and the pitting of the nail.

absence of overt skin lesions, but this is rare and other causes of arthropathy must first be carefully excluded.

It has been suggested that hair growth is abnormal in psoriatic patients and the term 'psoriatic alopecia' has been proposed for the diffuse thinning of scalp hair seen in a proportion of psoriatics. However, further work is needed to establish whether this is due to the disease or to its treatment.

Differential diagnosis

This includes Reiter's disease, lichen planus, seborrhoeic dermatitis, pityriasis rosea, and pityriasis rubra pilaris. Reiter's disease (p. 139) can usually be excluded in the absence of genitourinary, rheumato-logical, or gastrointestinal complaints. The histological features are diagnostic in lichenoid reactions including lichen planus. The histology of seborrhoeic dermatitis will usually, but not always, differentiate between this and seborrhoeic psoriasis. Biopsy and histological examination will differentiate pityriasis rosea and pityriasis rubra pilaris from psoriasis.

Be cautious about diagnosing an isolated plaque on the trunk of an elderly patient as psoriasis. Bowen's disease (p. 289) may look very similar. A diagnostic incisional biopsy will establish the correct diagnosis.

Treatment

Appropriate treatment of the patient with psoriasis will vary greatly according to (1) the age of the patient, (2) the type of psoriasis, (3) the extent of cutaneous involvement, and (4) past experience with various remedies. The extremes are at one end the patient with small scaling plaques on knees and elbows, and at the other end the erythrodermic 'homme rouge' with life-threatening pustular psoriasis causing high output cardiac failure.

The first point, when the diagnosis is made in the surgery, is to spend some time with the patient, explaining the essentially benign but usually chronic nature of the condition. Many patients believe that any skin disease is contagious and the *non*-infective, but sometimes inherited nature of psoriasis should be explained. The fact that regular therapy is likely to be needed to maintain an apparently normal skin must be emphasized, and the need for the patient to take some responsibility himself for psoriasis treatment explained. Many patients with psoriasis have a real, but unexpressed fear that it is a form of skin malignancy. Reassurance should be offered on this score.

Once the nature of the disease is fully understood, many patients with mild psoriasis may prefer to leave small plaques on knees and elbows untreated. There is no evidence that this will cause extension of psoriasis and it is an entirely acceptable option. A mild emollient, such as emulsifying ointment BP or white soft paraffin, will minimize scaling.

The majority of patients with psoriasis, however, will require a more active treatment programme. Methods of managing psoriasis have advanced considerably in the past few years, and the range of available topical and systemic therapies are itemized in Table 3.2.

Table 3.2. Topical and systemic preparations used in the management of psoriasis

	Preparation	Advantages	Disadvantages
Topical therapy	Dithranol-based	Safe	Some staining and irritation common
	Tar	Safe	Messy and cosmetically relatively unacceptable
	Salicylic acid	Useful, particularly for scalps, and hyperkeratotic palms and soles	Danger of salicylicism if high concentrations used on large areas of the body
	Topical steroids	Clean and cosmetically acceptable	Can cause severe side effects. To be used with caution
	Ultraviolet light UVB—natural sunlight wavelengths	Cosmetically acceptable	Unknown future risk of malignancy. Improvement in psoriatic lesions tends to be associated with some redness
Systemic therapy	Photo-chemotherapy (Psoralens + UVA = PUVA)	Cosmetically very acceptable	Not suitable for potentially pregnant women. Regular treatment at PUVA centre needed. Unknown future risk of malignancy
	Cytotoxic drugs (Methotrexate, azathioprine, hydroxyurea)	Rapidly effective	Teratogenicity. Liver and marrow toxicity
	Retinoid group of drugs. Etretinate (Tigason) or 13-*cis*-retinoic acid (Ro-accutane)	Effective in 50% of chronic plaque psoriasis. Very effective in 80% of pustular psoriasis of palms and soles	Teratogenicity. Raised serum lipids. Cheilitis. Bony changes

Topical therapy

Dithranol (anthralin). Preparations containing dithranol act in psoriasis by inhibiting mitosis. They are widely used and are useful for most types of psoriasis. The concentration of dithranol used may vary from 0.1 to 3 per cent or higher in an appropriate base. This is commonly Lassar's paste (zinc paste with 15 per cent salicylic acid added). Traditionally, this paste has been applied to psoriatic plaques night and morning under a stockinette gauze dressing after protecting surrounding normal skin with white soft paraffin. The Ingram regime combines topical dithranol applications with tar baths and ultraviolet light therapy (UVB). This treatment is safe and effective, with psoriatic plaques clearing in 2–3 weeks. If too high a dithranol concentration is used initially, there may be some irritation and, as the lesions clear, the skin may become stained a grey-brown colour. This staining wears off 7–10 days after stopping treatment.

At present there is considerable interest in the use of dithranol in a new 'short contact' or even 'minutes' treatment regime. The principle is that when dithranol is applied to psoriatic skin, a considerable amount is retained in or on the scaling psoriatic plaque after normal washing which removes it from surrounding normal skin. It has been established that it is possible to treat patients by applying stronger concentrations of dithranol for much shorter time periods and achieve clearance of psoriasis almost as rapidly as with the old continuous treatment regimes.

A representative 'short contact' treatment regime is the application of 1 or 2 per cent dithranol in a cream or ointment base to the skin for 30 minutes. During this time the patient need not apply any dressing. After 30 minutes the patient washes off the dithranol and leaves the skin free of dressings. This treatment can easily be applied either first thing in the morning or in the evening, and is obviously a much more socially acceptable method of using dithranol than the traditional continuous contact and dressings. If too high a concentration of dithranol is chosen initially, there may be some irritation. Although staining of clothes and skin is reduced, the bath may become stained—no treatment is perfect!

Tar preparations. These have been used to treat psoriasis for over 100 years although the rationale for their effect is not clearly understood. They are available in concentrations of 1–20 per cent in pastes and ointments, and need to be covered with stockinette dressings. The higher concentrations of the crude tar preparations are extremely messy to use and really only suitable for in-patient care. A few patients develop a sterile folliculitis when tar is applied to hair-bearing areas. This is self-limiting. The traditional Goeckermann regime includes the use of both tar and ultraviolet light (UVB).

There are a large number of cleaner proprietary tar preparations available. These are slightly less effective than crude coal tar preparations, but for out-patient use this is more than compensated for by their cosmetic acceptability. These include 5 per cent tar and 2 per cent allantoin in a 'vanishing cream' base (Alphosyl), 5 per cent tar in a wax stick (Meditar), and 10 per cent tar in a water miscible base (Carbodome).

There are no clear guidelines as to whether dithranol or tar-containing preparations are more effective at any point in time or for any particular patient. Current practice favours the use of dithranol for out-patients, and tar for some in-patients and those who do not tolerate dithranol. Although tar has been known for many years to act as a carcinogen, careful epidemiological studies have produced no evidence of any increase in the incidence of cutaneous or other malignancy in psoriatics who have used tar for many years.

Salicylic acid-containing preparations. These are most commonly used on the scalp, and on very thick hyperkeratotic areas on the palms and soles. Salicylic acid is a keratolytic and is used on the scalp in concentrations of 10–20 per cent in aqueous cream or emulsifying ointment and in lower concentrations for the palms and soles. If it is used over large body areas in high concentrations it can be absorbed and cause salicyism.

Topical steroids. Sensibly used, topical steroids are useful in the management of psoriasis in certain body sites. They should never, however, be the mainstay of treatment of chronic plaque psoriasis. Although the plaques will initially respond, in time many patients will develop 'irritable' or erythrodermic psoriasis. Other problems of inappropriate long-term steroid use are described on pp. 234–6.

Weak topical steroids are, however, useful for the management of flexural psoriasis provided the duration of use is carefully controlled. Pustular psoriasis of the palms and soles may respond to stronger topical steroids [e.g. beclomethasone dipropionate (Propaderm) or fluocinolone acetonide (Synalar)] and here also the quantity of steroid used and the duration of treatment should be carefully monitored.

Combinations of topical steroids and other anti-psoriatic preparations described above can be useful. The combination of a topical steroid and salicylic acid (Diprosalic) is particularly useful as a lotion for stubborn scalp psoriasis.

Shampoos. While it is traditional to prescribe tar-based shampoos for mild psoriasis, there is little proof of their efficacy by comparison with regular use of a standard shampoo. Some patients find them soothing, but to be effective they must be left on contact with the scalp for several minutes.

Systemic therapy

Topical therapy properly applied will control the great majority of psoriatic lesions. A small proportion of patients require more potent systemic therapy. The choices here lie between photochemotherapy (PUVA), the retinoid group of drugs (currently only available in the U.K. on hospital prescription), and cytotoxic drugs, including methotrexate and hydroxyurea. These treatments should not be considered until a very adequate trial of topical treatment has failed. None are safe for women in the child-bearing years without adequate (usually oral) contraception. Systemic steroids should not be used to control psoriasis.

Photochemotherapy (PUVA). This treatment involves the use of an oral photosensitizing agent, a psoralen, and subsequent total body exposure 2 hours later to ultraviolet light in the UVA range (320–365 nm; psoralen + UVA = PUVA). This form of therapy can be used either for clearing psoriasis—induction—or for maintaining the skin in a clinically normal state—maintenance. Treatment two or three times weekly is needed for the former and usually only once weekly for the latter.

Patients suitable for PUVA therapy require to live within reach of a centre with appropriate facilities. Immediate side effects are few, although some patients experience slight nausea. The main drawback at present to PUVA therapy is the possible future risk of skin cancer. PUVA has been available for 10 years and early figures show a slight increase in the incidence of skin cancer in PUVA-treated patients. More time is needed to assess the magnitude of this increased risk, but at present most centres try to restrict PUVA to patients over 40 years of age. Psoralens are teratogenic. PUVA is therefore not suitable for potentially pregnant females.

Psoralen is deposited in the lens of the eye and PUVA-treated patients must therefore wear dark glasses during treatment and for 24 hours thereafter.

Retinoids. These are synthetic vitamin A-like derivatives. Two drugs of this type are currently commercially available and many more will become available in the near future. The retinoid of greatest value in the treatment of severe psoriasis is etretinate (Tigason). This drug is taken orally in doses not usually exceeding 1 mg/kg/day. Trials have shown slow improvement over weeks or months of the majority of patients with plaque psoriasis, and a much more rapid improvement over a period of days in pustular psoriasis of the palms and soles. At present etretinate is available in the U.K. only on hospital prescription.

Side effects include skin thinning and cheilitis, and in some cases elevation of serum lipids. Recently, bony changes have been recorded in a very few patients. Patients on etretinate must therefore be monitored for these changes. The drug has a very long half-life and is teratogenic. Women of child-bearing potential must therefore use adequate contraception for the duration of therapy and for one year after therapy is discontinued.

Cytotoxic drugs. Cytotoxic drugs, particularly methotrexate, were until recently the mainstay of treatment of the patient with very severe psoriasis. The availability of PUVA and retinoids has reduced the number of patients requiring methotrexate, but it still has a part to play in certain cases. Its particular advantage is its speed of action, as improvement of psoriasis may be seen within 48 hours of administration of methotrexate.

Methotrexate can be given orally, intramuscularly, or intravenously. The usual dose required varies from 5 to 25 mg weekly. Careful monitoring of haematological and hepatic function is essential. A liver biopsy should be performed prior to starting methotrexate therapy and repeated every 18–24 months or more often if liver function tests show any abnormalities. Patients receiving methotrexate should be prepared to abstain from alcohol for the duration of therapy, and should try to maintain their weight within the normal range as liver function is more likely to become deranged in the obese.

Alternative cytotoxic drugs for use in psoriasis include hydroxyurea and azathioprine. Both require careful haematological monitoring and neither has any significant advantage over methotrexate.

Management of psoriasis of the nails and of psoriatic arthropathy

The management of psoriatic nails is unsatisfactory, but steroids injected into the posterior nail fold using a pressure gun such as the 'Dermojet' may be of some benefit. The management of psoriatic arthritis is also unsatisfactory, but the use of rest, heat, salicylates, and a variety of the currently available antirheumatic preparations may be helpful. There is no current evidence that antimalarials, gold, or indomethacin have any particular advantages in the management of psoriatic arthropathy. It is recommended that the management of patients with severe skin and joint disease should be shared by a dermatologist and a rheumatologist.

It can be seen that appropriate management of the patient with psoriasis requires careful initial consideration and constant reassessment. Table 3.3 illustrates a variety of clinical situations and appropriate initial therapy.

The Psoriasis Association has branches in many countries and publishes useful literature for patients. Many psoriatics find membership of this Association of value.

LICHEN PLANUS

Definition. This is a purely cutaneous disorder composed of pruritic, flat-topped papules most commonly seen on the inner surfaces of the wrists and the lower legs. The mucous membranes are usually affected. Spontaneous resolution usually takes place in a period of 3 months to 2 years.

Incidence

This disease accounts for 0.2–0.8 per cent of dermatological outpatients in Britain and North America.

Table 3.3. Appropriate treatment for psoriasis of different types in different age ranges

Patient	Type of psoriasis	Special considerations	Treatment	Comments
Boy aged 10	Guttate psoriasis	Usually self-healing type of psoriasis	0.1% dithranol in a cream base or simple white soft paraffin	Check for recurrent sore throats and enlarged tonsils
Married woman aged 28	Chronic plaque	Wishes to add to family	Short contact dithranol 2% 30 minutes daily	No currently available systemic treatment is appropriate for women who wish to become pregnant
Male aged 40	Severe pustular lesions palms and soles	Hand lesions causing concern over losing job	Trial of topical dithranol. If not successful try topical steroids. If these fail, consider for systemic Tigason therapy	
Female aged 56	Widespread plaques	Four recent hospital admissions. Post-menopausal. Relatively dithranol-resistant	Consider for PUVA therapy	Appropriate only if patient lives reasonably close to PUVA centre
Male aged 72	Erythrodermic psoriasis	Severe chronic. Obstructive airways disease makes home use of topical preparations very difficult	Consider for methotrexate	Possible hepatic toxicity may be outweighed by improved quality of life

Aetiology

The aetiology of lichen planus is unknown. As in psoriasis, the 50 Koebner or isomorphic phenomenon (p. 37) is a feature of the active disease, lesions appearing at sites of trauma.

Pathology

'Liquefaction degeneration' or selective destruction of the basal layer of the epidermis gives the dermo-epidermal junction a ragged, 'saw-toothed' outline. A mixed cell infiltrate is seen in the papillary dermis. This infiltrate varies in density, but tends to be found in close contact with the overlying epidermis, and to contain some free melanin. Discrete round deposits of amorphous pink material may also be observed in the papillary dermis. These so-called 'colloid bodies' are thought to consist of disintegrating basal cells. There is a prominent, sometimes wedge-shaped granular layer, and the epidermis is thinned in the atrophic and thickened in the hypertrophic form of the disease.

Immunofluorescence studies show large quantities of immunoglobulin on the colloid body surface. This is usually IgM and although the resulting 'bunch of grapes' immunofluorescent pattern is striking, it is not diagnostic, as colloid bodies can be seen in a variety of states associated with basal cell degeneration.

Clinical features

Classically, the onset is acute with intensely itchy, red or violet, shiny, flat-topped papules. The flexor surfaces of wrists, the forearms and legs are sites of predilection (Fig. 3.4). The oral mucous membrane is often affected at this time with white, spongy, slightly raised lesions, sometimes with a trabecular appearance, on the inner surfaces of the cheeks (Fig. 3.5). These lesions are commonly asymptomatic and unless specifically looked for they may well be missed. They are, however, an important point in establishing the diagnosis. Similar lesions may be seen on the genitalia.

The cutaneous lesions may persist for many months. With time they tend to become more violaceous, even blue in colour, and characteristically develop a fine white network on their surface—a pattern called Wickham's striae. Pruritus generally tends to diminish in time although some unfortunate individuals have itchy persistent lesions which last for many years. Rarer variants of lichen planus

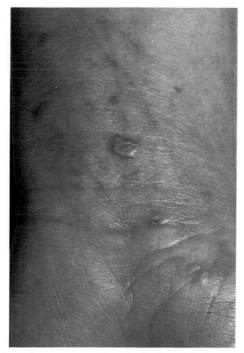

Fig. 3.4. Lichen planus seen on the classic site of the inner wrist area. Note the bluish-red, flat-topped papule with an overlying white network. This pattern is referred to as Wickham's striae.

include those with an annular or linear distribution, and the atrophic, ulcerative, and hypertrophic forms. All of these tend to be more persistent and resistant to therapy than the classical type.

Involvement of the nails is seen in about 10 per cent of patients, usually those with the more chronic skin lesions. Fine ridging or grooving, severe dystrophy, and even complete destruction of the nail bed may occur.

Differential diagnosis

Lichen planus is normally fairly easily diagnosed on clinical grounds and histological confirmation is not always required. It is essential to take a good history to exclude the possibility of a lichenoid eruption due either to drugs (thiazides, antimalarials, and gold) or to external

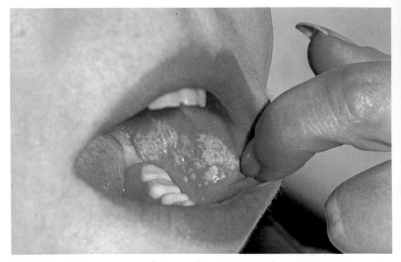

Fig. 3.5.   Lichen planus of the oral mucous membranes. Note the white, web-like pattern on the inner surface of the cheek.

contact with photographic colour developers. Occasionally, when the clinical picture resembles psoriasis, histological differentiation will be required. Persistent ulcerative or hypertrophic lesions should be biopsied to confirm the diagnosis.

Therapy

The most important aspect of treatment of lichen planus for the patient is control of what is usually severe and persistent itch. Systemic antihistamines, topical preparations such as 1–2 per cent menthol in calamine lotion or aqueous cream, topical steroid preparations and weak tar formulations are all traditional remedies. Stubborn lesions associated with very severe and persistent itch may be responsive to intralesional injections of a corticosteroid preparation. Some dermatologists advocate a short course of systemic steroids for early severe cases, but there is no place for systemic steroid administration on a long-term basis or for chronic lesions.

In the past, vitamin A acid (retinoic acid) has been used topically and systemically with some success. More recently, synthetic retinoids have been used but the results are in general disappointing and use of this group of drugs in lichen planus is not currently common practice.

PITYRIASIS ROSEA

Definition. A self-limiting disorder characterized by the development of asymptomatic erythematous scaling macules on the trunk.

Incidence and aetiology

Pityriasis rosea is most commonly seen in children and young adults. An increased incidence in spring and autumn, and outbreaks in institutions suggest that an infective agent, possibly viral, may be the aetiological agent.

Pathology

This is non-diagnostic, and an accurate history and careful clinical examination are more reliable aids to diagnosis. If a biopsy is performed, a moderately dense, mainly lymphocytic dermal infiltrate, papillary oedema, and a few extravasated red blood cells may be seen. Spongiosis may be seen in the epidermis at the edge of a developing lesion. This histological picture is very similar to that of secondary syphilis and as the clinical picture may also be similar, the pathologist must be given an accurate clinical history or unfortunate confusion may arise. If there is any doubt, serology should be performed.

Clinical features

The first clinical lesion in pityriasis rosea is the *herald patch*, an isolated erythematous patch with a peripheral collarette of scale. This is usually seen on the trunk, and precedes by 2–4 days or more the development of oval macules also with peripheral scaling on the trunk, thighs, and upper arms. The trunk lesions tend to have their long axes parallel to the ribs, giving a so-called 'Christmas tree' distribution of the lesions. Involvement of the hands, feet, or scalp are rare, and lesions are usually asymptomatic although there may be mild pruritus. Severe cases may have associated purpuric lesions.

Pityriasis rosea generally remits spontaneously in 4–8 weeks, but atypical or severe forms may be more persistent.

Differential diagnosis

Secondary syphilis, drug eruptions, pityriasis versicolor, and occasionally guttate psoriasis must be considered. Serological studies will exclude syphilis and negative mycological examination will exclude pityriasis versicolor. A good history will eliminate a drug eruption and occasionally a biopsy may be required to rule out psoriasis.

Therapy

Once the diagnosis is established all that may be needed is reassurance of the benign and self-limiting nature of the disease. Troublesome itch can be relieved by a topical antipruritic such as 1–2 per cent menthol in calamine or aqueous cream, and occasionally a systemic antihistamine may be needed. Topical steroids do not shorten the duration of the lesions and systemic steroids are not indicated.

PITYRIASIS RUBRA PILARIS

Definition. A rare erythematosquamous cutaneous eruption with characteristic follicular papules.

Incidence and aetiology

Pityriasis rubra pilaris is relatively rare. It is thought to be associated with abnormal vitamin A metabolism because low serum levels of vitamin A have been reported in this condition, and some patients show clinical benefit after systemic therapy with vitamin A acid (retinoic acid) or the newer synthetic retinoids.

Pathology

The striking histological features in a typical lesion are hyperkeratosis, with prominent parakeratosis around follicular openings, a mild inflammatory infiltrate in the papillary dermis, and apparent enlargement of the arrector pili muscles. As this is a non-specific picture, diagnosis should be based on clinical rather than on histological appearances.

Clinical features

In typical cases there is, on the trunk, a striking erythema in which occasional islands of normal skin can be seen. Follicular papules reminiscent of a nutmeg grater appear on the dorsa of the fingers, and a striking yellow-coloured hyperkeratosis develops on the palms and soles. There are no symptoms and the patient is well. In general, spontaneous resolution occurs in 6 months to 2 years.

Differential diagnosis

Psoriasis and seborrhoeic dermatitis, especially when atypical, may cause serious difficulty and justify a biopsy.

Therapy

In the past, treatment has been unsatisfactory and, although topical preparations including tars and topical steroids have been used, none has led to a dramatic improvement or shortening of the clinical course. Similarly, systemic administration of potent preparations such as steroids and cytotoxic drugs has not had any significant effect. Recently, synthetic retinoids given systemically have produced encouraging results in some patients.

DARIER'S DISEASE

Definition. A genetically determined disease characterized by abnormal keratinization based mainly on the hair follicles and causing a greasy reddish-brown papular eruption.

Pathology

Abnormalities of keratinocytes are seen in the lower layers of the epidermis. Prematurely keratinized cells (corps ronds) and distorted keratinocyte nuclei ('grains') are seen causing parakeratosis.

Clinical features

This rare disease is transmitted by autosomal dominant inheritance, and presents commonly in young adults as greasy brown papules on the chest and scapular area. It may be aggravated by sunlight and may have an acute onset after sunburn. Other features are the presence of small pits on the skin of the palm of the hand and irregularities of nail formation. There would appear to be a local immune defect in this condition as cutaneous infections with herpes simplex or, in the past, vaccination against smallpox may give rise to very severe widespread infection—so-called Kaposi's varicelliform eruption.

Treatment

Some patients with very mild Darier's disease may require no specific treatment. For others with the more severe forms of the disease the synthetic retinoid etretinate (Tigason) given systemically in doses of up to 1 mg/kg/day is very effective.

As with the treatment of severe psoriasis with retinoids, caution must be taken to ensure that the drug is not given to pregnant 56 women, and that contraception is maintained for one year after stopping the drug because of teratogenicity and a long half-life. Cheilitis is a common minor side effect and temporary elevation of triglycerides may occur, particularly if the patient is obese.

Traditional topical remedies have been based on the keratolytic action of salicylic acid and these have been superseded by the retinoids.

GROWTH POINTS

Psoriasis and the arachidonic acid metabolic pathways

Each decade a new observation in relation to psoriasis raises the hope that we will at last understand the aetiology of this common skin problem. Currently, a lot of research interest is centred around the role of certain products of arachidonic acid metabolism. There are two distinct pathways of arachidonic acid metabolism, the lipoxygenase, and the cycloxygenase pathways. Many non-steroidal anti-inflammatory drugs such as indomethacin act predominantly on the cycloxygenase pathway. There have been a number of reports over the years suggesting that patients with psoriasis incidentally given indomethacin and similar drugs experience a deterioration of their psoriasis. In the early 1980s, a rather different non-steroidal anti-inflammatory drug, benoxaprofen (Opren) was briefly available in the U.K. This drug inhibited both the cycloxygenase and the lipoxygenase pathways, and it was observed that many patients with psoriasis receiving it for other problems experienced clearing of their psoriatic lesions. These observations have stimulated intense interest in the role of lipoxygenase pathway metabolites in psoriasis. One of these, leukotriene B4, is a very potent polymorph chemo-attractant and if applied to the skin surface will cause aggregation of polymorphs in the epidermis.

This area of interest is important both for our understanding of the cause of psoriasis, and also for useful and appropriate use of the newer, relatively specific non-steroidal anti-inflammatory drugs in psoriasis.

The synthetic retinoid drugs

In the past 5 years, decades of work first on natural vitamin A derivatives and thereafter on synthetic vitamin A-like molecules have resulted in the availability of the two first generation retinoids for clinical use. The first of these, etretinate (Tigason), has been discussed in the sections on the management of psoriasis and Darier's disease. The second, 13-*cis*-retinoic acid (Ro-accutane), will be discussed in the next chapter on the management of acne vulgaris. Although both these drugs are effective, their use is limited by side effects and, in particular, by their teratogenicity. In the next few years, the second and third generation retinoids with fewer side effects will become available for clinical use.

FURTHER READING

Ashton, R. E., Andre, P., Lowe, N. J., and Whitefield, M.: Anthralin: historical and current perspectives. *Journal of the American Academy of Dermatology* **9**, 173 (1983).
A very comprehensive review with 161 references containing everything anyone would possibly need to know about dithranol.
Baker, H. and Ryan, T. J.: Generalized pustular psoriasis. *British Journal of Dermatology* **80**, 771 (1968).
Now a classic paper on all types of pustular psoriasis.
Bedford, C. J., Young, J. M., and Wagner, B. M.: Anthralin inhibition of mouse epidermal arachidonic acid lipoxygenase *in vitro*. *Journal of Investigative Dermatology* **81**, 566 (1983).
A useful scientific paper.
Cunliffe, W. J. and Miller, A. J. (eds): *Retinoid Therapy. A Review of Clinical and Laboratory Research*. Proceedings of an International Conference held in London, 16–18 May, 1983. MTP Press Limited, Lancaster (1984).
This book gives some insight into the range of conditions for which retinoids are being used and their relative benefits.

NOTES

4

Facial dermatoses

Several dermatological disorders which predominantly affect the face are considered together in this chapter. They are an important group, as patients with facial dermatoses tend to seek medical help earlier and for milder conditions than is the case with other body sites. Prompt therapy and vigorous reassurance are therefore often required for what may appear to be a trivial complaint. The conditions discussed are acne vulgaris and the other predominantly facial conditions from which it may require to be differentiated, perioral dermatitis, and light sensitive dermatoses.

ACNE VULGARIS

Definition. A disorder characterized by comedones, papules, and pustules centred on the pilosebaceous follicles.

Incidence and aetiology

Acne vulgaris is an extremely common problem. Surveys of school children in the U.K. suggest that almost all those between the ages of 12 and 17 experience some degree of acne. As a rule, however, only those with more severe or persistent lesions seek medical advice. Males and females are affected with equal frequency, but more females seek the help of family doctor or dermatologist. Rarely some may present in infancy and in relatively few cases lesions persist beyond the mid-twenties.

The lesions of acne result from obstruction of the pilosebaceous follicle. Oxidization of the follicular contents at the skin surface produces comedones (blackheads) which impair the normal flow of sebum to the skin surface, with stagnation within the pilosebaceous canal. Secondary infection may supervene and, if there is seepage of pilosebaceous contents into the surrounding dermis, a brisk and prolonged inflammatory response will develop. The initial step in this chain of events is associated with an elevated sebum excretion rate and possibly also abnormal keratinization within the excretory part of the pilosebaceous duct. Free flow of sebum is obstructed and the typical acne lesion develops. The timing of the onset of acne at puberty and the partial response of some cases to endocrine manipulation clearly illustrates that sebum production is under endocrine control.

Propionobacterium acnes is found in large quantities in the sebaceous glands of acne patients, but whether it is a primary aetiological factor or a secondary invader is debatable.

Pathology

Classical acne vulgaris is rarely biopsied as it is easily diagnosed clinically and because dermatologists are reluctant to cause facial scarring. Histological examination will, however, reveal the gross distension of the pilosebaceous follicle with a surrounding mantle of inflammatory cells. Both polymorphonuclear leucocytes and lymphoid cells are seen in this infiltrate, and in a particularly severe or chronic lesion foreign body giant cells, granulation tissue, and scar formation may also be seen.

Clinical features

When first seen the patient with acne vulgaris usually has open and closed comedones (blackheads and whiteheads), papules and pustules on the forehead, nose, and chin (Figs 4.1 and 4.2). In more severe cases the entire face with the exception of the periorbital skin may be affected, often with additional involvement of the upper chest and back. These sites are most densely populated with well developed sebaceous glands. Most acne patients seek help between 10 and 20 years of age, and girls tend to have problems 2–3 years earlier than boys. Generally, acne is associated with clinical signs of excessive sebaceous secretion, and a greasy facial skin and scalp. This interrelationship is not, however, exclusive because in other conditions (notably Parkinson's disease) associated with excessive sebaceous secretion there are no accompanying acne lesions.

The natural history in both sexes is for acne to improve spontaneously, but slowly over a period of several months to 2–3 years. Some women experience significant premenstrual deterioration. Use of the oral contraceptive pill has a variable effect depending on the oestrogen/progesterone ratio in the preparation used. There is a

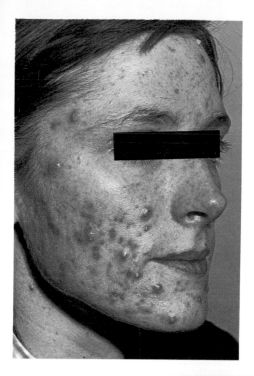

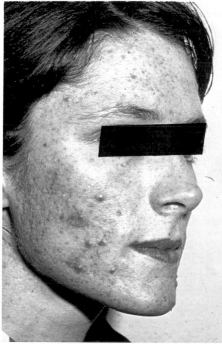

Figs 4.1 and 4.2. Typical acne vulgaris of moderate severity before and after 4 months treatment with systematic tetracycline (250 mg b.d.) and topical benzoyl peroxide preparations.

general tendency for acne to improve during pregnancy and lactation.

Severe acne in which there has been rupture of follicle and significant inflammation leading to dermal damage will cause scarring, but mild to moderate lesions will heal without scarring. At times it can be difficult to persuade both patient and parents of this fact.

Variants

Tropical acne affects young Caucasians in a hot humid environment such as the Far East. They develop gross acne lesions, mainly on the trunk, which can be disabling and resistant to all therapy other than return to a temperate climate.

Steroid acne appears in some patients on systemic steroid therapy. This acneiform eruption tends to affect the trunk rather more than the face and, although papules and pustules are present, comedones are notably absent.

Chemical acne is due to cutting oils and chlorinated hydrocarbons. This acneiform eruption is usually met in young people handling these substances at work. They develop some lesions on atypical sites, such as the legs, due to protracted contact with oil in saturated working clothes. Attention to hygiene will lead to a swift cure.

Chloracne, a very disfiguring disorder, is fortunately rare, but the leakage of dioxin gas at the Seveso chemical plant brought publicity and recognition. Dioxin and chlorinated hydrocarbons are absorbed in the body, and cause an acneiform eruption, characterized by large numbers of occluded whiteheads and inflamed cysts. These may persist for very many months after only transient exposure.

Infantile acne is a rare variant in which acne lesions are seen in male infants, usually between the age of 3 and 12 months. If severe, endocrine studies should be undertaken to exclude an androgen-secreting lesion. There is some evidence that infants affected with acne are prone to develop severe lesions in the teenage years.

Differential diagnosis

The clinical diagnosis of acne is usually simple, and is often made by the patient prior to seeking advice. Acneiform drug eruptions should be considered, particularly in any patient presenting outwith the normal age range. Antituberculous and antiepileptic drugs are both responsible not only for aggravating pre-existing acne, but also for provoking an acneiform eruption. Rosacea may give rise to confusion, but generally it is seen in an older age group. Although pustules may be present, there are no comedones and there is associated erythema.

Therapy

The management of young people with acne requires the patient's complete co-operation, but this is difficult for those who lead a busy life, often based on lodgings or halls of residence. At the outset, it is necessary to explain clearly the nature of acne and the need to treat it continuously for long periods of time. It is important both to stress the need to prevent scarring and also to encourage optimism by highlighting the usual improvement with age. Without doubt, some patients will co-operate more readily in their therapy if they are seen regularly and by the same doctor, but this is not always feasible.

Successful acne therapy depends on judicious use of topical and systemic preparations. There is little evidence that significant benefit can be gained from dietary measures. A few older women with resistant acne appear to benefit from hormonal manipulation. The results of application of topical erythromycin and tetracycline are encouraging. Both preparations are commercially available in the U.S. and will be available in the U.K. in late 1985.

Mild acne. The young teenager presenting with mild acne may need only a topical preparation, and commonsense advice on the avoidance of greasy cosmetics and face-concealing hair styles, often much favoured as camouflage by some sufferers. The use of a detergent cleanser may be of value, and 'picking' and self-trauma, which can lead to infection, can be discouraged. Active ingredients of topical preparations include salicylic acid, retinoic acid, resorcin, and benzoyl peroxide. Proprietary preparations frequently contain a mixture of these, the aim being to produce a keratolytic and bacteriostatic effect.

The most commonly prescribed preparations for mild acne are those containing 5–10 per cent benzoyl peroxide in a clear gel base (e.g. Panoxyl 5 and 10, Quinoderm, Benoxyl). These preparations are clear-coloured and odourless, and therefore acceptable by both sexes. There may well be some initial mild inflammation and desquamation, particularly in fair-skinned patients. They should be warned of this and encouraged to persevere. True sensitization to benzoyl peroxide is rare, but has been recorded.

Topical vitamin A-containing preparations (e.g. Retin-A gel) are particularly useful if the main problem is closed comedones (whiteheads). Here again some inflammation and irritation is very common. In the past, sulphur-containing preparations have been widely prescribed. While they are undoubtedly effective in mild acne, they are less cosmetically acceptable and therefore may not be used by the patient. Two to six per cent sulphur and 2–6 per cent resorcin in zinc paste is effective and can be used overnight. It is particularly effective on lesions on the back.

Topical steroids should not be used on acne lesions as they will aggravate the problem although steroid suspensions are occasionally injected intralesionally into cysts. Girls should be encouraged not to use greasy cosmetics to camouflage their acne lesions, but to substitute an appropriate tinted preparation if it is considered necessary.

Moderate acne. Patients with extensive involvement of the facial skin with acne or those who have not responded to topical therapy should be started on a systemic antibiotic without delay. The two antibiotics of choice are tetracycline and erythromycin, with tri-methoprim co-trimoxazole (Septrin) as a third choice. Clindamycin (Dalacin C) is no longer prescribed because of the risk of pseudo-membranous colitis. Tetracycline or erythromycin should be given in full doses of 1 g/day for at least 3 months. Much the commonest reason for apparent non-response of acne to systemic antibiotic therapy is the prescription of too low a dose for too short a period of time. Tetracycline should be given 30 minutes before meals on an empty stomach and should be washed down with water, not milk which interferes with absorption. Tetracycline should not be given concomitantly with oral iron which will also hinder absorption.

This regime supersedes older treatment schedules which suggested that lower doses of 500 mg/day were adequate. Recent studies have clearly demonstrated a more rapid and complete response to the higher dose of 1 g/day. If the antibiotics require to be continued for longer than 3 months, and this is common, the dose can at this stage be reduced with no loss of benefit to the patient.

The mode of action of systemic antibiotics in acne is not understood. While a part of their action may be in reducing the *P. acnes* colonization of pilosebaceous follicles, it is also postulated that they may affect chemotaxis of polymorphonuclear leucocytes and thus reduce the inflammatory response. Side effects of long-term antibiotic therapy for acne are rare, possibly due to the fact that the patients are otherwise healthy. Overgrowth with *Candida* is unusual. Girls should be warned that tetracycline will be deposited in bones and teeth of a foetus, should they become pregnant, and erythromycin should be given rather than other antibiotics to women who require acne therapy during pregnancy.

In the past, ultraviolet light in the natural sunlight UVB range (290–320 nm) has been prescribed for some acne patients. The mode of action is probably due to the desquamation induced by mild erythema causing unblocking of the blocked acne follicles. Effective modern topical and systemic therapy has resulted in a decreased need for ultraviolet light as an additional therapeutic aid, but a few patients will benefit. If prescribed, the dose of UVB should be carefully controlled and the patient must protect the eyes with goggles.

Severe or recalcitrant acne. There are two distinct problems here. One is very severe papulopustular acne with nodules and scarring in a teenager. The second is the persistence of mild acne long after the teenage years. This is commoner in women than men and tends to affect the chin. A premenstrual flare is a frequent association of this type of case.

The very acute severe type of acne can now be well controlled in almost all cases by the use of 13-*cis*-retinoic acid, a synthetic retinoid which is given systemically. In the U.K. this drug is available only on hospital prescription, but in the U.S. it is freely available. 13-*cis*-retinoic acid (Ro-accutane, Accutane) appears to have a very specific effect on the pilosebaceous gland and measurements of sebum excretion show a dramatic reduction in outflow of sebum. If the acne-bearing skin is biopsied, the pilosebaceous follicles will be seen to have shrunk to the vestigial structure seen prior to puberty.

If 13-*cis*-retinoic acid therapy is considered necessary it is prescribed in doses varying from 0.5 to 1.0 mg/kg body wt/day for 3 months. Although the higher 1 mg/kg dose is associated with a higher incidence of minor side effects, the benefit of therapy persists for much longer after the end of the 3-month course.

Minor side effects include dry skin, cheilitis, and, in some cases, a temporary elevation of serum lipids which revert to normal at the end of the course. A few patients on therapy for varying periods of time have been found to have bony abnormalities in the form of hyperostosis and the development of bony spurs around the wrists and ankle areas. By far the most serious problem, however, in the use of 13-*cis*-retinoic acid is its teratogenicity. It is essential if it is to be prescribed that females understand that pregnancy is absolutely contraindicated. There are reports of foetal abnormalities in children born to women who only took the drug for 1 or 2 months. A pregnancy test prior to starting therapy and continuation of contraceptive measures for the month after stopping therapy is therefore mandatory. Very severe facial acne responds more rapidly to 13-*cis*-retinoic acid than lesions on the back.

It must be stressed that 13-*cis*-retinoic acid therapy is currently only advocated for the more severe forms of acne. Patients with mild acne should not be referred for hospital prescription of the drug.

The second problem group in the management of acne are the women whose acne persists into their late twenties and thirties, despite adequate topical therapy and repeated courses of systemic antibiotics. These women frequently have mild hirsutism and a very clear premenstrual flare of their acne. For this group a trial of hormonal therapy is justified. Cyproterone acetate is currently available in a dose of 2 mg combined with ethinyl oestradiol as an essential contraceptive (Diane). This combination may be of value in mature female acne. Table 4.1 outlines the currently available acne treatments.

Acne scarring. The aim of modern acne therapy is to prevent scarring. In some patients scarring has developed before the patient seeks medical advice. In such cases, once all acne activity has ceased, it may be possible to reduce scarring by chemical peeling techniques or dermabrasion. Results, however, are often disappointing and patients must be warned that a perfect, smooth complexion cannot be guaranteed.

Table 4.1. Management strategies for varying types of acne

Type	Management
Mild teenage acne	Topical benzoyl peroxide Advice about non-greasy cosmetics Add systemic tetracycline or erythromycin if persistent after 3 months topical therapy
Moderately severe acne	Topical benzoyl peroxide Tetracycline or erythromycin 1 g/day for a minimum of 3 months Enquire about response to natural sunlight: consider artificial ultraviolet light
Severe acne	Topical benzoyl peroxide and systemic antibiotics. If no response to full doses of antibiotics for 3 months, refer for consideration for 13-*cis*-retinoic acid
Persistent acne in mature females	Consider for hormonal therapy (Diane)

ROSACEA

Incidence and aetiology

Rosacea is relatively common and affects 1 per cent of dermatological out-patients in Britain. It is commoner in women, although men tend to have more severe facial lesions and a higher incidence of the associated complications of keratitis and rhinophyma.

The aetiology of rosacea is unknown. The sebaceous hyperplasia, vasomotor instability, and tendency to facial flushing following physical or emotional stimuli are unexplained, but suggest lack of normal homeostatic control of blood vessels supplying the pilosebaceous follicle. Despite earlier teaching there is no evidence of any associated gastro-intestinal disorder. Although large numbers of the mite *Demodex folliculorum* can be found on the face in rosacea, its role in the pathogenesis of the disease is speculative. The application of potent or fluorinated topical steroids will aggravate pre-existing lesions of rosacea.

Pathology

Dilatation of the vessels in the papillary dermis and sebaceous hyperplasia are hallmarks. A granulomatous dermal inflammatory infiltrate containing giant cells may be seen in chronic cases.

Clinical features

Flushing and erythema begin typically on the forehead, the bridge of the nose, and cheeks—the so-called butterfly area of the face (Fig. 4.3). It may, however, be more widespread and spread to the neck, and occasionally beyond the face and neck areas. Over a period of months or years transient flushing is replaced by persistent erythema on which papules and pustules develop. Unlike acne, there are neither comedones nor seborrhoea.

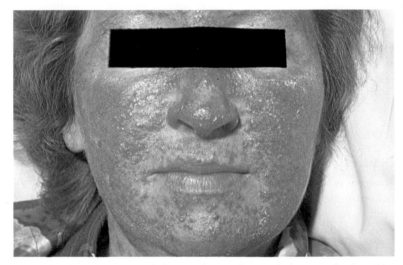

Fig. 4.3. Rosacea. Note inflammation and pustulation on cheeks, chin, and forehead. Comedones are absent.

In severe chronic cases, particularly in males, the sebaceous gland hypertrophy is concentrated on the nose, and produces gross soft tissue overgrowth and hypertrophy. The resulting appearance, termed *rhinophyma*, can be disfiguring and at times grotesque (Fig. 4.4).

Ocular involvement is a potentially serious complication. It presents as a sense of 'grittiness' or other discomfort in the eyes. Clinically, there may be a mild blepharitis and conjunctivitis, but if

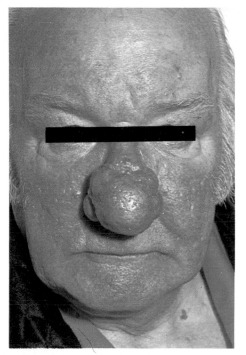

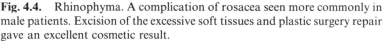

Fig. 4.4. Rhinophyma. A complication of rosacea seen more commonly in male patients. Excision of the excessive soft tissues and plastic surgery repair gave an excellent cosmetic result.

the more grave keratitis develops, corneal ulceration, vascularization, and visual impairment may supervene. Rosacea keratitis may develop in those with relatively mild cutaneous lesions.

Differential diagnosis

The commoner facial dermatoses to be considered in the differential diagnosis of rosacea include acne vulgaris, light sensitivity, contact dermatitis, lupus erythematosus, and perioral dermatitis. Acne usually affects younger patients and is distinguished by comedones. Both facial photosensitivity and contact dermatitis are more rapid in onset than rosacea and lack pustules. Chronic discoid lupus erythematosus is characterized by discrete scaly lesions, and in the systemic variety of lupus erythematosus the rash has a rapid onset and the patient is generally unwell. Perioral dermatitis may cause confusion but its distribution on chin and upper lip is characteristic.

Treatment

Topical therapy is of doubtful value in rosacea although weak concentrations of sulphur (2 per cent) or ichthyol (2 per cent) in a cream or paste can be prescribed for nocturnal use. While low potency corticosteroids (e.g. 1 per cent hydrocortisone) may reduce inflammation and relieve symptoms, long-term use of stronger steroid preparations will undoubtedly aggravate pre-existing rosacea and lead to skin atrophy with telangiectasia. Moreover, a degree of cutaneous dependence on these preparations appears to develop, as their withdrawal is frequently followed by a severer 'rebound' phenomenon with temporary deterioration. This can be so severe and distressing that it may be necessary to admit the patient to stop her/him from applying the steroid and to allow the exacerbation to settle. In this situation cold compresses of either saline or cold water are soothing and beneficial.

The cornerstone of therapy in rosacea is the use of low dose long-term systemic antibiotics, commonly tetracycline. Oxytetracycline 250 mg q.i.d. for 2 months reducing to b.d. 30–60 minutes before food for 3–6 months is usually effective. 13-*cis*-retinoic acid (Roaccutane) appears to be of value in this condition in reduction of papules and pustules, but not of erythema. Because of side effects and in particular teratogenicity, its use should be restricted to those who do not respond to tetracycline.   *Ice chips to.*

Severe rhinophyma should be treated surgically. Shaving or excision of the excess soft tissue on the nose and skin grafting can be most effective. This should be done while the patient is receiving systemic tetracycline to reduce the chance of recurrence.

Any patient with rosacea and ocular symptoms, however mild, should be referred to an ophthalmologist without delay. As there is no clear relationship between the severity of cutaneous lesions and the risk of developing ocular lesions, all patients without exception should be asked about ocular symptoms.

PERIORAL DERMATITIS

Definition. A facial disorder characterized by erythema, papules, and pustules on the lower face and chin.

Incidence and aetiology

Perioral dermatitis has been recognized by dermatologists only since the advent of topical corticosteroids, and as its incidence was relatively high when potent and fluorinated steroids were generously prescribed, and is decreasing now that the use of such preparations is more restricted, the condition may be at least in part iatrogenic and steroid-provoked. There is a very marked female preponderance (7–10 females to 1 male).

Other recent environmental changes suggested as a cause of perioral dermatitis include oral contraceptives and fluorinated toothpastes. Neither of these are used by all sufferers from the condition, whereas a history of prior application of topical steroid is obtained in all cases.

Clinical features

The chin and upper lip area are the sites of predilection (Fig. 4.5). Frequently, a narrow band of circumoral pallor is surrounded by an area of erythema and scaling, surmounted in more severe cases by papules and pustules. The individual lesions closely resemble those of rosacea, but the distribution is different. The tendency of both conditions to be aggravated by potent topical steroids strongly suggests a common aetiological factor and some workers consider perioral dermatitis to be a variant of rosacea.

The majority of patients are young women who present after having applied topical steroids to a mild and banal pre-existing condition. The topical steroids may have been specifically prescribed or acquired from friends or relatives. The usual sequence of events is for mild lesions to persist as long as the potent steroid is used, but for 'rebound deterioration' to occur when this is withdrawn. Slow spontaneous recovery will then usually take place. The principal symptoms are discomfort and pruritus.

Treatment

Systemic antibiotics, generally tetracycline, administered as for rosacea are the most effective method of treatment. Oxytetracycline should be prescribed in a daily dose of 250–500 mg for 2–4 months. Potent topical steroids should be withdrawn when the patient is first seen and a weak hydrocortisone preparation substituted temporarily (usually for a few days only). Cold compresses may give symptomatic relief.

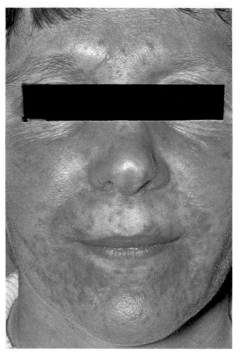

Fig. 4.5. Perioral dermatitis. The typical patient is a young female and the usual site of involvement is the upper lip and chin. Note the relative sparing of the immediate circumoral area.

LIGHT SENSITIVE ERUPTIONS

Photosensitive eruptions generally appear first on the face. They may be the cutaneous marker of systemic disease, as in systemic lupus erythematosus (p. 142) or porphyria (p. 248), or be due to photosensitizing drugs such as the phenothiazines (Fig. 4.6). There is a rare group of purely cutaneous disorders characterized by extreme sensitivity to a variety of wavebands of ultraviolet and visible light. These patients present with itch, erythema, papules, and even blisters after exposure to only mild sunlight. Specialized photobiological investigation is required to establish the diagnosis and to plan logical treatment which may include avoidance of light, and the use of both physical and chemical barrier preparations on exposed skin.

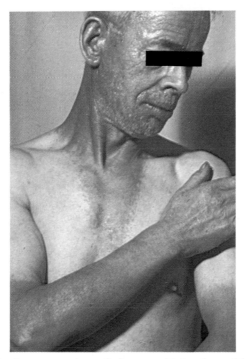

Fig. 4.6. Classic presentation of photosensitivity dermatitis showing involvement of face, neck, and arms from below the level of shirt sleeves.

LUPUS ERYTHEMATOSUS (LE)

This condition is discussed in full on p. 142. As, however, the face commonly is affected first, brief mention is necessary in this chapter. *Chronic discoid LE*, a purely cutaneous disorder, is characterized by well-demarcated, red, circular lesions with adherent scales. These are generally provoked or aggravated by sunlight, and heal with scarring. The facial lesions of *systemic LE* may also be aggravated by sunlight, but can be much less striking than those of the chronic discoid variety despite the multisystem involvement and more serious nature of the disease. Morphologically, there may be a diffuse macular erythematous eruption on the 'butterfly area' of the cheeks, nose, and forehead. Other light-exposed areas, such as the V of the neck or the arms, may also be involved.

FACIAL CONTACT DERMATITIS

Allergic contact dermatitis is fully discussed on pp. 88–92. Contact dermatitis involving only the face is generally due to cosmetics, toiletries, or medicaments. A rapid onset of facial discomfort, erythema, and swelling may be seen, and a careful history will elicit the likely aetiological agents.

GROWTH POINT

The most exciting advance in the management of facial dermatosis in the past 5 years has been the introduction of the 13-*cis*-retinoic acid or Ro-accutane and its dramatic effect in severe acne. The striking comparison between the effect of 13-*cis*-retinoic acid and the very mild effect of the other commercially available retinoid, the aromatic retinoid Tigason, shows very clearly the specificity of the effect of 13-*cis*-retinoic acid on the pilosebaceous follicle. This observation should lead to greater understanding in time of the actual mechanism underlying the production of the acne lesions, and with newer and more specific retinoids control of acne lesions without the problems of side effects of currently available retinoids seems likely in the next few years.

FURTHER READING

Cunliffe, W. J. and Cotterill, J. A. *The Acnes. Major Problems in Dermatology, Vol. 6*. W. B. Saunders Company Ltd, London and Philadelphia (1975).
A well-written, though now slightly dated text on all types of acne.
—— and Miller, A. J. (eds): *Retinoid Therapy. A Review of Clinical and Laboratory Research*. MTP Press Ltd, Lancaster (1983).
An excellent update of work currently in progress covering both acne and psoriasis.
Plewig, G. and Kligman, A. M.: *Acne. Morphogenesis and Treatment*. Springer-Verlag, Berlin (1975).
Beautifully illustrated 'coffee table' book on all aspects of acne.

NOTES

5

Dermatitis and eczema

Dermatological terminology can be confusing and usage of the words 'dermatitis' and 'eczema' is no exception. To some dermatologists the term eczema implies an endogenous process, and dermatitis a cutaneous reaction caused by one or more external factors. In this book dermatitis and eczema will be used synonymously, as recent work on interaction between the Langerhans cell and the lymphocyte has emphasized the fact that it is no longer possible to divide types of dermatitis and eczema into exogenous and endogenous processes. The fact that the histological pattern of 'eczema' has never been satisfactorily described is a reason for preferring to use the term 'dermatitis' in dermatopathology. In choosing which term to use when talking to patients, however, discretion should be exercised, for to many industrial workers the word dermatitis suggests an occupational dermatosis and possible litigation. On the other hand, parents of atopic children often dread the term 'eczema' and are less distressed by the use of 'dermatitis'. Some degree of flexibility in the use of the terms is therefore desirable.

CLINICAL VARIETIES OF DERMATITIS

1 Atopic dermatitis
2 Contact dermatitis—direct irritant and allergic contact
3 Dishydrotic eczema (cheiropompholyx)
4 Neurodermatitis and nummular dermatitis
5 Stasis dermatitis
6 Seborrhoeic dermatitis

These disease entities are all discussed in this chapter, but first, for convenience, there is a description of the clinical and histological features of the dermatitis reaction in all its phases, for they may be seen in any form of dermatitis.

The dermatitis reaction

This reaction can be divided rather arbitrarily into three phases: the acute, the subacute, and the chronic. It is important, however, to realize that on the skin of a patient with dermatitis, particularly of the atopic or the contact varieties, all three phases may coexist on different body sites.

The *acute* phase is characterized clinically by erythema and serous exudate on the affected area. Oedema is common, and large amounts of serous fluid may quickly saturate clothing or dressings. Secondary infection can quickly develop on such a site if hygiene is poor. In the flexures, it can be particularly difficult to treat the contiguous areas of skin which become adherent and crusted, with painful erosions and fissures. At this stage, the usual symptoms are pain, heat, and tenderness, although itch may predominate, and promote scratching and excoriation despite the pain. This picture is most commonly seen in acute contact dermatitis, and in severe atopic and seborrhoeic dermatitis.

The term *subacute dermatitis* is used when erythema and crusting are present without the extreme oedema and exudation of acute reactions. It may develop either *ab initio*, or as an acute phase resolves, or again as a chronic dermatitis exacerbation. Patients with predominantly subacute lesions tend to complain more of itch than of pain. Excoriations and secondary infection are common complications of subacute dermatitis.

Chronic dermatitis refers generally to long-standing lesions which take at least 3 months to develop. They are due to constant scratching and rubbing which elicit a reactive and possibly protective acanthosis. The resulting thickening of the skin and accentuation of normal skin markings is termed *lichenification*, and is seen most commonly in chronic atopic dermatitis in the limb flexures and in neurodermatitis. Itch rather than pain is the cardinal symptom, and gives rise to the continual rubbing and scratching which perpetuates the lesions. In an effort to avoid excoriations, the patient tends to rub the lesion with the flat of the nail rather than with its free edge. Consequently, the nail plate becomes shiny and polished, as if nail-varnished.

The histological features of acute, subacute, and chronic dermatitis merge into a spectrum of activity. The striking histological feature of the severe acute phase is *spongiosis* which consists of severe intercellular oedema in the epidermis with relative separation of keratinocytes. When adhesion between adjacent cells is retained, the desmosomal connections are clearly seen, even on light microscopy, but if these connections are broken by fluid pressure, intraepidermal vesicles will develop. There are variable numbers of inflammatory cells within the epidermis and such vesicles, and if secondary infection has supervened larger numbers of polymorphonuclear leucocytes may be present. Bacteria can be identified within these lesions by specific staining (e.g. Gram stain). On the palms and soles the thick horny layer forms a strong roof resulting in large tense bullae.

In subacute dermatitis there is histologically less extravasation of fluid into tissue spaces although a degree of spongiosis and a moderate inflammatory cell infiltrate are common. In addition, however, there are the beginnings of epidermal thickening (*acanthosis*) with an increase in the number of intraepidermal cells and loss of the regular rete ridge pattern. Some of the corneocytes of the horny layer retain their nuclei (*parakeratosis*). In chronic dermatitis this parakeratosis may be very marked over areas of gross acanthosis, but spongiosis and an epidermal infiltrate may still be observed.

Although various types of dermatitis may show subtle histological differences distinguishing the one variety from another, the pathologist will give a general report describing the histology as consistent with acute, subacute or chronic dermatitis reaction. Clinical features and results of other investigations will therefore determine whether it has developed on a background of, for example, atopy or contact allergy.

The practical importance of recognizing the clinical and histological phases of the dermatitis reaction lies in each requiring a distinct approach to therapy. In the acute phase, the primary aim is to reduce oedema and exudation, whereas in chronic lesions the need is to control the thick lichenified epidermis.

ATOPIC DERMATITIS

Definition. A chronic remitting pruritic cutaneous disorder with a strong genetic aetiological component, frequently associated with asthma or rhinitis.

Incidence and aetiology

Atopic dermatitis affects 1–3 per cent of all infants in the U.K. In later childhood and certainly in adults the incidence is lower. In Scotland it is seen in 30–40 per cent of young children attending paediatric dermatological clinics. In certain ethnic groups, such as the Chinese, it seems to be rarer, but more severe and persistent than in Caucasians.

Most patients with atopic dermatitis have a positive family history of the atopic triad—dermatitis, asthma, and allergic rhinitis—and although the exact mode of inheritance is obscure, autosomal dominance with variable penetration is postulated. In this triad, serum levels of reaginic antibodies—immunoglobulin E—are elevated and in atopic dermatitis they may be very high indeed. The results of radioallergosorbent testing (RAST) to determine the specific antigens against which this IgE is being synthesized indicate that they are the house dust mite (*Dermatophagoides pteronissinus*), pollens, cat, and dog hair, and food allergens. The elevated serum IgE levels appear not to be a primary aetiological factor and may be secondary to loss of suppressor lymphocyte activity. The excessive IgE production is manifest *in vivo* by the high incidence of positive prick tests to a battery of common allergens.

Striking seasonal variation is seen in some patients with deterioration in either very warm or very cold climatic conditions. Geographic variables may also affect the condition and there are many reports of complete clearance of severe atopic dermatitis at high altitudes.

In atopic disease the cutaneous vasculature responds abnormally to stimulation. Instead of a normal 'weal and flare' response, firm rubbing of the skin elicits *white dermographism* as a simple white linear streak along the site of pressure with no oedema or erythema. The typical facies seen in patients with atopic disease may reflect this associated paradoxical cutaneous vascular response. This and other features have given rise to the suggestion that one of the basic defects in atopic disease may be blockade of surface β-adrenergic receptors, preventing stimulation of second messenger. However, the role of this and other reported immunological abnormalities in the pathogenesis of atopy are not yet fully established.

Clinical features

Most patients with atopic dermatitis present in infancy between the ages of 3 and 6 months, with apparently itchy scaly lesions on the scalp, face, and trunk. The infant may be irritable, restless, and wakeful, and tries to rub the affected areas. In babies the cheeks, wrists, and hands are usually red, scaling and scratched. In toddlers and older children, the common sites of involvement are the elbow and knee flexures, the ankles, the dorsa of the feet under straps of shoes, and the retroauricular fold (Fig. 5.1). In severe cases there may be extensive involvement of all four limbs with gross excoriation and secondary infection.

Dryness of the skin is common, and a mild degree of ichthyosis and 'keratosis pilaris' may be seen. This consists of horny papules of the orifices of the hair follicles, and is most readily seen and felt on the outer surface of the upper arm.

Respiratory manifestations may co-exist and vary in severity either coincident with or alternating with fluctuations in the dermatitis.

In a large proportion of affected children the disease remits spontaneously between the ages of 2 and 5 years, but if it continues into adolescence and adult life it enters the chronic phase with striking lichenification in the popliteal and antecubital fossae and on the nape of the neck (Fig. 5.2). Prominent infraorbital creases are also seen, giving a weary and prematurely aged expression. Thinning of the lateral half of the eyebrows (Hertoghe's sign) is frequently

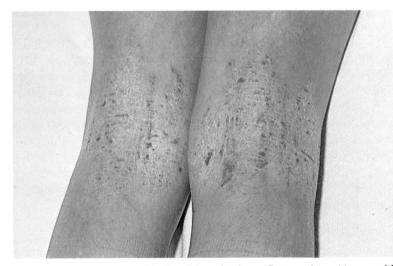

Fig. 5.1. Atopic dermatitis involving the knee flexures in a 10-year-old child. Note both lichenification and recent excoriations.

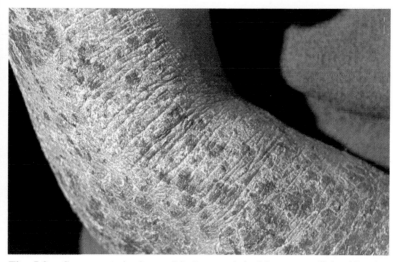

Fig. 5.2. Severe atopic dermatitis in an adult. Note gross lichenification and superimposed excoriations.

present, probably due to continual rubbing. Shiny fingernails result from buffing rather than scratching the lesions.

Patients with atopic dermatitis are reported to have a lower incidence than expected of allergic contact dermatitis, but they are more susceptible than non-atopics to irritant contact dermatitis. It is most important therefore to offer atopic adolescents guidance about careers and to indicate those occupations which are inadvisable. Many atopic girls are interested in a nursing career because of their knowledge of hospital life, but this is to be discouraged as continual exposure to soap and water causes exacerbation of hand lesions.

Complications and associations

Clinical conditions seen in atopic patients strongly suggest a minor, but specific defect in cell mediated immunity. Patients with atopic dermatitis have a higher incidence of viral warts and of fungal infections than do age-matched controls, and show abnormal response to contact with certain other viruses. These viruses are herpes simplex and vaccinia, and exposure to either may result in very widespread cutaneous lesions with, in some cases, involvement of the central nervous system. This complication, termed *Kaposi's varicelliform eruption*, is serious and may be life-threatening. In the past, it was advised that no patient with active or recently active atopic dermatitis should be vaccinated against smallpox. This advice is now superfluous, however, as smallpox is now thought to have been eradicated. The more common risk is dissemination of herpes simplex virus (Figs 5.3 and 5.4). Parents should be warned about it and instructed to keep their child away from persons with active 'cold sores'. Similarly, anyone who works in or visits a dermatology department and who has active herpes simplex should avoid contact with atopic dermatitis patients.

Treatment

The management of a young baby with atopic dermatitis requires the full understanding and co-operation of the parents. In many cases the family will already have had experience of the disease, but even then time is well spent explaining such features as the need to

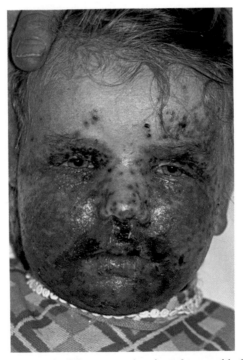

Fig. 5.3. Kaposi's varicelliform eruption in a 3-year-old child with mild atopic dermatitis. Herpes simplex virus was isolated from the lesions.

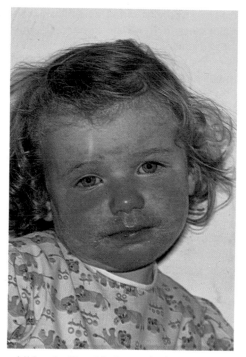

Fig. 5.4. Same child as in Fig. 5.3, 3 months later. Note complete healing and absence of scarring.

avoid sudden temperature changes, and the relative susceptibility of the skin to irritation by woollen garments and cat or dog hair.

Itch may be partially controlled by systemic antihistamines such as promethazine or trimeprazine, in syrup form, prescribed in 5–10-ml doses at night and also, if necessary, by day. It is wise to change the antihistamine prescribed fairly frequently as otherwise loss of effect even at high doses will be seen. Topical therapy will depend on the phase of the dermatitis and sites involved. Acute weeping lesions require wet dressings impregnated with a bland preparation such as isotonic saline or 1 per cent ichthyol in calamine lotion. The evaporation from these dressings assists in rapid control of the oozing surface. Most lesions in the infant are subacute and a steroid-antibiotic combination topically is usually beneficial. Suitable preparations include hydrocortisone combined with vioform or fucidin, and clobetasone butyrate with oxytetracycline (Trimovate). The use of potent steroids must be avoided as much as possible in small children, and they should never be applied to children's faces as telangiectasia and striae may develop very rapidly. Preparations containing tar or ichthyol applied over the milder steroids reduce the quantity of topical steroid required: 1–2 per cent tar or ichthyol in zinc ointment can both be used in this way. Tar acts as a mild antiseptic and is antipruritic. The bandaging over the dressings is important as it will prevent further scratching. For older children and adults the use of higher concentrations of tar (2–5 per cent) in an ointment or paste base will help minimize lichenification. If pruritus and excoriation are particularly troublesome features, occlusive bandages impregnated with ichthyol or tar (Ichthopaste, Colta-paste, Tarband) applied for days at a time may result in dramatic improvement.

It is extremely important to treat the associated dry skin with simple emollient preparations as this may significantly reduce the quantity of topical steroid required. Dispersable bath oils (Oilatum, Aveeno oilated oatmeal sachets, Alpha-Keri bath oil) are of value and emulsifying ointment BP after bathing is beneficial. Soap should be restricted or avoided and emulsifying ointment BP used instead. Some patients find urea-containing preparations (e.g. Calmurid) beneficial, as they theoretically help the skin to retain moisture, but in young children they should be used with caution initially as they can cause a temporary, but severe 'stinging' sensation. Woollen garments frequently irritate the skin of atopics: cotton garments are much more suitable.

There is currently considerable controversy over the role of diet in atopic eczema. There are two specific questions:
1 Does modification of the diet as a young infant, or even by the pregnant mother, modify or prevent the onset of atopic dermatitis?
2 In established atopic dermatitis, does dietary modification or restriction help to control the condition?

As far as the first question is concerned, it has been suggested in the last decade that exclusive and prolonged breast feeding could reduce the incidence of or even prevent atopic dermatitis. Carefully controlled epidemiological studies have not confirmed this sugges-tion and, although breast feeding of the infant in an atopic family should be encouraged for all the usual reasons, the parents can be given no reassurance that this will prevent the onset of atopic dermatitis. The role of maternal diet during pregnancy and breast feeding is currently under investigation.

The role of dietary manipulation in established atopic dermatitis is currently an interesting and somewhat controversial problem. A number of children with atopic dermatitis do show clinical improvement if cow's milk products are removed from their diet and occasionally withdrawal of other foods such as citrus fruits is associated with benefit. Soya milk-based products can be substituted for cow's milk (e.g. Prosobee, Wysorb) for a month's trial if the mother is keen to try dietary treatment, but it is strongly recommended that the expert advice of a dietitian be sought if extensive and prolonged dietary restrictions are planned as deficiencies of protein, calcium, or essential vitamins can quickly develop.

At present it would appear that only a small proportion of children with atopic eczema benefit from dietary restriction. It must be emphasized that dietary management of the atopic requires the full co-operation of the child and parent.

Other useful measures for control of some cases of atopic dermatitis include removal of common allergens from the environment. Some atopics react badly to cat hair, dog hair, feathers in pillows and quilts, and pollens. A dust-free, pet-free, plant-free house may help some patients. The house dust mite is ubiquitous, but measures to reduce the numbers present may also be useful.

CONTACT DERMATITIS

Contact dermatitis can be divided into two distinct groups, the one caused by a *direct irritant* action of a substance on the skin, the other *allergic contact dermatitis* which occurs only in patients whose skin has previously been sensitized by contact with an allergen. Fresh contact with the antigen elicits a dermatitis reaction mediated by specifically sensitized T lymphocytes. The role of the epidermal Langerhans cells in presenting the allergen and in making subsequent contact with T lymphocytes either in the skin or local lymph nodes is currently the subject of active investigation.

Some of the salient differences between direct irritant contact dermatitis and allergic contact dermatitis are enumerated in Table 5.1. Current figures show that in the U.K. direct irritant dermatitis is a much commoner problem than the allergic contact variety.

Table 5.1.   Differences between direct irritant and allergic contact dermatitis

	Direct irritant	Allergic contact
Prior exposure to substance	Not required	Essential
Affected sites	Sites of direct contact with little extension	Sites of contact and distant sites
Susceptibility	Everyone susceptible in varying degrees to appropriate concentrations	Only some patients susceptible
Other associated skin diseases	Atopy predisposes	Prolonged use of topical medicaments for chronic skin disease (e.g. leg ulcers) predisposes
Timing	Rapid onset 4–12 hours	Onset generally 24 hours or longer after exposure
	Lesions develop at first exposure	No lesions on first exposure

DIRECT IRRITANT CONTACT DERMATITIS

Definition. Dermatitis caused by exposure to a substance which has a damaging effect on the normal barrier function of the epidermis.

Incidence and aetiology

Irritant dermatitis may be an *acute reaction* to one single exposure to a strong skin irritant such as acid, alkali, phenol, halide, or quaternary ammonium compounds. The onset is rapid and lesions appear at sites of contact.

A second variety of irritant dermatitis results from *cumulative exposure* to a mild cutaneous irritant. The classic example is 'washerwoman's hands' due to continual contact with detergents and/or alkalis which degrease the skin and remove the protective lipid film. Chronic skin damage then develops.

Mild examples of cumulative insult irritant dermatitis are extremely common among persons regularly exposed to detergents and degreasing agents either at work or at home, and patients with atopic dermatitis are particularly susceptible.

Clinical features

After exposure to a strong irritant the affected skin becomes reddish-brown and vesicles develop. The lesions appear rapidly, usually within 6–12 hours of contact, and are painful and itchy. If there is no further contact with the irritant, recovery is rapid and it is unusual for lesions to develop at distant body sites. Identification of the aetiological agent depends on a careful history, and as the site and timing of the lesions are clear-cut the patient himself will usually identify the substance in question.

Chronic irritant dermatitis tends initially to present as dry, hacked, or fissured areas of skin which are susceptible to secondary infection. This is seen typically in housewives and young mothers whose hands are repeatedly exposed to soap, detergents, and water. These substances tend to accumulate under rings and, with the added effect of local trauma, may provoke severe reactions which are clinically very similar to those seen as a result of allergic contact sensitivity to metals.

Treatment

Identification of the irritant and its subsequent avoidance is the cornerstone of successful therapy. The aetiological diagnosis here is made on the patient's history, not on patch testing, which will give false positive results as the majority of the population will react to those irritants if tested at appropriate concentrations.

For the active phase, a topical steroid cream or ointment is the mainstay of treatment. If the lesions are particularly acute with vesicles and weeping, wet dressings in the form of soaks or lotions may be needed until the more subacute phase is reached, when topical steroids can be substituted. Suitable wet dressings and lotions include aluminium acetate lotion 5 per cent in sterile water and calamine lotion BP (15 per cent calamine, 5 per cent zinc oxide, and 5 per cent glycerine). Prior soaking of the area in a weak solution of 0.01–0.1 per cent potassium permanganate in water for 5 minutes may be soothing and help to prevent secondary infection. The choice of topical steroid for the subacute phase is wide and as the surface area involved may be small, and the condition of short duration, the use of a relatively strong steroid is justified. Suitable examples are 0.1 per cent betamethasone 17-valerate with 3 per cent clioquinol in a water miscible base (Betnovate C), fluocinolone acetonide (Synalar), or beclomethasone dipropionate 0.025 per cent (Propaderm). As acute reactions seldom become chronic, keratolytics are rarely indicated.

Prevention of irritant dermatitis is simple and all individual workers at risk should be issued with appropriate protective clothing. Chronic detergent contact with hands should be prevented by using occlusive vinyl (not rubber) gloves and underneath these a thin pair of cotton gloves to absorb perspiration. This is much more effective than flock or cotton-lined gloves. Thorough rinsing of the hands after essential soap and water exposure is important as is the regular use of emollient preparations to hydrate the skin (e.g. emulsifying ointment BP, Ung. Merck). Routine use of topical steroids for this purpose is not advised.

ALLERGIC CONTACT DERMATITIS

Definition. Dermatitis caused by prior exposure to an allergen leading to specific cell-mediated sensitization.

Incidence and aetiology

This form of dermatitis is extremely common and affects 1–2 per cent of the population overall. Certain groups, however, are at greater risk. Patients with chronic skin conditions such as leg ulcers tend to become sensitized to medicaments, and workers exposed to common sensitizers such as chromates in the building industry, or dyes and tanning agents in leather manufacture, have a higher incidence than the population at large.

The commonest senitizing agents in Europe and North America have been identified, and they are used as a routine battery of 20 patch tests for investigating patients with this type of dermatitis. Substances in this battery are listed in Table 5.2. In addition, smaller groups of relevant allergens are used when investigating specific problems, e.g. a 'footwear battery' for chronic foot dermatitis.

In theory, once the offending allergen has been identified by patch testing, and thereafter avoided, rapid clearance of the skin lesions should occur, but in practice this is not always the case. Certain common allergens are very difficult to avoid in the course of everyday life and nickel is a good example. It is found in cutlery,

Table 5.2. Substances currently used in the European standard battery of patch tests

Potassium dichromate 0.5% in
 petrolatum
Cobalt chloride 1% in petrolatum
Nickel sulphate 2.5% in
 petrolatum
Formaldehyde 2% in water
p-Phenylenediamine (PPD) 1% in
 petrolatum
Balsam of Peru 25% in
 petrolatum
Turpentine peroxides 0.3% in
 olive oil
Neomycin sulphate 20% in
 petrolatum
Parabens (methyl-, ethyl-,
 propyl-, butyl-, benzyl-) 3%
 each, 15% in petrolatum
Chinoform 5% in petrolatum
Colophony 2% in petrolatum
Wood tars (pine, beech, juniper,
 birch), 3% each, 15% in
 petrolatum
Wool alcohols 3% in petrolatum
Epoxy resin 1% in petrolatum
Mercapto-mix 2% in petrolatum
Thiuram-mix 1% in petrolatum
PPD-mix 0.6% in petrolatum
Naphthyl-mix 1% in petrolatum
Carba-mix 3% in petrolatum
Ethylenediamine 1% in
 petrolatum

coins, cooking implements, gardening and motoring equipment, jewellery, household furniture, and many other items, and it can be extremely difficult, even for an intelligent and motivated patient, to lead a life devoid of external nickel contact. Moreover, there is evidence that even trace amounts of nickel in the diet may play a part in perpetuating the skin lesions.

Medico-legal consequences of allergic contact dermatitis acquired through exposure to allergens at work are considerable, but are beyond the scope of this book. Prevention is both vital and feasible. The decline of chromate dermatitis in building workers in Scandinavia following removal of chromates from cement illustrates the value in this respect of collaboration between dermatologists and industry.

Clinical features

Allergic contact dermatitis usually presents with acute or subacute dermatitis lesions at sites where the allergen was in direct contact with the skin and also with milder involvement of more distant areas. As hypersensitivity may develop after many years of trouble-free daily contact with the allergen, the patient may be completely unaware that he is reacting to this particular substance and even after positive patch testing it may be very hard to convince him that a material handled regularly for many years is now to be avoided.

Common sites of involvement are the ear lobes and nape of neck (nickel in jewellery), the wrist (metal or leather watch straps or bracelets), and the feet (tanning agents used in curing leather, adhesives used for fixing insoles, dyes used for leather or socks, glue used in assembling shoes) (Figs 5.5 and 5.6).

In the early stages the affected area is inflamed and itchy, with papules and vesicles. Continued exposure to the allergen will lead to

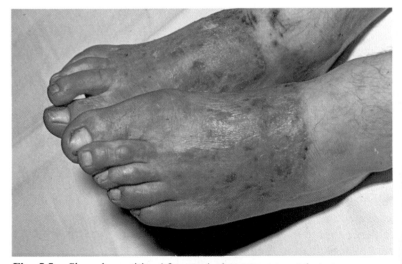

Fig. 5.5. Shoe dermatitis. After topical treatment patch tests were performed and a positive result obtained to chromium.

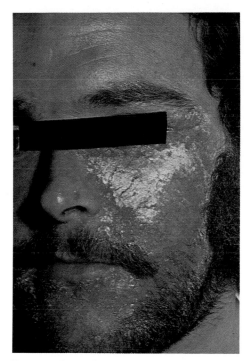

Fig. 5.6. Medicament dermatitis. This patient had recently received an eye ointment containing neomycin.

dryness, scaling, and fissuring. This picture may be complicated when renewed exposure causes an acute or subacute exacerbation to develop on the background of a long-standing chronic dermatitis. The lesions frequently spread well beyond the area of contact with the allergen and also even to distant body sites which have not been in contact with the allergen. The main site of involvement may give a useful clue to the cause and Table 5.3 lists such common sites and likely agents. Exposure to sensitizing plants, particularly to primula, tends to cause a blistering eruption relatively rapidly on the sites of actual contact and also a general facial erythema due to airborne allergen.

Hand dermatitis tends to be a common and persistent problem in individuals sensitive to nickel. It is good practice to patch test in all cases of persistent hand dermatitis.

Table 5.3.   Principal sites of allergic contact dermatitis and likely causes

Site	Likely cause
Face	Cosmetics, perfume in toilet soap, nickel, plastic spectacle frames, medicaments (e.g. antibiotics in eye or ear drops)
Scalp	Hair dyes (paraphenylenediamine—PPD), lotions and tonics containing Balsam of Peru
Mouth	Denture materials
Neck and ear lobes	Nickel
Wrists	Nickel, PPD, chromates
Hands	Plants (e.g. primulas), nickel (begins under rings), material handled in occupation or recreation, lanolin (hand creams, medicaments)
Body	Nickel clips or rubber material in underwear
Feet	Dyes used in socks and shoes; glues, chromates, etc., in shoes

Treatment

The management of allergic contact dermatitis is divided logically into four stages.

1 *Detection of the likely sensitizing agent* by taking a careful occupational, recreational and medicament history. Knowledge of the common sensitizers and the sites they may affect is obviously useful at this stage.

2 *Preparation for valid patch testing* to identify the allergen. It is essential to avoid all materials thought to be possibly responsible for the eruption while applying a topical steroid preparation to clear the dermatitis. The presence of active lesions even at distant body sites while patch testing is carried out will result in both false positive and false negative results, and all lesions must therefore be cleared *before* patch tests are performed. Appropriate topical therapy, as in other types of dermatitis, will vary according to the degree of activity. For acute weeping lesions wet soaks or shake lotions are soothing, and in the subacute phase topical steroid preparations are helpful. The strength of steroid used should be chosen according to the site involved—facial lesions should receive a mild preparation (e.g. clobetasone butyrate, Eumovate) while the thicker skin of the hands and feet require a stronger preparation (e.g. fluocinolone acetonide, Synalar).

3 *Patch testing* to the suspected substances (for the technique, see p. 12). In practice it is common to test patients with all substances in the European standard battery plus any other likely allergens, e.g. small pieces cut from the inner aspects of shoes in foot dermatitis. Patch testing is, in theory, deceptively simple. However, the snags are many, and even basic aspects, such as allergen presentation and concentration, are critical and require expert consideration. Moreover, the interpretation of patch test results can be far from straightforward as some allergens are also irritants.

4 *Counselling on avoidance of responsible allergens* following patch test results. This is not always straightforward. For example, although it may be easy to avoid the plant in primula dermatitis, it is much more difficult to obtain appropriate footwear in shoe dermatitis. Difficulties can be formidable in industry when a skilled worker finds it hard to avoid exposure to an allergen, and factory or industrial medical officers may be of great assistance in such cases.

It is essential that these four stages of treatment and investigation be followed. A delay in response to treatment prior to patch testing (stage 2) may be due to continuing exposure to the aetiological agent. This is particularly common in medicament-induced contact dermatitis and in such cases topical preparations containing lanolin or preservatives (e.g. parabens) should be avoided.

POMPHOLYX (dishydrosis or dishydrotic eczema)

This term is used to describe a very characteristic pattern of intensely itchy vesicles in the skin of the hands—cheiropompholyx—and occasionally also the feet—cheiropodopompholyx. The sides of the finger are frequently involved and clinically the individual lesions have a 'sago grain' or 'frog spawn' appearance due to translucent deeply-set papules.

The cause of this pattern of dermatitis is not understood. In some cases there is a history of or even concomitant allergic contact dermatitis, especially to nickel. In other cases no specific allergen is found, but the problem appears to be aggravated by stress.

Treatment
Systemic antihistamines will help control the need to scratch and

thus prevent secondary infection. The intense, but usually short-lived discomfort is best controlled by frequently applied lotions to allow maximum cooling. One per cent calamine lotion is an appropriate application.

ASTEATOTIC ECZEMA (eczema craquelé)

This term is used to describe the dry irritable skin seen mainly on the limbs of elderly patients. The skin is dry and has large scales with a 'crazy-paving' appearance. It appears to be the result of loss of epidermal lubrication together, in many cases, with inadequately removed soap after a bed bath. The problem is extremely common in communities of elderly people.

Treatment

This consists of replacing the missing lubrication. Soap should be withdrawn and emulsifying ointment B.P., Ung. Merck, or a similar preparation used. Adequate lubrication may require very regular application of emollients and a reduction in bathing. Topical steroids should be avoided as the underlying skin is already thin and fragile.

NEURODERMATITIS (circumscribed lichen simplex)

Definition. A well-demarcated area of chronic lichenified dermatitis which is not due to either external irritants or identified allergens.

Incidence and aetiology

In predisposed persons the lesions are induced by continual scratching or rubbing of a localized area of itchy skin. The initial pruritic stimulus, which seems to be related to stress or emotional disturbance, generates an itch-scratch-itch cycle. This, in turn, stimulates a reactive epidermal hyperplasia recognized clinically as lichenification.

Neurodermatitis is relatively uncommon and the diagnosis should be made after excluding commoner causes of dermatitis, e.g. irritant or allergic contact dermatitis. It is commoner in women than in men.

Clinical features

Usually the isolated, well-circumscribed, lichenified, slightly elevated plaques are seen on the nape of the neck, the forearms, or the legs. They have a characteristic mauve colour and accentuation of normal skin markings. Affected patients are often tense and obsessive, and there appears to be an association with atopy.

Diagnosis and treatment

A biopsy may occasionally be necessary to confirm the diagnosis when individual lesions resemble psoriasis or even lichen planus. An atypical fungal infection could also cause confusion. Mycological examination will exclude this possibility.

Treatment is designed to break the itch-scratch-itch cycle and consists of antihistamines by mouth to reduce pruritus, topical corticosteroids to suppress inflammation, and tar or ichthyol-containing preparations for their antipruritic and keratolytic effects. Occlusive dressings prevent scratching and can produce dramatic improvement. They are much the most effective treatment. For lesions on a limb, a tar or ichthyol impregnated bandage (e.g. Coltapaste, Ichthopaste) applied for a week may totally clear the lesion. Unfortunately, however, recurrence after removal of occlusion is frequent. In some cases intralesional injections of a steroid preparation such as triamcinolone may be beneficial.

NUMMULAR OR DISCOID DERMATITIS

Definition. A chronic, recurrent pattern of dermatitis with discrete coin-shaped lesions tending to involve the limbs.

Incidence and aetiology

This variety of dermatitis usually affects adults although a small number of children with atopic dermatitis may present with or develop discoid lesions in the course of their disease. The aetiology is unknown and, although secondary infection is common, a primary infective cause has not been proven.

Clinical features

The lesions arc circular, ranging from 4 to 10 cm or more in diameter and are often distributd symmetrically on the legs (Fig. 5.7). They are usually subacute with erythema, mild oedema and, in some cases, vesiculation. The surface may be moist and appear infected. Pruritus is variable and can be absent, in marked contrast to neurodermatitis.

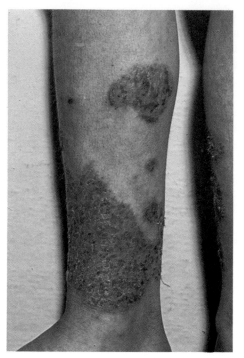

Fig. 5.7.   Nummular dermatitis involving both lower legs.

Diagnosis

Classic nummular dermatitis is generally easy to diagnose, but atypical cases may resemble neurodermatitis, psoriasis, or allergic contact dermatitis. The lack of pruritus and lack of lichenification will distinguish the condition from neurodermatitis. The distribution of the lesions, generally sparing the knees, elbows, and scalp, is unlike psoriasis. Patch testing will identify most patients with allergic contact dermatitis, a few of whom, particularly women with nickel dermatitis and hand lesions, have a nummular pattern of dermatitis.

Treatment

Topical corticosteroids are the most effective means of controlling this condition. As secondary infection is relatively common, the use of a steroid-antibiotic combination [e.g., betamethasone valerate + chinoform (Betnovate C)] is logical and may clear the lesions. In more persistent cases the application of 0.5–2 per cent tar or ichthyol in zinc paste will be beneficial. Systemic antipruritics are rarely required.

STASIS DERMATITIS

Definition. An area of dermatitis on the lower legs, commonly seen in association with venous innsufficiency or frank ulceration.

Incidence and aetiology

A large number of obese, usually female, patients have a degree of venous insufficiency or frank varicose veins of the lower limbs. Prior to the development of frank stasis ulcers (p. 164) a mild dermatitis reaction associated with epidermal atrophy, purpura, and pigmentation due to haemosiderin may develop. These changes are related to extravasation of blood into the tissues and poor oxygenation.

Clinical features

The inner aspects of both lower legs above and around the medial malleolus are chiefly involved. Pruritus may be severe and cause scratch marks which are slow to heal. Other less severe lesions may be seen on the calves and thighs.

Treatment

Treatment of the underlying venous insufficiency is the most important form of therapy. The use of topical steroids, although symptomatically valuable, is not to be recommended as it will accelerate the development of atrophy of what is already thin epidermis. Protective ichthyol or tar-impregnated bandages are useful both in preventing scratching and in protecting from other forms of minor trauma.

SEBORRHOEIC DERMATITIS

Definition. A form of dermatitis of unknown aetiology, mainly affecting areas of maximum concentration of sebaceous glands.

Incidence and aetiology

This condition is found especially in adult males and should not be confused with infantile seborrhoeic dermatitis (p. 264) which seems to be unrelated. Seborrhoeic dermatitis was much commoner in the U.K. 20–30 years ago, and the decreasing incidence has been attributed to factors such as improved hygiene and dietary changes.

Qualitative and quantitative changes in sebaceous secretion have not been reported, and although secondary infection or colonization of the sebaceous glands with *Pityrosporum ovale* has been suggested as a cause, this organism is commonly found in normal skin.

Clinical features

The eruption consists of discrete, commonly asymptomatic, red to yellow, glazed-looking lesions, mainly on the trunk. The presternal area, the axillae, submammary folds, groins, and external ear are common sites. Facial lesions are commoner in men and may be very persistent (Fig. 5.8).

The scalp is frequently involved, and the presenting complaint may be of severe and persistent dandruff (pityriasis capitis, seen as scaling and erythema on the scalp). Eyebrow and eyelid involvement is common, and this blepharitis can be very unresponsive to therapy. Overall, seborrhoeic dermatitis tends to be chronic with seasonal variations peculiar to the individual.

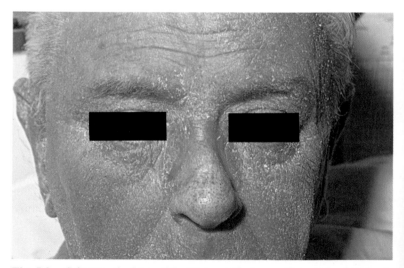

Fig. 5.8. Seborrhoeic dermatitis. Note erythema, scaling, and seborrhoeic blepharitis.

Diagnosis

Confusion may arise with allergic contact dermatitis, psoriasis, and pityriasis versicolor. Patch testing will generally exclude a true contact allergy, and the greasy yellow appearance of the lesions and their distribution are pointers against psoriasis, but this may easily be confused particularly when there are only scalp lesions present. In psoriasis, however, the lesions are easily palpable and well delineated with large coarse silvery scales, whereas in seborrhoeic dermatitis they are more diffuse with finer smaller scales. Mycological examination of scrapings from individual lesions will exclude pityriasis versicolor and other fungal infections.

Treatment

This is difficult and often unrewarding. Lesions on the trunk and limbs can be improved, and on occasion cleared with a mild steroid preparation, but the constant use of topical steroids in a chronic, relatively asymptomatic condition should be discouraged. Some patients derive benefit from salicylic acid 1–2 per cent in an aqueous cream base, while others find coal tar or ichthyol 1–2 per cent in zinc paste helpful. The use of broad spectrum antifungal preparations such as clotrimazole, miconazole, or econazole may also be beneficial.

Adverse reactions to topical preparations are common, as many of these patients find even weak preparations of tar or salicylic acid to be irritant. The persistent scalp lesions can be treated with weak concentrations of salicylic acid (1–5 per cent) either in aqueous cream as a hair-dressing for men or in higher concentrations for 8–12 hours before shampooing for women. These will generally control the scaling, but erythema and discomfort of the scalp may necessitate intermittent application of a steroid lotion or gel (e.g. Betnovate scalp application, Diprosalic scalp lotion).

DERMATITIS ARTEFACTA

The term 'dermatitis' is used inappropriately to describe this disease, as it does not aetiologically belong to the dermatitis/eczema group of disorders. A more accurate descriptive term is 'cutaneous artefactual disease' and it is discussed further on p. 255.

PATIENT ASSOCIATION

The Eczema Society is a large and well organized self-help group with branches in many countries. Although initially mainly composed of patients with atopic eczema or parents of children with this problem, the membership is now wider. Useful newsheets and information are produced at regular intervals.

GROWTH POINTS

1 *Atopic dermatitis.* The observed defects in cell mediated immunity in patients with atopic dermatitis have led to the search for a specific T lymphocyte defect. Current studies suggest that T suppressor lymphocyte numbers and function are low in these patients. This relative lack of T suppressor cells could also explain the high levels of IgE seen in these patients.

2 *The Langerhans cell and allergic contact dermatitis.* The evidence that the epidermal Langerhans cell has many of the features of a macrophage has led to the theory that it is responsible for antigen presentation of material absorbed through the epidermis. Studies on experimental models of nickel dermatitis have demonstrated the avidity of the cell for such molecules and movement of the Langerhans cell from the epidermis to the draining nodes is postulated. Study of this chain of events should lead to a clearer understanding of the events taking place during the development of hypersensitivity to an allergen and possibly thereafter to means of inducing tolerance. This is obviously of great importance in the prevention and treatment of allergic contact dermatitis, but possibly of even greater long-term significance in approaching the problem of skin allografts for burns patients.

FURTHER READING

Cronin, E.: *Contact Dermatitis.* Churchill Livingstone, Edinburgh (1980).
    The current reference book in this field.
Epstein, E.: Hand dermatitis: practical management and current concepts. *Journal of the American Academy of Dermatology* 10, 395 (1984).
    A useful update on hand problems. 66 well-chosen references.
MacKie, R. M.: *Eczema and Dermatitis,* Positive Health Guide Series. Martin Dunitz, London (1983).
    An inexpensive paperback designed mainly for patients or parents of atopic children.

Larsen, W. G.: Perfume dermatitis. *Journal of the American Academy of Dermatology* **12,** 1 (1985).
An excellent review illustrating the current problems with sensitization to perfumes and cosmetics.

NOTES

6

Cutaneous infections and infestations

In Britain, Europe and North America the problem of cutaneous bacterial infection has decreased in recent years, and is now relatively easily controlled with topical and systemic antibiotics. It is still important, however, to be able to recognize and treat these conditions promptly. Unfortunately there has been no such decline in the incidence of viral or fungal cutaneous infections, although their control too is now easier with modern medicaments. Cutaneous infestation continues to be a problem of poor hygiene and overcrowding, and there is currently a rising incidence of various forms of sexually transmitted disease. All of these will be discussed in this chapter.

Bacterial infections

IMPETIGO

Definition. A superficial cutaneous infection caused by either staphylococci or streptococci.

Incidence and aetiology

Impetigo is nowadays a relatively rare disease although in situations where hygiene is poor and direct contact between individuals frequent, the causative organism can spread quickly, particularly between children, causing an outbreak of the disease.

The organisms commonly identified in impetigo are *Staphylococcus aureus* and group A streptococci. The disease is much commoner in children, and can present as a very thin-roofed, quickly ruptured blister, especially when caused by staphylococci.

Clinical features

The hallmark of impetigo is a lesion covered with a heavy honey-coloured crust. The face and hands are the sites of predilection. Lesions can develop with great rapidity, and may complicate a pre-existing skin condition such as atopic dermatitis or even acne (Fig. 6.1).

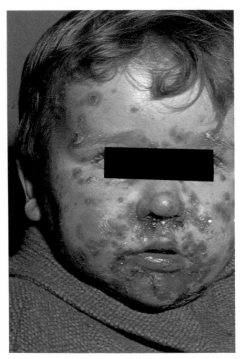

Fig. 6.1.   Staphylococcal impetigo superimposed on mild atopic dermatitis. Note gross honey-coloured crusting.

Management

Removal of crusts with warm saline or olive oil soaks and the application of a topical antibiotic, such as aureomycin or fucidin, are the essential points of management. The infection in impetigo is extremely superficial and therefore most cases will respond to these measures alone.

While the use of systemic antibiotics in impetigo is only essential if streptococci have been shown to be present, as the aim is to prevent post-streptococcal glomerulonephritis, it is common practice in the majority of severe cases to routinely prescribe full doses of oral penicillin or erythromycin. While, in theory, it is possible to swab the lesions and wait for a bacteriology result before deciding on whether or not an antibiotic is essential, in practice the result will rarely be available in time to avert streptococcal glomerulonephritis if streptococcus is causing the lesions.

ERYSIPELAS

Definition. A cutaneous streptococcal infection characterized by sharply demarcated unilateral lesions, commonly on the face.

Clinical features
Erysipelas presents as a bright red, brawny, oedematous area. The

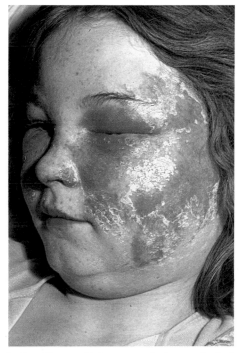

Fig. 6.2. Erysipelas. Note well-demarcated edge to the lesion. Response to oral penicillin within 24 hours is normal.

face is most frequently affected. The organism gains entry through a minor abrasion and infects the superficial lymphatic vessels. The lesions are unilateral, and associated with leucocytosis and fever 105 (Fig. 6.2, p. 105).

Diagnosis and treatment

Prompt response to full doses of oral penicillin is the most useful diagnostic test for erysipelas. Although swabs should be taken routinely for bacteriological confirmation, the results should not be awaited before starting therapy. Topical therapy other than simple hygiene is unnecessary.

In a proportion of cases recurrent erysipelas develops on the same site, leading in time to chronic lymphoedema. Management of this complication is difficult and, although long-term antibiotic therapy is used, results are not always satisfactory.

CELLULITIS

Definition. A cutaneous infection, usually due to streptococci, but with deeper involvement of the subcutis than in erysipelas.

Clinical features

Cellulitis presents as a raised, hot, tender, erythematous area of skin. The organism enters through a cut or abrasion, or a pre-existing dermatological disorder such as a leg ulcer. The affected area is larger and more diffuse than in erysipelas and the edges are not so well demarcated. Fever and leucocytosis are common. The draining lymph nodes are usually palpable and tender.

Diagnosis and treatment

Diagnosis is usually straightforward and therapy should be commenced immediately with full doses of a systemic antibiotic. Bacteriological swabs should be taken to identify the causative organism and to test for its antibiotic sensitivity. When these results are available the antibiotic can if necessary be changed. The initial choice of antibiotic will depend on the patient and his environment. In an otherwise healthy young person seen outside hospital the streptococcus is likely to be the cause and full doses of penicillin V are appropriate. On the other hand, in the elderly or in patients who have impaired immunity, a variety of organisms may be responsible and a broad-spectrum antibiotic (e.g. flucloxacillin) should be used. Blood cultures should be taken before starting therapy in this situation.

ERYTHRASMA

Definition. A cutaneous infection caused by *Corynebacterium minutissimum.*

Clinical features

Erythrasma causes an asymptomatic, reddish-brown area of skin, commonly in body flexures, particularly the groin. It does not appear to be contagious and, if untreated, it spreads slowly with a well demarcated advancing edge.

Diagnosis and treatment

Erythrasma can be diagnosed both by bacteriological identification of *Corynebacterium minutissimum* and by the coral-red fluorescence seen under Wood's light. Clinical confusion with a superficial fungal infection is resolved by these procedures.

Full doses of erythromycin by mouth (250 mg q.i.d. for 7 days) will effect a cure. Topical therapy is not essential, but fucidin ointment or Whitfield's ointment may accelerate clearance of lesions.

Tuberculosis of the skin

Although tuberculosis is now uncommon in Britain, it must still be recognized and promptly treated in the elderly, in the immunosuppressed, and in immigrant populations with less natural resistance to *Mycobacterium tuberculosis.* Current figures for the U.K. suggest that atypical forms of tuberculosis, involving the joints, the genitourinary system, and the skin, are becoming relatively commoner as classical respiratory tuberculosis declines.

LUPUS VULGARIS

Definition. The commonest form of cutaneous tuberculosis occurring after primary infection in individuals with good natural resistance to *M. tuberculosis*.

Incidence and aetiology

Lupus vulgaris (LV) is most common in the cool damp climate of Northern Europe and affects females more often than males. Children are frequently affected and in the elderly it may present with reactivation of old lesions following inadequate treatment in the past.

Pathology

Discrete, well-formed, tuberculoid granulomata are seen in the mid-dermis. Caseation is rare and the mycobacteria will only exceptionally be identified in Gram-stained sections, or by culture or guinea-pig inoculation.

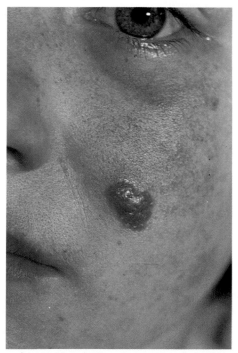

Fig. 6.3.   Lupus vulgaris. Note yellow-brown translucent tinge to lesion.

Clinical features (Fig. 6.3)

Lupus vulgaris most commonly affects the face and neck and is seen initially as firm, translucent, brown nodules. These are called 'apple jelly nodules' because of their appearance on *diascopy*. This is gentle pressure on the lesion with a transparent glass slide or coverslip to impede local blood flow.

Untreated, the lesions will slowly spread laterally, giving rise to disfiguring scarring and contractions. Malignant change has been reported in these scars, even in patients who have not received therapeutic X-rays or large doses of UV light in the past (Fig. 6.3).

Diagnosis and treatment

Biopsy should be performed to confirm the diagnosis and then the patient should receive full antituberculous therapy for at least one year. At least two antituberculous drugs should be used, and if there is any doubt about the organism's sensitivity or any delay in response to therapy, three drugs should be given. The current drugs of choice are rifampicin, isonicotinic acid hydrazidc (INAH), and para-amino salicylic acid (PAS). Local ultraviolet light as supportive topical therapy is of doubtful value, but plastic surgery may be needed eventually to correct the disfiguring contracted scars caused by the condition.

SCROFULODERMA

Definition. Cutaneous tuberculosis due to spread of the organisms via sinuses from underlying caseous lymph nodes.

Recognition is easy as *M. tuberculosis* can be identified both in the nodes and in the material draining onto the skin surface.
Full antituberculous therapy is required.

LEPROSY

Air travel and the presence of a large immigrant population in parts of the U.K. make it important for both the family practitioner and the dermatologist to be familiar with the commoner modes of presentation of leprosy. Although the condition is rare in Europe and North America, the epidemiological consequences of undiagnosed cases of leprosy can be far-reaching.

Infection with *Mycobacterium leprae* produces a range of clinical reactions, the polar varieties being *tuberculoid* and *lepromatous*. The tuberculoid form is associated with low infectivity and a high degree of natural resistance to the organism, whereas the lepromatous type is associated with large numbers of easily identified micro-organisms, a high degree of infectivity, and little natural resistance to the mycobacteria. In between these two extremes lies a range of presentations combining features of both polar forms. Borderline or dimorphous leprosy and indeterminate leprosy are terms used to cover clinical presentations of this type.

Pathology

In tuberculoid leprosy well-formed granulomata invade the dermis from within the nerve trunks which are the primary site of infection. Cutaneous nerves may have been destroyed by this process and a search for *M. leprae* is generally unrewarding.

In lepromatous leprosy the granulomata generally lie deeper in the dermis and contain a large proportion of foamy histiocytes (macrophages). *M. leprae* are present in large numbers in these cells and can be easily identified with special stains (e.g. Ziehl–Neelsen).

Clinical features

In tuberculoid leprosy the brunt of the infection is borne by peripheral nerves and the cutaneous manifestation is likely to be an anaesthetic macule or plaque with pigmentary changes. On white skin this may show as an erythematous or brown discoloration, and on coloured skin depigmentation is commonly seen. Palpable peripheral nerves may be identified adjacent to the plaque. As skin appendages are damaged by the process, sweating and hair growth are diminished or absent. The lesions tend to develop adjacent to scars and vaccination sites, and they are sparse in the pure tuberculoid type (Fig. 6.4).

In borderline cases the lesions are similar but more numerous.

In lepromatous leprosy macules, papules, nodules, and ulceration develop at sites where tissue temperature is low. Thus, the nostrils are frequently involved, leading to septal perforation, collapse of the nasal bones, and a characteristic deformity. Hair growth and sweating over the lesions is not impaired, and normal sensation is

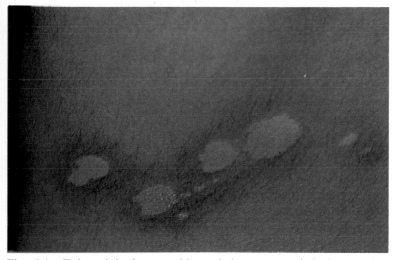

Fig. 6.4. Tuberculoid leprosy. Note obvious areas of depigmentation which were also anaesthetic.

preserved. A generalized thickening of the involved facial tissues gives rise to a leonine facies, and severe and intractable leg ulcers may develop.

Diagnosis and treatment

It is preferable to confirm the diagnosis and institute therapy at a centre which has some experience of the disease. A full-thickness skin biopsy, skin snips, a peripheral nerve biopsy, and the lepromin test are all diagnostic aids. The choice of which of these to use in individual cases depends on the clinical presentation.

Treatment is based on systemic sulphones, rifampicin, and clofazimine, and in the initial stages it can be complicated by reactions, particularly in lepromatous leprosy. As resistance to sulphones is now well recorded they are no longer the first line drugs of choice. The duration of treatments varies. The tuberculoid variety should be treated for 1–2 years after disease activity has ceased, but in the lepromatous variety treatment should continue for life. Children who are household contacts should be followed up as they can harbour the organism for many years and develop the disease in adult life. Adult contacts rarely become infected.

Viral infections

WARTS

Definition. Common benign cutaneous tumours initiated by the human wart virus.

Warts are usually self-limiting cutaneous tumours caused by a DNA virus, the human papilloma virus (HPV). They vary significantly in their clinical presentation and recently several different types of wart virus have been identified, some associated with specific clinical presentation (e.g. genital warts). The wart virus is transmitted by direct contact.

Common wart (Verruca vulgaris). These easily identified lesions are usually multiple, raised, hyperkeratotic, and are commonly found on the hands. They are particularly common in children aged 5–10 years and may be painful, especially when periungual. Common warts demonstrate the *Koebner phenomenon* and develop on sites of trauma.

Plane warts. These occur most frequently on the face and the backs of the hands. Each is a slightly raised circular or oval plaque. Despite their relatively banal appearance, they are surprisingly resistant to therapy (Fig. 6.5).

Plantar warts (Verruca plantaris). Constant pressure and friction on the soles prevents the normal outward expansion of warts in this site, and instead they grow inwards towards the dermis. Pressure on nerves can cause considerable pain. Children, sportsmen, athletes, and others who use communal showering facilities are particularly at risk.

Genital warts. These warts tend to develop in large clusters. They affect the penile and vulvar skin, mucous membrane, and also the perianal area. Lesions in this site are more common in homosexuals. Sexual partners should attend for examination and treatment, as otherwise reinfection is very common. All patients with perianal

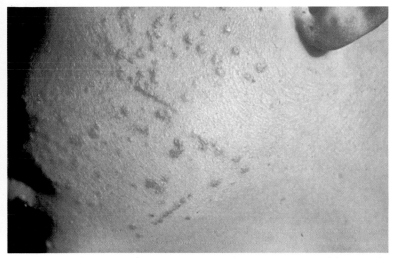

Fig. 6.5. Plane warts. Note the Koebner phenomenon caused by scratching.

warts should have a proctoscopic examination to exclude rectal involvement.

Pathology

Biopsy is rarely required to confirm the clinical diagnosis. The histopathology is, however, characteristic. Hyperkeratosis and acanthosis are accompanied by large numbers of keratohyalin granules in the Malpighian layer. Some epidermal cells are vacuolated and may also contain basophilic inclusions. The wart virus can be clearly seen and identified by electron microscopy.

Diagnosis

Diagnosis of warts is usually straightforward. Occasionally, the periungual fibromata of tuberous sclerosis are misdiagnosed as periungual warts, but close examination and a search for other signs of this condition (p. 253) should clarify the situation. Plantar warts may be confused with either corns or, if haemorrhage into the lesion has occurred causing discoloration, with invasive malignant tumours such as malignant melanoma.

Paring down the lesion with a sharp scalpel blade can be of

diagnostic help as in plantar warts punctate bleeding points will be seen. In corns one sees only a thickened epidermis while in a malignant tumour such as melanoma dark friable vascular tissue will be revealed. If a malignant tumour is suspected the patient must be referred without delay for a diagnostic excision biopsy. It is preferable to excise unnecessarily the occasional plantar wart than to treat a malignant melanoma inappropriately.

Genital warts may be confused with condylomata lata of syphilis, and as both conditions are transmitted by sexual contact, they may co-exist. Full serological screening for venereal diseases should therefore be performed routinely on all cases of genital warts.

Treatment

A large proportion of *common warts* will involute spontaneously and therefore either no treatment or placebo treatment for the first 3–4 months after presentation is quite acceptable, particularly in the case of small children. If therapy is deemed necessary, a salicylic acid paint (e.g. 12 per cent salicylic acid, 10 per cent acetone, and collodion to 100 per cent, Salactol, Duofilm) is recommended. 114 Paints containing glutaraldehyde (Glutarol) are also useful. For lesions persisting despite a 3–4 month trial of such paints, cryotherapy with liquid nitrogen, or a slush of carbon dioxide snow and acetone can be used. Warts should be frozen for sufficient time to cause the surrounding skin to develop a white halo. Some discomfort is inevitable, and blistering may develop 24–48 hours after treatment. The procedure should be repeated at 3 weekly intervals until the warts are gone. Curettage, or electrocautery, or diathermy under local anaesthesia are standard methods for dealing with more persistent warts. Radiotherapy has been used in the past, but nowadays is not to be recommended even for persistent lesions.

With all forms of therapy the recurrence rate is relatively high.

Plane warts, particularly on the face, should be treated by bland, non-scarring preparations. Salicylic acid paints may accelerate spontaneous clearance.

For *plantar warts* slightly different methods are more likely to be successful. The first step is to pare away as much of the overlying hard skin as possible, and then apply salicylic acid or gluteraldehyde-containing paint (Salactol, Glutarol), and covering with occlusive plaster. In some countries 25–50 per cent podophyllin in liquid paraffin or white soft paraffin is used. This causes tissue necrosis if an occlusive bandage is kept in place for 10–14 days. The remaining wart virus-infected tissue can be curetted away after this period. Formalin soaks are also of value. The patient applies a protective layer of Vaseline to the surrounding normal skin, then immerses the wart for 10–20 minutes in a saucer containing 3–6 per cent formalin in an aqueous solution. This is repeated daily, and after 2–3 weeks warts become smaller and desiccated, and can be curetted out with ease and little pain.

Genital warts can be persistent and difficult to treat. Full vaginal and/or rectal examination should be performed to establish the extent of the problem before starting to treat the visible lesions. Cryotherapy can then be commenced, and used weekly or twice weekly for as long as is necessary. This is at present the best method of outpatient management, causing relatively little discomfort. Alternatively, daily applications for 3–4 days of podophyllin 25–50 per cent in soft paraffin is effective, but it leads to considerable maceration and discomfort. It is difficult to use on an out-patient basis.

Situations in which warts must be regarded as a more serious problem are pregnancy and immunosuppression. Young pregnant women with a few mild genital warts tend rapidly to develop large, fungating, cauliflower-like masses of lesions. The use of podophyllin in pregnant women is *not* recommended because of sporadic case reports of foetal damage. Early and efficient treatment of small lesions with cryotherapy is the treatment of choice.

In the immunosuppressed patient also warts can grow with alarming speed and give rise to major problems. Children on long-term chemotherapy for leukaemia, and other malignancies tend to develop large and very persistent lesions. Such patients should be treated promptly and effectively as spontaneous resolution is most unlikely to occur. It is also good practice to examine such children for warts prior to commencing chemotherapy and treat any lesions before further chemotherapy-induced immunosuppression develops. Very persistent warts in immunosuppressed patients may require specialist measures such as intralesional bleomycin or systemic interferon.

MOLLUSCUM CONTAGIOSUM

Definition. An infectious cutaneous lesion caused by a pox virus.

This benign, but troublesome condition is a common cause for dermatological out-patient referral in the under-fives, and occasionally in older children and adults. Multiple lesions are common in young children, but in adults isolated lesions, sometimes of considerable size, are more common.

Pathology

Biopsy is rarely required and is usually performed on a large isolated lesion to exclude other more serious conditions. The histological changes are confined to the epidermis and consist of acanthosis, hyperkeratosis, and an increase in the numbers of keratohyalin granules. As epidermal cells in the centre of the lesion are destroyed they are replaced by large amorphous eosinophilic structures, the molluscum bodies, which are the histological hallmark of this condition.

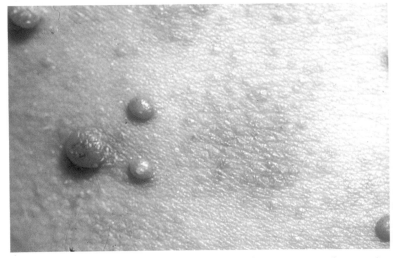

Fig. 6.6.   Molluscum contagiosum. Note central punctum, seen best on the largest lesion.

Clinical features

The lesions are most commonly seen on the face and neck, although the trunk may also be involved. The lesions are elevated, smooth, reddish papules and all have a small central punctum which is an important diagnostic point to be sought. Troublesome lesions may develop around the eyelids and at the vermilion border of the lip. In adults, isolated lesions may develop on any body site and in recent years crops of mollusca on genital skin have been seen more commonly (Fig. 6.6).

Diagnosis and treatment

Diagnosis is usually straightforward, but an isolated lesion may not be recognized until histological examination of curettings or of a biopsy.

The aim of treatment is to stimulate an inflammatory reaction in the dermis underlying the lesion. This can be achieved by puncturing the lesions individually with a curette or forceps, and applying iodine to the area. Liquid nitrogen or carbon dioxide/acetone slush can also be used, but are less effective.

ORF

Definition. A rapidly growing solitary cutaneous lesion caused by a pox virus.

Clinical features

The infection is contracted through contact with sheep, either directly or indirectly from barbed wire, grass, or other material adjacent to the animals. It is easily and quickly recognized by agricultural workers, country dwellers, and veterinary surgeons, but may dismay and alarm a town dweller who develops a rapidly expanding lesion on his hand 2 weeks after a visit to a farm in the country.

After an incubation period of 7–10 days a red papule develops, commonly on the sides of the fingers, rapidly grows, and finally reaches a size of 5–10 cm, with a central necrotic or bullous area. Lymphangitis, local lymphadenopathy, and fever are not uncommon. Spontaneous recovery takes place and one attack confers subsequent immunity.

Treatment

Topical antibiotics such as 3 per cent aureomycin ointment may prevent secondary infection but should this develop, a systemic antibiotic is recommended.

HERPES SIMPLEX

Definition. A cutaneous infection due to *Herpes virus hominis.*

Two types of *H. hominis* virus are currently recognized. Type 1 is the variety mainly responsible for recurrent 'cold sores' in the upper lip area, and type 2 is usually associated with genital herpes lesions. Carcinoma of the cervix is commoner in women with a high titre of antibody to the type 2 virus, but no putative or proven association with malignancy has yet been reported with the type 1 virus.

Primary infection with type 1 virus is almost universal in childhood or early adult life and is usually subclinical. Thereafter, most people have no further problems, but a few have exacerbations of *H. hominis* infection, usually on the upper lip, often in association with other viral infections. No specific immunological difference between these individuals and those without recurrent herpes simplex has yet been identified.

Pathology

The epidermis shows the significant changes. Gross intracellular oedema leads to balloon degeneration of the infected epidermal cells. The nuclei of these cells show specific intranuclear inclusions. Large multinucleate giant cells may also be seen in persistent infections.

Clinical features

The characteristic clinical picture of an active primary *H. hominis* type 1 infection is a miserable febrile child with a painful ulcerated mouth, and painful enlarged local lymph nodes (Fig. 6.7). The lesions persist for 3–6 days and subside spontaneously. They consist of a group of small blisters on the skin surface as well as on the buccal mucous membrane. If the cornea is involved, immediate ophthalmological care should be instituted, as corneal scarring and ulceration are common sequelae. *Herpetic whitlow* or inoculation herpes simplex is common in hospital workers and results from the virus entering through a small abrasion, usually on the fingers. Frequently misdiagnosed as a pyogenic lesion, it consists of a painful, indurated, and tender area, topped by blisters which initially are filled with clear fluid. Occasionally, primary infection on the trunk may have a linear distribution and cause confusion with herpes zoster.

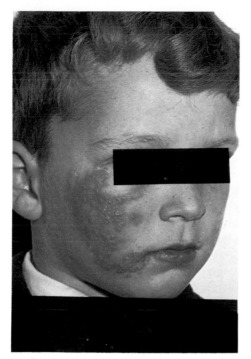

Fig. 6.7. Herpes simplex. Primary infection in an 8-year-old boy.

Recurrent herpes simplex attacks are ushered in by a tingling sensation, and then tender, painful lesions appear, usually on the upper lip.

Diagnosis and treatment

If there is doubt clinically, a thick smear from the surface of the lesion should be examined in the electron microscope to identify quickly the viral particles. Blood samples can be taken both at the time of presentation and 10–14 days later to demonstrate a rise in titre of antibody to the virus.

Management of severe primary infection is largely supportive, to maintain an adequate fluid balance. If necessary, systemic antibiotics can be administered to control secondary infection.

Recurrent herpes simplex lesions are difficult to control and impossible at present to prevent. The use of a spirit paint, a povidone iodine paint, or a specific antiviral agent such as 5–10 per cent idoxuridine in dimethylsulphoxide have all been recommended, but are of value in cutting short an attack only if used at the first hint of prodromal tingling or pain, and certainly before any epidermal damage is clinically apparent. Currently, povidone iodine (10 per cent) paint can be recommended as a relatively inexpensive application. The availability of the specific antiviral agent *acyclovir* has improved treatment for recurrent herpes simplex infections. Topical acyclovir is of little value, but oral or intravenous acyclovir given at the first sign of recurrent infection will diminish the duration and severity of the attack.

Herpes simplex infection in the immunosuppressed and in patients with atopic dermatitis can be serious and potentially life-threatening. Hospitalization and prompt supportive care are matters of urgency and systemic antiviral agents such as acyclovir may be required. It is important to protect these two groups of patients from herpes simplex infection and mothers of children with atopic dermatitis should be warned that persons with cold sores are hazardous to their child. At the present time in Britain, Kaposi's varicelliform eruption in patients with atopic dermatitis is usually due to herpes simplex. Once again systemic acyclovir has greatly improved the outlook for patients with this condition.

HERPES ZOSTER (shingles)

Definition. A cutaneous infection caused by the chickenpox virus, *Herpesvirus varicellae.*

Herpes zoster is a disease of adult life and old age, being very rare in children and healthy young adults. As with other viral infections, however, it can develop in a virulent and fulminating form in those who are immunosuppressed either by disease or by therapy. Patients with Hodgkin's disease are particularly prone to develop herpes zoster.

Pathology

As in herpes simplex, the striking histological feature of herpes zoster is balloon degeneration—the presence of grossly swollen, distorted cells in the epidermis. Because these two diseases have a similar histological appearance, clinical doubt about the diagnosis should be resolved by serology rather than by biopsy.

Clinical features

After a prodromal period of pain, usually in a dermatome distribution, malaise, and sometimes pyrexia, a linear erythematous band develops on this dermatome, usually on the trunk. Groups of small blisters then develop on the erythema. Some of these may become secondarily infected, and local lymphadenopathy is common. Pain may appear to be out of proportion to the other clinical signs, and when it persists and evolves into post-herpetic neuralgia, it is extremely difficult to treat (Fig. 6.8).

Certain clinical varieties require special management. These include involvement of the ophthalmic division of the trigeminal nerve, leading to ocular damage and the Ramsey–Hunt syndrome when the geniculate ganglia are affected, causing pain and blistering of the external ear. Involvement of the first and second sacral

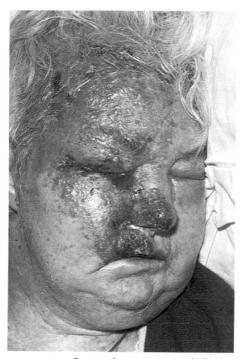

Fig. 6.8. Herpes zoster. Severe herpes zoster infection involving the trigeminal nerve.

ganglia may cause severe ulceration in the genital region and urinary retention. In the elderly, unfit, or immunosuppressed, more than one dermatome may be involved and when zoster is disseminated, it carries a significant mortality.

Diagnosis and treatment

The clinical appearance is usually diagnostic, but occasionally examination of a thick smear in the electron microscope, or serology, is required. Treatment of a classical case is symptomatic, and consists of bed rest, simple analgesics, maintenance of fluid balance, and soothing topical (drying) applications of lotions such as povidone iodine or ichthyol 1 per cent in oily calamine lotion. Topical steroids should *not* be applied to this or to any other lesion in which actively growing virus is present. Spontaneous resolution in 7–10 days can be confidently predicted.

In patients in poor health or immunosuppressed the administration of gamma globulin at the start of an attack may shorten the natural course of the disease, but in fulminating herpes zoster in an immunosuppressed patient it may be necessary to use specific systemic antiviral agents such as acyclovir (Zovirax).

The management of post-herpetic neuralgia is unsatisfactory. A 7–10-day course of systemic corticosteroids may help some otherwise healthy patients, but in others the pain is persistent and severe, and neurosurgical intervention may have to be considered.

Fungal infections

Two main groups of fungi infect man. The one comprises the *Candida* group of yeasts, the other the *dermatophytes. Candida albicans* is the most common species responsible for human infection and of the dermatophytes, *Trichophyton rubrum, Trichophyton mentagrophytes* var. *interdigitale, Trichophyton tonsurans*, and *Epidermophyton floccosum* are the commonest pathogens in the U.K. All these dermatophytes are transmitted directly from one human host to another. However, humans can contract animal ringworm from domestic animals, the usual dermatophytes responsible being *Microsporum canis* and *Trichophyton verrucosum*.

Pityriasis versicolor, due to a yeast, *Malassezia furfur*, is a superficial infection and will be discussed in this section.

CANDIDA INFECTIONS (candidiasis, thrush)

Candida albicans is a normal commensal of the gastrointestinal tract, and can be grown from apparently healthy normal mouths and perianal skin. In the very young, the elderly, and in those whose natural microbiological flora has been disturbed by disease, or by therapy such as antibiotics, it may become a pathogen.

Pathology

Candida albicans exists both as yeasts and in hyphal form. In pathological conditions budding yeasts and pseudohyphae are easily seen, and best visualized by staining with periodic acid Schiff (PAS). They lie in the stratum corneum. Persistent lesions may be associated with abscess formation, acanthosis, and, in more severe cases, with a granulomatous reaction.

Clinical features

Cutaneous lesions due to *Candida albicans* present in infants as napkin candidiasis and in the elderly as intertrigo affecting the submammary folds, the axillae, and the groins (Fig. 6.9). In both situations the lesions are a glazed brick-red and are characterized by

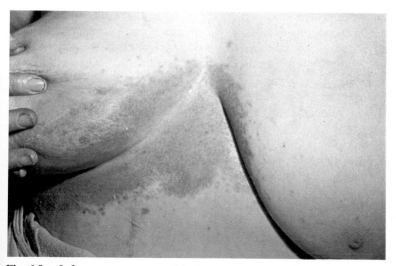

Fig. 6.9. Inframmammary candidosis in an obese diabetic patient.

'satellite lesions' and occasionally pustules around the main area of involvement. These are isolated individual lesions which have the same colour and appearance as the main lesion. Painful fissures frequently develop in the affected body folds and may be resistant to therapy.

In those whose hands are habitually immersed in water, candidal paronychia is an occupational hazard. Initially, the protective cuticle between nail and nail fold is lost, allowing *Candida* to invade the space thus created. The resulting inflammation produces a 'bolstered' posterior nail fold from which beads of pus can be expressed.

Chronic candidal granuloma, most commonly on the lips, may develop in patients who have a long history of candidiasis. This consists of a firm, indurated area and must not be mistaken for a developing malignancy.

Lesions due to *Candida* on the mucous membranes may involve the mouth, the urogenital area, the oesophagus, and the alimentary tract. Oral candidiasis produces adherent white patches on the tongue and inner surfaces of the cheeks. If scraped off, a raw bleeding area will be revealed. In the elderly these lesions are fairly common under dental plates and may be very difficult to cure as the plate itself is frequently colonized by the organism. Candidal vulvovaginitis causes an irritable erythema associated with a copious discharge. There is no convincing evidence that oral contraceptives predispose to this condition, but pregnant and diabetic women are more at risk. *Candida* infecting the bronchial or alimentary mucous membranes is less common but should always be borne in mind when infants with napkin *Candida* have persistent diarrhoea.

Generalized systemic infections due to *Candida* are rare and usually associated with intense immunosuppression or antibiotic therapy. Chronic mucocutaneous candidiasis is rare, but of great interest to dermatologists and immunologists as it appears to be an excellent model for establishing the relative value of cell-mediated and humoral immunity in the host response to *Candida*.

Diagnosis and treatment

All lesions thought to be due to *Candida* should be swabbed and examined for the presence of the organism. In typical cases this serves merely to confirm a clinical impression, but in less classic presentations it is essential. It must be remembered, however, that the presence of the organism does not of necessity imply a pathogenetic role, and also that *Candida* may colonize a pre-existing skin condition such as seborrhoeic dermatitis and cause an opportunistic secondary infection rather than primary disease.

Treatment depends firstly on removing the damp, moist, warm microclimate in which *Candida* thrives. Thus napkin candidiasis will not clear as long as the infant is swathed in damp napkins beneath occlusive plastic pants. Similarly, obese females with pendulous breasts will retain their inframmammary *Candida* as long as the two apposing skin surfaces remain in close contact, Soaks or swabs should therefore be used to separate skin folds in such situations.

Moist lesions on skin or mucous membrane will respond rapidly to gentian violet 0.5–1.5 per cent in aqueous solution. This is effective, but understandably unpopular among out-patients because of the persistent blue staining on both skin and clothing. The same applies to Castellani's paint (magenta 0.4 per cent and phenol 4 per cent with boric acid, resorcinol, acetone, industrial methylated spirit, and water), another useful preparation. The more modern colourless preparations, such as econazole lotion or spray or clotrimazole solution are therefore more likely to be used. For drier lesions nystatin ointment or miconazole cream are effective. *Candida* paronychia is relatively slow to respond to therapy, but good results will be achieved by instructing the patient to work nystatin ointment well into the nail fold and to keep the hands dry. If working conditions necessitate rubber gloves, a separate pair of cotton gloves should be worn next the skin and changed frequently. 'Denture mouth' due to *Candida* requires concomitant treatment of the mouth with nystatin suspension, miconazole gel, or amphotericin B lozenges and also nightly soaking of the dentures in an antifungal solution.

Infants with persistent napkin *Candida* should be given oral nystatin drops as a high proportion will have involvement of the alimentary tract.

Topical steroids are an excellent growth medium for *Candida* and are contraindicated.

In the past few years a new systemic antifungal agent, ketoconazole (Nizoral), has become available. Extensive studies of its *in vivo* activity suggest that it is very effective against *Candida*, but is less effective against dermatophytes. Initial enthusiastic prescribing of ketoconazol has recently been modified after reports of non-reversible hepatic toxicity in a very small number of patients given ketoconazole, usually for periods of months to treat persistent nail infections. At present patients should be very carefully selected for either long- or short-term ketoconazole therapy. Patients with the rare, but life-threatening problem of chronic mucocutaneous candidiasis respond very well to oral ketoconazole, and for those with chronic paronychia non-responsive to topical anti-*Candida* therapy, a 2–month course of ketoconazole is justified. Patients receiving oral cytotoxics or corticosteroids in high doses who develop secondary oral candidosis also merit short-term oral ketoconazole therapy if topical therapy is not effective. A short course of the drug is also extremely effective in clearing persistent vaginal candidosis. The recommended dose of ketoconazole is 200 mg daily. Patients receiving oral ketoconazole must avoid pregnancy, should avoid alcohol, and should have regular liver function tests carried out.

DERMATOPHYTE INFECTIONS

Definition. Cutaneous lesions due to dermatophytes, presenting most commonly as athlete's foot, nail infections, tinea corporis, and scalp ringworm.

Pathology

These pathogenic fungi inhabit the keratinized tissue of skin, hair, and nails, and generally do not invade living tissue. In active infections they are seen as branched hyphae. They grow down the pilosebaceous follicles towards the hair bulb, but are arrested before reaching the bulb itself and fan out to form multiple hyphal fronds known as *Adamson's fringe*. The hair shaft is invaded.

Dermatophytes can be seen on *direct examination* by taking skin scrapings or nail clippings from the affected area and mounting them on a slide with coverslip in 10–20 per cent potassium hydroxide, which is gently warmed and examined microscopically. To identify the particular dermatophyte present it is necessary to culture the samples for up to 3 weeks on a suitable medium such as Sabouraud's. These techniques rather than biopsy constitute the correct method of identifying fungi, but if it is necessary to look for fungi in a histological section it should be stained with periodic acid

Schiff (PAS) or methenamine silver to show them in the stratum corneum.

Clinical features

Tinea pedis (athlete's foot). This common condition is found in adolescents and young adults, particularly those who use communal changing facilities, showers, and swimming pools. The usual site of infection is the toe webs, especially the fourth, where moist, white 'blotting-paper' skin will be seen. Pruritus is common. The instep, and in persistent cases the nails, may also be involved and therapy then poses considerable difficulties (Fig. 6.10).

The organisms most commonly found are *Trichophyton rubrum, Trichophyton mentagrophytes* var. *interdigitale*, and *Epidermophyton floccosum*.

Tinea corporis (ringworm). Infection of the trunk frequently begins in the body folds such as the groins or axillae and presents as an itchy erythematous area with a raised advancing edge. Scrapings will be most likely to yield positive results if taken from this edge.

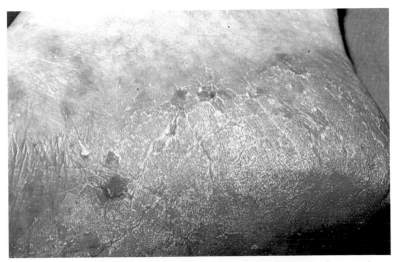

Fig. 6.10. Tinea pedis involving the instep and heel. *Trichophyton rubrum* was cultured from scrapings.

Diagnosis is not always straightforward. Isolated scaling lesions on the trunk may resemble psoriasis. If tinea corporis has been treated with topical steroids, its presentation may be atypical. Persistent hand dermatitis may be due to dermatophytes, most commonly *Trichophyton rubrum*, in which case the palm is dry with itchy, scaly creases. Mycological examination should be routine in such circumstances.

Dermatophyte infection of the hair shaft on the scalp or beard area may be due to *T. tonsurans*, *M. canis*, *T. rubrum*, or *T. verrucosum* (Fig. 6.11). Usually, the first sign is a well-circumscribed pruritic scaling area of hair loss, with a variable inflammatory response. Suspected hair infection should always be examined under Wood's light (ultraviolet light > 365 nm) as lesions due to *M. canis* and *M. audouinii* will show a diagnostic brilliant green flurescence. Those

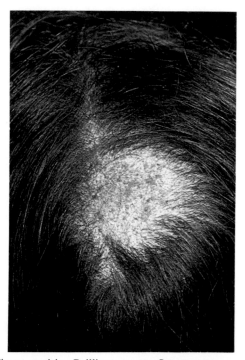

Fig. 6.11. Tinea capitis. Brilliant green fluroescence was seen under Wood's light and *Microsporum audouinii* isolated in culture.

due to *Trichophyton* species do not give rise to this degree of fluorescence, although *T. schoenleinii* causes a dull green flurescence and gives rise to the distinctive clinical entity called *favus*. This condition is now most common in North America, around the Mediterranean and in the Middle East. The characteristic features are extensive—even complete—hair loss, scalp atrophy leading to permanent alopecia, and the presence of adherent scales (scutulae) on the remaining hairs. Infection of the hair shaft with *T. verrucosum* may cause a very brisk inflammatory reaction, termed a *kerion*, seen commonly in children after contact with cattle or other domestic animals. There is a dramatic, acute folliculitis with pustules and swelling forming a boggy mass on the scalp. Hair loss and eventual scarring alopecia are common, but one attack usually confers subsequent immunity.

Diagnosis and treatment

Direct microscopy of scrapings in potassium hydroxide and the use of Wood's light in the clinic or consulting room will immediately confirm the clinical diagnosis in a high proportion of dermatophyte infections. The remainder will require culture of skin scrapings or nail clippings. Any persistent scaling lesions should be scraped and examined in this way as atypical fungal infections may mimic psoriasis, seborrhoeic dermatitis, or mycosis fungoides. Overdiagnosis of dermatophyte infections may also occur, particularly in the case of lesions on the feet when the true cause may be simple maceration from hyperhidrosis or allergic contact dermatitis to footwear. Any persistent lesions on the feet which do not respond to antifungal therapy should be carefully reviewed, particularly if there is no involvement of the interdigital clefts.

Cutaneous dermatophyte infections should be treated with topical antifungal preparations. Moist lesions require a drying agent such as a magenta paint (magenta 0.4 per cent and phenol 4 per cent in spirit Castellani's paint or, if a colourless preparation is preferred, econazole, or miconazole lotion, or spray. Drier lesions will respond better to creams or ointments, Miconazole and econazole are useful preparations (Daktarin, Ecostatin, Dermonistat, Exelderm).

Oral griseofulvin, which is effective against dermatophytes, but not *Candida* species, should be reserved for more severe cutaneous infections involving body sites other than or in addition to the interdigital clefts. It is, however, the treatment of choice for widespread or persistent tinea corporis, tinea capitis, and tinea unguium. The dose is 500 mg–1 g of griseofulvin daily for adults. This should be given orally during a fatty meal. Duration of treatment varies with site of involvement, but in general 4–6 weeks for scalp and body lesions, and 6 months, or until mycological cure, for finger nails is recommended. Established toe-nail infection is almost impossible to eradicate as toe nails take 18–24 months to grow out completely. 130 Even if systemic griseofulvin is given for this period, infection in the nail bed may not be eradicated. In such cases avulsion of the toe nails and systemic griseofulvin for 18–24 months offers the greatest hope of cure. Ketoconazole is less effective than griseofulvin in this situation.

Prevention of tinea pedis can to a large extent be achieved by simple hygiene, footbaths, and the use of an antifungal dusting powder after using communal baths and showers.

PITYRIASIS VERSICOLOR

Definition. A persistent, usually asymptomatic, fungal infection of the trunk due to *Malassezia furfur*.

This infection is relatively common in tropical countries and is seen with increased frequency in Britain during spells of hot humid weather. The causative organism is known as *Pityrosporum orbiculare* in its yeast-like form, and as *Malassezia furfur* when it becomes hyphal. These hyphae and yeasts can be recognized in skin scrapings, or Scotch tape strippings, or on biopsy material using PAS stain. The hyphae are found in the horny layers and there is little underlying reaction.

Clinical features
The lesions are asymptomatic, mainly on the trunk and proximal parts of the limbs, with a fine superficial scale seen best after gently scraping the surface with a fingernail. Untanned white Caucasian skin shows an increase in pigmentation in the affected areas with a yellowish-brown scale, but in darker skin or heavily tanned skin there is depigmentation. The overall effect is a dappled appearance (Fig. 6.12).

Diagnosis and treatment
Skin scrapings for direct microscopy and examination under

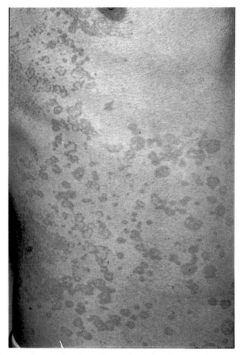

Fig. 6.12. Pityriasis versicolor. On pale skin these lesions appear as darker macules, but paradoxically on darker skin some depigmentation is seen.

Wood's light for pale yellow fluorescence can both be used to 131 identify the organism. Vitiligo (p. 183) is frequently confused with pityriasis versicolor and scrapings should be taken from all atypical cases.

Many topical preparations have been recommended for therapy, but recurrences are common. Useful preparations are 2.5 per cent selenium sulphide suspension applied once overnight to the whole body and washed off after 12 hours. Clotrimazole solution, miconazole cream, and econazole cream and lotion are also effective, but more expensive remedies. Benzoic acid-salicylic acid ointment (Whitfield's ointment) is a traditional remedy now to a large extent superseded by these more modern preparations. Oral ketoconazole given for 1 week should be reserved for persistent recurrences.

To minimize reinfection, clothes, bed clothes, and bath towels should be boiled and all family members with lesions treated simultaneously.

Cutaneous infestations

The Commonest infestations in man are due to lice and scabies.

SCABIES

Definition. A persistent pruritic skin eruption caused by cutaneous infestation with the mite *Sarcoptes scabei.*

The female inhabits a burrow in the stratum corneum and eventually dies after laying her eggs there. The eggs hatch and the new generation matures in 14 days, when the cycle is repeated.

The incidence of scabies varies on a world scale with hygiene, housing conditions, and population movements. Epidemics are associated with world wars, and recent local increases in incidence in Europe have been attributed to changing social habits and increasing body contact. Frequently, whole households and infested, although only one member may complain of symptoms.

Pathology

A local hypersensitivity reaction to the female scabies mite is assumed to cause release of lymphokines and other substances, giving rise to severe and persistent itch.

If scabies lesions are biopsied, usually in error, the female mite and her eggs may be seen in a burrow high in the stratum corneum. Occasionally, nodular lesions persist after successful therapy and these consist of a chronic inflammatory reaction with many lymphocytes in the dermis.

Clinical features

Patients complain bitterly of severe and persistent itch, worse after bathing and at night. In those who have a high standard of personal hygiene, lesions may be very sparse, but the classical sites of involvement are the finger webs, the sides of the fingers, the flexor aspects of the wrists, the points of the elbows, the anterior axillary fold, the periumbilical area, the penile or scrotal skin in males, and the areolae of the nipple in females (Fig. 6.13). In infants who are not yet walking, striking involvement of the soles is common (Fig. 6.14). The individual lesions may seem superficially to be excoriated

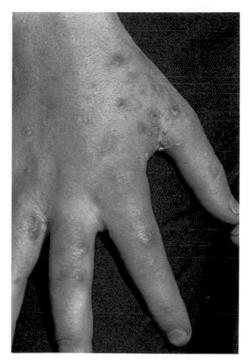

Fig. 6.13. Scabetic lesions on the hands. An acarus was extracted from the raised lesion on the third (middle) finger.

papules, but on closer inspection a linear burrow may be seen extending from this papule. The mite can frequently be extracted from this burrow with a needle, and painting the area with Indian ink, then washing off the excess on the skin surface will demonstrate dramatically the extent of the burrows. In long-standing cases secondary infection with pustule formation, crusting is common, and nodular lesions which persist for months after successful therapy may be seen. These are commonest on the buttocks and the male genitalia.

A moist oozing infected dermatitis may develop on top of scabetic burrows and dermatitic lesions on scabetic sites of predilection should be very carefully examined for underlying burrows.

Diagnosis and treatment

In all cases demonstration of the acarus by extracting it from a

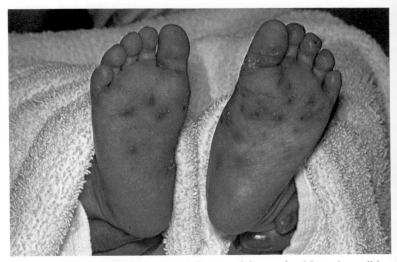

Fig. 6.14.   Scabetic lesions in an infant aged 9 months. Note the striking involvement of the soles of the feet.

burrow should be attempted as this is the cardinal diagnostic test. The most common mistake is to misdiagnose scabies either as contact dermatitis or as dermatitis herpetiformis. All cases of presumed scabies in which the acarus has not been identified, and which do not respond to therapy should be reassessed and biopsy considered.

The most useful acaricides are 1 per cent gamma benzene hexa-chloride, 25 per cent benzyl benzoate emulsion, and sulphur preparations. Sulphur preparations such as 2.5 per cent sulphur ointment are recommended in many centres for infants because of the risk of percutaneous absorption of the first two preparations. It is essential that the *entire body* from the neck to the soles of the feet be treated and that the hands are re-treated during the course of the 24 hours for which the preparation should remain on the skin. A 2-inch paintbrush or cotton wool swabs are useful applicators. After 24 hours the application can be washed off in a hot bath. If gamma benzene hexachloride is used, one application is adequate, but if benzyl benzoate is chosen, two or three applications should be applied, each at 24-hour intervals. Twenty-four hours after the last application the patient should bath, and all clothing and bed linen be washed. Boiling or fumigation is not required. Pruritus may continue for a few days even after successful therapy, and crotamiton cream will minimize this.

All household and other close contacts of a confirmed case of scabies should be warned that they are likely to be infested, and should be treated at the same time as the patient, even if they are asymptomatic. The usual cause of persistent scabies is either inadequate application of topical therapy or reinfestation from contacts. Written instructions to patients on how to treat themselves and their families will increase the likelihood of the correct procedures being followed.

PEDICULOSIS CAPITIS

Pediculosis capitis is a relatively common problem in schoolchildren in various parts of the world, and at present it is prevalent in certain large cities in the U.K. Pediculosis corporis is less common, and is most frequently seen in vagrants and others living in very poor social circumstances.

The well-known nit is a head louse egg, stuck firmly to scalp hair by its capsule. Nits may look like fine adherent dandruff particles. There are no associated symptoms until the louse hatches, when an irritant dermatitis on the scalp develops. Scratching leads to secondary impetiginization, particularly at the nape of the neck and behind the ears.

Diagnosis and treatment

Identification of the nit or of the adult head louse with the naked eye is straightforward. Shaving the head is not required, but cutting the hair short will facilitate treatment and lessen the risk of reinfestation.

Resistance of head lice to gamma benzene hexachloride is now reported from many centres, and to deal with this 'superlouse' 0.5 per cent malathion lotion, applied to the entire scalp and left for 12–24 hours, is recommended. The hair should then be shampooed and dead nits combed out. Treatment may have to be repeated after 7–10 days in a few cases. As with scabies, all affected family members should be examined and treated simultaneously if required. Other contacts in schools should also be checked for infestation.

PEDICULOSIS CORPORIS (body lice, vagabond's disease)

Patients infested with body lice usually present with pruritus, excoriations and secondary infection. Weals and erythematous macules may also be seen, but the source of the problem should be sought and identified by examining the seams of clothing worn next the skin. This is the site where they are likely to be found. In chronic cases striking pigmentation may be observed on the trunk and limbs.

Treatment

Infested clothing should be removed and fumigated with gamma benzene hexachloride or other parasiticide. The patient should be examined for concomitant infestation with scabies and head lice. One treatment with 0.5 per cent malathion to the body is recommended, followed by the use of a topical steroid/antibiotic preparation to accelerate relief of symptoms.

PEDICULOSIS PUBIS

The pubic louse is transmitted by close body contact and qualifies as a sexually transmitted disease. Patients complain of pruritus and have the characteristic blue-black 'dots' in their pubic hair. These are the pubic lice, engorged after sucking blood from their host.

Treatment

One or two applications of gamma benzene hexachloride lotion will kill the lice. Sexual partners should be treated simultaneously.

The sexually transmitted diseases

In most European countries, dermatology and venereology are combined specialities, but in the U.K. the two subjects are divided into separate specialities. In practice, however, patients with venereal disease may well present initially to a dermatological clinic. A brief mention of the cutaneous manifestations of syphilis and gonorrhoea is therefore included in this chapter. For a more comprehensive account the reader is referred to a specialist textbook.

SYPHILIS

The patient with syphilis may present with dermatological manifestations in any of the three stages of infection. In the primary stage there is a *primary chancre* at the site of sexual contact and from it the causative organism, the *Treponema pallidum*, can be isolated. Local lymphadenopathy is common. Four to eight weeks after an untreated primary chancre, secondary syphilis will develop. The dermatological reaction consists of a maculopapular, sometimes lichenoid, rash which affects the whole body including the palms, soles, and mucous membranes. It is generally asymptomatic. Tertiary syphilis is fortunately much rarer than the other stages, but may present to the dermatologist as an isolated, painless, ulcerating lesion, a *gumma*.

The primary chancre. One to four weeks after infection a moist, ulcerating lesion develops on or near genital mucosa. The ulcer has a sharply demarcated edge, and is both indurated and infiltrated. As serology does not become positive until about 4 weeks after contact, all serological studies at this stage may be negative, but *T. pallidum* can be identified by dark field illumination of a thick smear from the ulcer. Untreated, 20–30 per cent of these patients will develop secondary syphilis.

Secondary syphilis. As secondary syphilis develops 4–8 weeks after primary infection, the primary chancre may still be visible when secondary lesions appear (Fig. 6.15). These are small maculopapules seen on the trunk and limbs, associated with generalized lymphadenopathy, and, if profuse, with *condylomata lata* on the genital mucosa. Lesions on the palms and soles are important in aiding clinical distinction from other dermatological disorders, such as pityriasis rosea and seborrhoeic dermatitis. Loss of scalp hair and eyebrows may be present, and the pattern of loss is described as 'moth-eaten'.

During this period all patients will have positive serology. *T. pallidum* may be identified in lesions, particularly of the mucosa, and a biopsy will show a perivascular infiltrate, often with many plasma cells, and endarteritis of the small vessels. In cases with untreated lesions, oedema is a common feature. The histological changes are

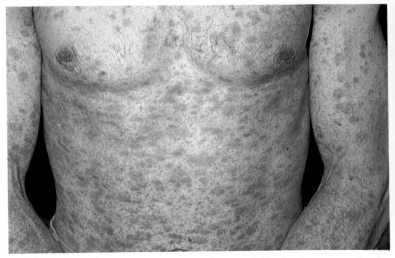

Fig. 6.15. Macular eruption of secondary syphilis. Lesions may also be seen on the palms of the hands.

non-specific, although suggestive, and therefore serology must be used for confirmation.

Tertiary syphilis. Cutaneous lesions of tertiary syphilis can appear after a latent period of many years, or even decades. At this stage serology is not reliable. Histologically, there is expansion of granulation tissue, stimulated by the presence of *T. pallidum*, through the dermis and epidermis, leading to ulceration. This is seen clinically as a *gumma*, a painless lesion whose healing is slow and incomplete, with scarring. On the oral mucosa this will ulcerate the soft palate, leading to perforation.

Treatment

Patients with primary or secondary syphilis should be treated with large doses of penicillin G. Commonly, 3–5 megaunits over 3–4 days are used. Sexual contacts should be traced and treated simultaneously.

GONORRHOEA

Cutaneous manifestations of infection with *Neisseria gonorrhoeae* are most commonly superficial erosions on the genital mucous membrane. They appear up to 14 days after sexual contact, and are associated with urethritis and a urethral discharge in men. Women, however, may be asymptomatic. The organisms can be identified on thick smears from the affected area.

Treatment

High doses of penicillin and contact tracing are the important points in management.

REITER'S SYNDROME

The triad of arthritis, urethritis and conjunctivitis is known as Reiter's syndrome. A proportion of patients have in addition gastrointestinal symptoms. Cutaneous involvement can occur and consists of heaped-up scaling lesions on the feet, termed *keratoderma blenorrhagica*, circinate balanitis, and occasionally lesions on the oral mucous membrane. No causative organism has yet been identified, and there is debate as to whether it should be grouped with sexually transmitted disease or with psoriasis as the lesions on the feet are strikingly similar to rupioid psoriasis both clinically and histologically (p. 37).

Treatment

Cutaneous lesions respond to conventional topical psoriasis therapy (p. 42) and the urogenital lesions to systemic tetracycline.

GROWTH POINT

Cutaneous lesion associated with the Acquired Immunodeficiency Syndrome (AIDS)

The early reports of the first cases of what is now known as AIDS came from New York and San Francisco. In the early cases a high proportion of cases suffered from Kaposi's sarcoma, a malignant proliferation of small vascular and/or lymphatic channels in the skin. The important point about AIDS-related Kaposi's sarcoma, which is at present seen in approximately half the patients reported with AIDS, is that the individual lesions are not the gross lesions of classic Kaposi's sarcoma which is endemic to certain parts of Africa.

Classical Kaposi's - older male of Mediterranean origin. Often associated c̄ long-term immuno-suppression (COPDers on prednisone; transplant patients)

In contrast, AIDS-related Kaposi's sarcoma lesions may be very small, insignificant, often solitary vascular papules. Because of this, and because of the current awareness and concern on the part of populations at increased risk of AIDS, family doctors and dermatologists may be asked to biopsy insignificant angioma-like lesions on the skin of these individuals. Histology is not always diagnostic. The availability of a test for the human T cell leukaemia virus III *140* (HTLV III) antibody will be of some value in this respect. A large number of other skin lesions have been reported in association with the AIDS complex, but most are relatively non-specific. Persistent *Candida* infection in an at risk patient is also a possibly associated factor and should arouse suspicion.

FURTHER READING

Alexander, J. O. D.: *Arthropods and Human Skin*. Springer-Verlag, Berlin (1984).
　A first class scholarly work with abundant references.
Bhutani, L. K.: *Colour Atlas of Dermatology*. Interprint, New Delhi, India (1982).
　This is an excellent collection of pictures of both common and rare skin diseases on coloured skin. Many illustrations are of skin infections.
Bunney, M. H.: *Viral Warts: Their Biology and Treatment*. Oxford University Press, Oxford (1982).
　A very useful small book by an individual who has many years experience of running a wart clinic.
Miller, D., Weber, J. and Green, J. (eds): *The Management of AIDS Patients*. Macmillan Press, Basingstoke (1985).
Nicholson, K. G.: Antiviral agents in clinical practice. *Lancet* **ii**, 736 (1984).
　A useful account of the indications for acyclovir therapy.
Roberts, S. O. B., Hay, R. J. and McKenzie, D. W. R.: *Infectious Diseases and Antimicrobial Agents: Volume 5*. Marcel Dekker, New York and Basel (1984).
　A readable introduction to diseases caused by fungi. Both laboratory and clinical aspects are covered.

NOTES

7

Autoimmune diseases and disorders of collagen and elastic tissue

The so-called 'collagen' or connective tissue diseases frequently present dermatologically and three of them, discussed in this section, have a relatively benign, purely cutaneous variant. The term 'collagen' disease is unfortunate and inaccurate, for among the diseases discussed in this chapter only systemic sclerosis and the Ehlers–Danlos syndrome have recognized biochemical abnormalities of collagen. The principal factor that several of the other diseases discussed here have in common is an unexpectedly high incidence of autoantibody formation. Currently, this is thought to be due to loss of suppressor T lymphocyte control of antibody production by B lymphocytes so that the term 'autoimmune' is more appropriate than 'connective tissue'.

Table 7.1 lists the conditions discussed in this chapter. Pseudoxanthoma elasticum (PXE) is discussed here as it occurs in association with the Ehlers–Danlos syndrome more frequently than can be attributed to chance. Although polyarteritis nodosa and its cutaneous variant are included in Table 7.1 they will be found in Chapter 8 under disorders of vasculature.

Lupus erythematosus (LE)

Lupus erythematosus exists in two varieties. The systemic form (SLE) can affect the skin, the joints, and the haemopoietic, cardiovascular, respiratory, and central nervous systems, and is well recognized by general physicians. The other form, chronic discoid lupus erythematosus (CDLE), is a purely dermatological disorder. The general rule is that patients have either SLE or CDLE, and in only 5 per cent or so of patients does CDLE progress to SLE.

Table 7.1. Connective tissue diseases

Systemic disease	Indeterminate	Cutaneous variant
Systemic lupus erythematosus		Chronic discoid lupus erythematosus
Systemic sclerosis	?'Mixed connective tissue disease'	'Scleroderma', morphoea
Polyarteritis nodosa	CRST† syndrome	Cutaneous polyarteritis
Dermatomyositis		—
Rheumatoid arthritis		—
—		Lichen sclerosus et atrophicus
—		Ehlers–Danlos syndrome
—		Pseudoxanthoma elasticum

†See p. 152.

Pathology

Cutaneous lesions in CDLE and SLE have similar pathological features and therefore cannot be distinguished one from another on skin biopsy alone.

Findings in the epidermis include hyperkeratosis, follicular plugging, and striking damage to the basal layer, in which the individual basal cells are destroyed by a process termed 'liquefaction degeneration'. The resulting deposit of amorphous material stains bright pink with conventional haematoxylin and eosin, and is termed a colloid body. Within the dermis there is a mixed infiltrate of lymphocytes and histiocytes, and the basal cell degeneration may be seen in the skin appendages, particularly the hair follicles. In certain rare forms of CDLE the pathological activity appears to be centred deeply around the skin appendages—the so-called subcutaneous or dermal CDLE.

The important differential diagnosis histologically is lichen planus, which may be indistinguishable on light microscopy. Immunopathological techniques more easily make the distinction.

Immunopathology

If frozen sections of skin from a *CDLE lesion* are treated with antibody raised against human IgG, IgM, and C_3, and linked to a fluorescent dye, a broad irregular band of fluorescence is seen in the region of the dermo-epidermal junction when the sections are examined under a fluorescence microscope (Fig. 7.1).

In SLE the situation differs in that deposits of immunoglobulin and complement are observed at the dermo-epidermal junction not only of clinically abnormal skin but also of clinically normal skin if taken from a sun-exposed site (e.g. wrist). Some SLE patients also have these deposits in clinically normal skin from covered sites (e.g. buttocks) and there are some indications that this is associated with a poor prognosis and renal complications of SLE.

In 80 per cent of patients with CDLE no circulating antinuclear antibodies are found, and DNA binding studies are therefore normal. The remaining 20 per cent may have circulating ANA, and it is within this group that the small fraction of patients who subsequently develop SLE are likely to be found. In contrast, 80–90

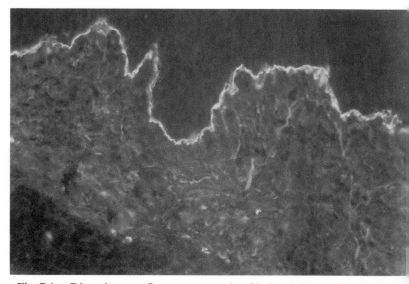

Fig. 7.1.   Direct immunofluorescence study of lesional skin in CDLE. Note the granular linear band of C_3 at the dermo-epidermal junction. IgM was also present in this site.

per cent of patients with SLE have circulating antinuclear antibodies in high titre and if these are present at serum dilutions of 1/256 or higher the DNA binding properties of the serum are also likely to be increased. Several different types of antinuclear antibodies exist and some are associated with specific clinical presentations.

SYSTEMIC LUPUS ERYTHEMATOSUS (SLE)

Women are more often affected than men, in a ratio of 8:1.

Paradoxically, SLE patients with this, the more serious and life-threatening form of the disease, have a less dramatic skin eruption than do CDLE patients. The classic SLE rash is a macular erythema over the cheeks and nose, the so-called 'butterfly area' (Fig. 7.2). This may be provoked by sun exposure, but a variety of drugs, listed in Table 7.2, are known to induce SLE, sometimes in association

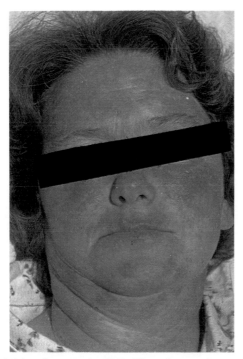

Fig. 7.2.   Facial involvement in SLE. There is macular erythema and no scarring results.

Table 7.2.   Some of the commoner drugs known to induce an SLE-like syndrome

Hydralazine	INAH
Methyldopa	Phenylbutazone
Griseofulvin	Procaine amide
Oral contraceptives	Sulphonamides
Penicillin	Diphenylhydantoin

with sunlight. The palms of the hands show a diffuse erythema (Fig. 7.3), not unlike that seen in patients with liver disease, and the backs of the hands may show a diffuse mottled pattern, particularly after sun exposure.

Patchy, diffuse hair loss is a common feature, but as there is no scarring or permanent damage to the hair bulbs, the hair will regrow normally after successful treatment.

These patients frequently have symptoms related to other systems, such as joint pain, fatigue, breathlessness, ankle swelling, and polyuria. Consequently, before they start treatment a detailed clinical and laboratory assessment is essential to establish the extent of disease involvement.

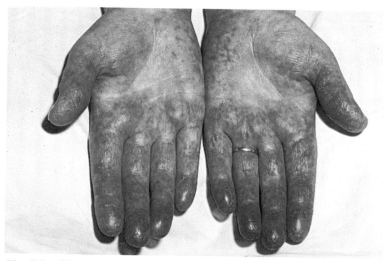

Fig. 7.3.   The palms in SLE. Note the erythema and telangiectasia.

Investigations

More specialized investigations will depend on the systems thought on the basis of history and clinical examination to be involved in the disease process, but the following are regarded as the minimum required to establish a baseline prior to therapy: e.s.r., haemoglobin, white blood cell and platelet counts (and, if indicated, bone marrow examination); blood urea, serum creatinine, and electrolytes; urinalysis, electrocardiogram, chest X-ray, and assessment of joint function; antinuclear antibody, rheumatoid factor, DNA binding, and complement screening profile (C_3 and C_4 levels, and CH_{50}). Other investigations (e.g. renal biopsy, brain scan, pulmonary function studies) may be required. Biopsy of skin, preferably of both an affected area and of clinically normal, but light-exposed skin, should be performed. These biopsies should be divided, one half being processed for routine histology and the other snap-frozen for immunopathological studies.

Diagnosis and treatment

In a patient who is obviously generally unwell, and who has a butterfly rash provoked by sunlight, SLE is a likely diagnosis. Antinuclear antibody and DNA binding determination are the most useful confirmatory laboratory tests. A careful drug history should be taken to exclude drug-induced SLE. Occasionally, other photosensitive eruptions may mimic SLE, but in these cases there is no systemic upset, and RNA and DNA binding will be normal.

Treatment of SLE is usually based on systemic corticosteroids together with, in some cases, an immunosuppressive agent such as cyclophosphamide, azathioprine, or chlorambucil as a steroid-sparing agent. The starting dose will depend on the patient's condition, but often a dose of 50–100 mg of prednisolone daily is required. It should be reduced as the patient's clinical condition improves. For monitoring disease activity DNA binding may be useful and a sudden rise may give warning of a relapse. Maintenance steroid therapy should be as low as possible to limit long-term side effects, and alternate-day regimes are of value. The addition of immunosuppressives is also helpful in this respect and some patients can be maintained on these drugs alone. Whichever regime is found best for the individual patient, all require careful fortnightly or monthly supervision to monitor activation of disease and to screen for treatment-induced side effects. Azathioprine, cyclophosphamide, and chlorambucil are most likely to produce haematological or renal toxicity, while hypertension, weight gain, glycosuria, and electrolyte imbalance are the principal hazards for the steroid-treated patient.

Topical therapy is a minor factor in managing these patients, although sun avoidance is important. A sun-screen with a sun protection factor (SPF) of 10 or more (e.g., Coppertone supershade 15, Roc A total sunblock) and a topical steroid by night may accelerate improvement of cutaneous lesions, even in patients receiving relatively high doses of systemic steroids.

CHRONIC DISCOID LUPUS ERYTHEMATOSUS (CDLE)

Definition. A chronic, relapsing and remitting, purely cutaneous disease mainly affecting light-exposed sites and characterized by plaques of scaling and erythema which progress to atrophy.

Patients with CDLE in the U.K. tend to present in the early spring and summer months. Females are affected twice as often as males.

Clinical features

Classically, CDLE affects the face, neck, scalp, and hands of young adults. The lesions are usually multiple and consist of raised, red, scaly, well-demarcated plaques (Fig. 7.4), although in the very early stages there may be only red, oedematous, raised areas. As the disease progresses new crops of lesions develop, commonly after sun exposure, while the older lesions heal with scarring, pigmentary change, and telangiectasia. Unlike SLE, lesions in the scalp can destroy the hair bulbs, leaving a permanent scarring alopecia. The scarred areas are often pigmented on white skin, but some loss of pigment is the rule in coloured skin. A proportion of patients have extensive lesions on the hands and feet, and some of these resemble chilblains. It is important to follow these patients carefully as they appear to have a strong tendency to develop SLE.

Diagnosis and treatment

Diagnosis is frequently made on clinical grounds, but should be confirmed by biopsy. The presence of red, scaly circular lesions on light-exposed skin is strongly suggestive and if a scale is removed

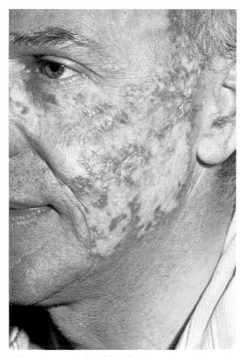

Fig. 7.4.   Facial involvement in CDLE. Contrast with Fig. 7.2 and note in this case scarring and pigmentary change.

from a lesion, its undersurface will show the pathognomonic plugs which have occupied the pilosebaceous follicles (the carpet tack scale). Biopsy will show a histology like that of SLE and lichen planus. Immunopathological findings are more specific. There is a coarse band of immunoglobulin, and usually also of C_3, in the region of the dermo-epidermal junction only in the areas of clinically affected skin. About 20 per cent of patients with CDLE will have circulating antinuclear antibody at titres of 1/16 or higher. This should alert the clinician that SLE may subsequently develop.

Initial treatment of CDLE consists of avoiding direct sunlight. Suitable clothing and the provision of a high SPF sun-screening agent (e.g., Roc 10 A + B, Spectraban 15). Topical treatment will suffice in some cases, one of these sun-screen preparations being used by day and a topical corticosteroid preparation at night. CDLE is one of the few exceptions to the rule that strong topical steroid preparations should not be used on the face, for it may well be necessary to use β-methasone 17-valerate 0.1 per cent (Betnovate, Valisone) or fluocinolone acetonide 0.025 per cent (Synalar, Fluonid). The use of a steroid-impregnated tape (Haelan tape), or intralesional steroid injections, may also be helpful.

In some patients systemic therapy is also required. The most useful group of drugs are the antimalarials chloroquine and mepacrine, but neither is without drawbacks. Mepacrine is probably less toxic, but causes a yellow discoloration of the skin. It should be used in a dose of 200–400 mg daily. Chloroquine should be given in similar doses, but only under strict ophthalmological supervision as a permanent retinopathy may develop. There is evidence that this is related to the total cumulative dose, and it is therefore essential to keep a careful record of the total quantity prescribed and to limit therapy to the spring and summer months. Even then, annual ophthalmological examination is mandatory.

Other complications of antimalarial therapy include pigmentation of the nails and palate, depigmentation of the hair, and exfoliating and lichenoid drug eruptions. Recently, the use of clofazimine (Lamprene) has been recommended. Experience with this drug is as yet limited.

Scleroderma

Scleroderma is the generic term for systemic sclerosis and morphoea. As with lupus erythematosus, there is a systemic form (systemic sclerosis) and a purely cutaneous or local form (morphoea). Unlike LE, however, the pathological features of the skin in the two forms are distinct and will therefore be considered separately.

SYSTEMIC SCLEROSIS (generalized scleroderma, acrosclerosis)

Definition. A systemic disease characterized by progressive accumulation of collagen, fibrosis, and loss of mobility of the skin and other organs, such as the respiratory and gastrointestinal tracts. The kidneys may also be involved and in rare cases this is fulminating and leads rapidly to death.

Pathology

The striking feature seen in fully developed systemic sclerosis is a reduction of the normal thickness of the dermis for the body site biopsied. Thus, the subcutaneous fat is seen to be much closer to the epidermis than is normally the case. Endarteritis and minor inflammatory changes are found around blood vessels in the dermis. In contrast to morphoea, skin appendages are generally present in normal numbers.

Clinical features

Females are more commonly affected (F:M = 4:1) and many initially have severe Raynaud's phenomenon. The affected hands and feet are initially swollen and have tight, slightly atrophic skin which is bound close to the subcutaneous tissue (Fig. 7.5). The soft tissue of the mouth and palate are similarly affected, causing denture wearers to complain of poorly fitting plates because the mouth gradually shrinks. The face is often characteristic, with a strikingly line-free forehead, a small beaked nose, a small mouth with radial furrowing around the lips, and, in advanced cases, multiple dilated capillaris

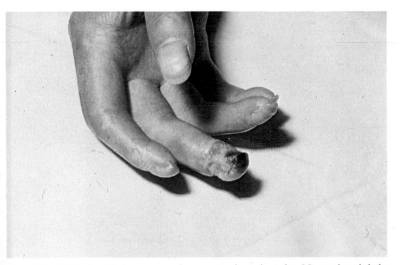

Fig. 7.5. The hand in progressive systemic sclerosis. Note the tightly bound skin, atrophy, and early gangrene in the middle finger.

(telangiectasia) (Fig. 7.6). Small calcified nodules may develop in longstanding cases, usually in the skin of the hands and feet. A variant of this disorder has been named the CRST or CREST *152* syndrome (C = calcification, R = Raynaud's disease, E = esophageal dysfunction, S = sclerodactyly, and T = telangiectasia) in which extensive multisystem involvement is said to be less common than in true systemic sclerosis.

Involvement of the gastrointestinal tract causes dysphagia and malabsorption through loss of peristalsis. Pulmonary involvement presents as dyspnoea and cardiovascular complications may lead to heart failure.

Laboratory findings

Most patients with progressive systemic sclerosis have high titres of circulating antinuclear antibody, usually of the speckled variety.

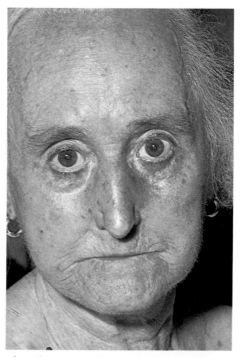

Fig. 7.6. The face in progressive systemic sclerosis. Note the unlined forehead, beaked nose, and radial furrowing around the mouth.

Radiologically, the jaw in dentulous patients shows a widened peridontal membrane, and the hands may show resorption of the distal phalanges and early flecks of subcutaneous calcification. On barium swallow there is loss of oesophageal peristalsis. Pulmonary function tests show impaired diffusion and serial renal function tests may show rapid renal failure, the most serious complication of this disorder.

Diagnosis and treatment

Diagnosis is often made clinically, simply on the appearance of the patient as she enters the clinic. Confirmatory tests include a skin biopsy, an autoantibody screen, hand and jaw X-ray, barium swallow, and respiratory function tests.

Treatment is largely symptomatic, but although there is little evidence that systemic steroids affect the course of this disease, they are certainly justified in patients with severe respiratory or renal involvement. The disease tends to progress slowly, but as some cases burn themselves out, it is difficult to assess the value of any therapeutic procedure. Hands and feet should be kept warm and regular professional chiropody offered. A trial of sympathetic blockade will indicate whether or not surgical sympathectomy is likely to be of value, but this is rarely the case.

Three preparations have recently been reported to be of value in the management of Raynaud's disease or Raynaud's phenomenon complicating one of the collagen disorders, usually systemic sclerosis or lupus erythematosus. These are the prostacyclins, ketanserin, and nifedipine (Adalat). The prostacyclins have been shown in small scale double blind studies to raise the temperatures of the hands and fingers, and bring about pain relief in patients with Raynaud's phenomenon. Initially, these were given intravenously, but oral preparations are now available. The 5-hydroxytriptamine receptor antagonist ketanserin has also been used in double blind studies in patients with both Raynaud's phenomenon and Raynaud's disease and significant improvement shown in both blood flow and skin temperature measurements. The dose required is 20 mg three times per day and no significant side effects are recorded.

Nifedipine, the calcium channel blocker, has also been reported to be of value in patients with Raynaud's phenomenon and Raynaud's disease. As yet there is no reported trial comparing these three new approaches in the management of Raynaud's disease.

MORPHOEA

Definition. A purely cutaneous disorder seen most commonly in children or young adults and characterized by the spontaneous appearance of a scar-like band or plaque on any body site.

Pathology

Loss of all skin appendages is the major feature in the histology of morphoea, thus imparting an 'empty' look to the dermis. Scrutiny of the size and distribution of the collagen bundles shows them to be larger than usual and to tend to run parallel to the skin surface. The normal difference between the papillary and reticular dermis is thus lost, and the overlying epidermis tends to be thin and atrophic.

Clinical features

Morphoea presents as a rather firm white or violaceous patch of skin on any body site, commonly the thighs, trunk, and upper arms (Fig. 7.7). In any developing lesion there is a well-marked red or viola-

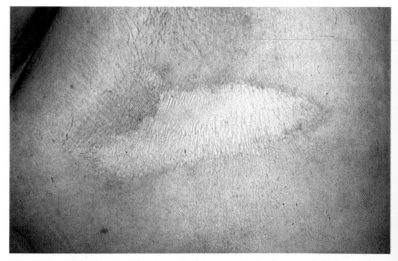

Fig. 7.7. Morphoea. The ivory white patch is firm and indurated on palpation, and has a slightly erythematous border.

ceous peripheral edge. As the disease activity burns out, this edge assumes the same colour as the central lesion and the white area becomes very firm with an atrophic glazed epidermis. Calcification within the lesion is not uncommon. A linear variant of morphoea is commonly seen on the scalp and face (so-called '*en coup de sabre*'), and gives rise to alopecia and to growth irregularities of the underlying skull if in a young child. In morphoea melanin pigmentation tends to develop in 'burnt out' lesions.

Diagnosis and treatment

The clinical appearance is commonly diagnostic and biopsy is rarely required. In very early lesions, when erythema rather than a firm white atrophic plaque is seen, the lesion may have to be observed for 2–3 months before a firm diagnosis can be made. Biopsy at this stage is not always helpful as the fully developed histological picture is not present.

There is no specific treatment. Intralesional corticosteroid injections into an active lesion may alter its final shape, but will not arrest its development.

LICHEN SCLEROSUS ET ATROPHICUS (LSA)
('white spot disease')

Definition. An atrophic condition commonly of the vulva, sometimes associated with morphoea on other body sites.

It is possible that LSA is a variant of morphoea as the two conditions are found together more frequently than can be attributed to chance. White, atrophic, glazed areas of skin with follicular plugging develop (Fig. 7.8), and may progress to extreme atrophy and shrinkage of genital tissue. The lesions may ulcerate and cause pain and pruritus, although some are asymptomatic. LSA usually affects the female genitalia. It rarely affects the penis in the male, when it is termed balanitis xerotica obliterans. Extragenital lesions are most common around the neck and upper back. There is a small reported incidence (around 5 per cent) of malignant change in vulvar LSA. This is not reported with prepubertal LSA which clears spontaneously at puberty.

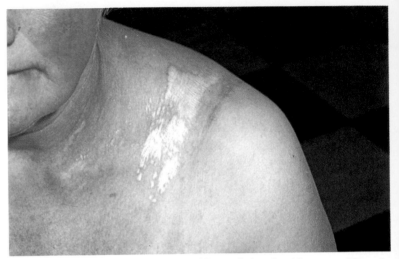

Fig. 7.8.   Lichen sclerosus et atrophicus of the shoulder area. Note the atrophic white macules. Vulvar lesions are very commonly seen in patients with these extragenital lesions.

Diagnosis and treatment

Diagnosis is usually made clinically although biopsy may be required in atypical cases.

Treatment is unsatisfactory and unnecessary for asymptomatic lesions. Pruritus and ulceration are helped by topical steroid preparations (e.g. vioform hydrocortisone cream) or topical oestrogens (e.g. Dinoestrol cream).

Long-term follow-up is required in all severe cases as malignancy may not supervene until the lesion has been present for 20 years or more.

DERMATOMYOSITIS (polymyositis)

Definition. A disorder of skin and muscle characterized by a specific skin rash and muscle weakness.

Dermatomyositis is relatively rare. There are two varieties, one affecting children, the other adults. Only in *the adult form* is there an association between the disease and an occult systemic malignancy.

The frequency of this association varies in different series, but may be as high as 25 per cent and is found more commonly in males in the sixth to eighth decades.

Pathology

The cutaneous lesions show histological changes similar to those seen in SLE. Liquefaction degeneration of the basal layer is common, and the overlying epidermis may be thin and atrophic. In the dermis large numbers of free melanin granules are seen due to pigmentary incontinence. Free red cells are also present, the result of capillary leakage.

The degree of muscle involvement is variable, but if affected, the muscle shows fibre degeneration and internalization of the sarcolemmal nuclei.

Clinical features

The typical rash of dermatomyositis is a macular erythema on the face, particularly marked in the periorbital area where it is heliotrope (blue violet) in hue. The dorsa of the hands and fingers are also involved and develop a very characteristic linear erythema. Nail fold haemorrhages may also be seen, but these are common to all the connective tissue disorders. Erythema can also appear on the neck and upper chest, and progress to *poikiloderma* (dappled skin) which consists of telangiectasia alternating with atrophy. Photosensitivity is also commonly seen.

Muscle weakness is very variable. It most commonly affects the proximal muscle groups of all four limbs, so that early weakness tends to be noted on climbing stairs or performing tasks with the hands at or above shoulder level. It may become very severe, and respiratory embarrassment can result from involvement of intercostal and diaphragmatic muscles.

In childhood, dermatomyositis tends to 'burn out', but may leave severe crippling and restriction of limb movement due to calcification in and around muscles.

Diagnosis and treatment

Diagnosis is usually based on the combination of a typical skin rash, muscle weakness, and raised circulating muscle enzymes (SGOT, SGPT, creatine kinase, and aldolase). If muscle biopsy is to be performed, electromyography will indicate a suitable area of involved muscle.

In an adult presenting with dermatomyositis, a search for occult malignancy utilizing all available non-invasive techniques should be instituted. Some authorities would even consider an exploratory laparatomy to be indicated. Unfortunately, failure to find an underlying malignancy does not rule out its development as the dermatomyositis can precede manifestation of the malignancy by several years. Removal of a malignancy if present may result in spontaneous, although usually temporary, improvement of the muscle weakness. If no malignancy is found, systemic steroid therapy may give symptomatic relief and a trial of prednisolone 20–60 mg/day is justified. Systemic azathioprine (150 mg/day) may also be of value either alone or as a steroid-sparing measure. Disease activity should be monitored by regular assays of muscle enzyme levels.

EHLERS–DANLOS SYNDROME (cutis hyperelastica)

Definition. A group of inherited disorders characterized by defects in dermal collagen.

At the present time at least five biochemical variants of this true 'collagen' disorder are recognized. The mode of inheritance is autosomal dominant in four and sex-linked recessive in one. The basic defects in collagen synthesis are both quantitative and qualitative, and can be accurately identified by fibroblast culture and biochemical assay. On light microscopy the collagen appears whorled and disorganized, and in some cases there is an associated increase in elastic fibres.

Clinical features

Clinically, the skin is hyperelastic, fragile, and bruises easily. The joints have lax capsules, are hyperextensible, and readily undergo subluxation. Poor posture and hernia formation may in part be due to muscular hypotonia. Poor healing of minor skin trauma leaves ugly scars (Fig. 7.9). In some cases the collagen of large vessels is also affected, and death due to dissecting aneurysm or spontaneous vessel rupture is recorded. A proportion of patients also have features of pseudoxanthoma elasticum.

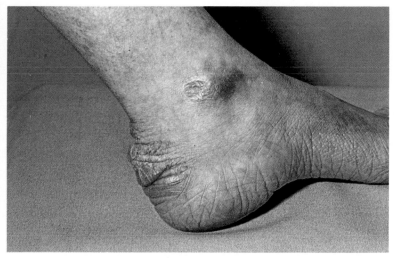

Fig. 7.9. Ehlers–Danlos syndrome. Note the ugly scars and 'pseudo-tumours' due to lax skin over sites of minor trauma.

Diagnosis and treatment

Diagnosis is based on the clinical appearance and a positive family history, and should be confirmed by biochemical studies on fibro-blast cultures. No treatment is yet available, but identification of the type of Ehlers–Danlos will aid genetic counselling.

PSEUDOXANTHOMA ELASTICUM

Definition. A hereditary disorder of elastic tissue.

Like the Ehlers–Danlos syndrome, there are genetically distinct variants. At present, two autosomal dominant and two autosomal recessive varieties are recognized.

Pathology

The characteristic pathological feature is the presence in the dermis of tangled degenerate elastic fibres on which calcification readily occurs. This abnormality is also found in elastic tissue of the blood vessels and the heart.

Clinical features

The cutaneous lesions are found in the axillae and groins and are soft, yellowish papules—'chamois leather' skin (Fig. 7.10). Ocular lesions are common and can be seen on ophthalmoscopy as angioid streaks, haemorrhage, and choroiditis. Some degree of visual impairment is common. Involvement of major blood vessels may give rise to hypertension, angina, and haemorrhage including haematemesis.

Diagnosis and treatment

Diagnosis is based on the clinical appearance, a positive family history, and the histology. No specific therapy is available.

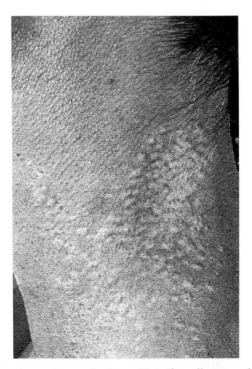

Fig. 7.10.   Pseudoxanthoma elasticum. Note the yellow papules on the side of the neck, a classic site of involvement.

GROWTH POINTS

1 *The use of thalidomide in severe chronic discoid lupus erythematosus*

Following the reports of foetal and neonatal abnormalities, the drug thalidomide has remained until recently virtually unused for the past twenty years. In the past 2 years three cutaneous indications have been suggested for thalidomide. The conditions suggested are severe intractable chronic discoid lupus erythematosus, polymorphous light eruption, and severe Behçet's disease. In all of these conditions significant response to oral thalidomide has been reported in patients who are resistant to other forms of therapy. Patients receiving thalidomide are at risk of developing a peripheral neuropathy which is not always reversible, and therefore must be carefully monitored and the drug given only for short periods. The ethical problems of giving a drug which is proven to cause foetal abnormalities has given rise to some discussion. There are no clear guide lines but it is obvious that if use of the drug is contemplated in an otherwise life-ruining dermatological situation the patient concerned must not be at any risk whatever of becoming pregnant.

2 *Neonatal heart block and congenital lupus erythematosus*

A number of papers in the past few years have indicated clearly that in infants born with congenital heart block, an irreversible condition which carries a high mortality in the first year of life, the majority of sufferers have an antinuclear antibody present to a soluble tissue ribonucleoprotein antigen called Ro (SS-A). These infants have transient erythematous cutaneous lesions similar to those seen in lupus erythematosus in older individuals. A large proportion of the mothers of these infants also carry antinuclear antibodies of the Ro (SS-A) type, but are in fact asymptomatic. This antibody crosses the placenta and is therefore if present in a pregnant woman a marker for the risk of congenital complete heart block.

FURTHER READING

Sontheimer, R. D.: Immunobiological significance of the Ro – SS-A antigen antibody systems. *AMA Archives of Dermatology* **121**, 327 (1985).
  A clinically orientated review: 38 relevant references.
Watson, R. M. *et al.*: Neonatal lupus erythematosus. A clinical, laboratory

and immunogenetic study with a review of the literature. *Medicine* **63,** 362 (1984).
An excellent study in linking the laboratory and clinical findings in children.
Weston, W. L.: The significance and characters of SS-A (Ro) and SS-B (La) antigens. *Journal of Investigative Dermatology* **84,** 85 (1985).
A succinct one-page review with 15 well chosen references.

NOTES

8

Disorders of the vasculature

Disorders of the arteries, veins, and capillaries may all present with skin manifestations, but whereas some are predominantly cutaneous disorders affecting only the cutaneous vasculature, others are more generalized, involving many systems, the skin included. The most common problem discussed in this section is lower leg ulceration which may be due to either venous or arterial malfunction. Capillary disorders often cause a purpuric eruption and vasculitis can produce painful nodular ulcerating lesions. Vascular pathology is most commonly seen on the lower legs as their circulation is subject to stasis. Biopsies from this site have to be interpreted with care, for histology of clinically normal skin of this area may show minor vascular changes due to gravity.

Leg ulceration

Seventy to eighty per cent of ulcers on the lower legs result from venous damage, usually consequent on the increased venous pressure associated with varicose veins and past venous thrombosis. The remaining 20–30 per cent result from arterial damage and tend to differ clinically. It is essential that all family doctors understand the basic principles of leg ulcer management.

VENOUS LEG ULCERS (stasis ulcers, gravitational ulcers)

Incidence and pathological features

Venous ulceration is very common in Britain and accounts for 3 per cent of all new cases attending dermatological clinics. The incidence in the community must, however, be much higher as many patients either attend their general practitioner or seek no medical assistance. Most patients are women.

The pathogenesis stems from incompetence of valves in the leg veins. There is secondary increase in capillary pressure, with stasis, capillary damage, fibrosis, and a poorly nourished skin which is easily damaged by minor trauma.

Clinical features

The typical patient is an obese, middle-aged woman. A past history of a deep venous thrombosis is common and varicose veins are usually present. Cutaneous lesions may be unilateral or bilateral (Fig. 8.1). The most common site of ulceration is over the medial malleolus, and the surrounding skin frequently shows gross fibrosis, purpura, and livedo due to extravasation of blood from damaged capillaries, an appearance termed '*atrophie blanche*'. The ulcer is frequently precipitated by minor local trauma. Stasis ulcers are commonly single and although they may be extremely large they are relatively pain-free, in contast to arterial ulcers. The surrounding skin is frequently oedematous, eczematous, and secondarily infected.

Diagnosis and treatment

The diagnosis of a leg ulcer is self-evident. It is necessary to

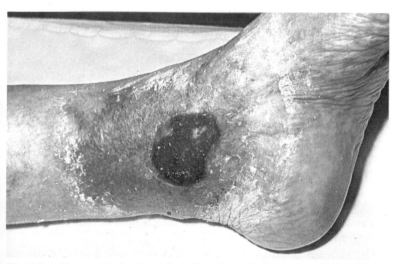

Fig. 8.1. Venous stasis ulceration. Note typical site over medial malleolus and trophic changes in surrounding skin.

establish, however, whether the lesion is of purely vascular origin or whether it is part of a generalized disease and, if vascular, whether it is due to arterial or venous disease.

Systemic diseases associated with leg ulcers include diabetes mellitus, syphilis, lesions of the spinal cord, rheumatoid arthritis, and polyarteritis nodosa. Sickle cell disease and other haemoglobinopathies must be considered in patients of Mediterranean origin. In a long-standing leg ulcer with atypical features the possibility of malignant change should be borne in mind and biopsy performed. Treatment of an established venous leg ulcer consists not only of symptomatic therapy designed to promote healing but also of prophylaxis to reduce the risk of recurrence. These measures include surgical treatment of venous varicosities if feasible, weight reduction, and the use of supportive elastic stockings and protective bandaging (e.g. blue-line bandages, Bisgaard bandaging).

The basic principles of management of an established venous leg ulcer are the maintenance of a clean healthy ulcer base free of infection, and protection of the surrounding skin to allow reepithelialization to take place. Unfortunately, this is easier to write than to practise as the damage resulting in the leg ulcer has usually built up over decades. The base of the ulcer is frequently a poor surface for new skin to grow on and even if healing can be achieved, breakdown of the healed area after minor trauma is all too common.

A variety of astringent preparations will help to maintain a clean healthy ulcer base. These include 20 per cent benzoyl peroxide (Benoxyl),sodium hypochlorite 1 in 4 (Milton solution), and a variety of brightly coloured paints such as magenta paint Topical antibiotics should not be used routinely on clinically clean ulcer bases. For very moist exudative ulcers 2–3 days treatment with absorbent dextranomer beads (Debrisan) will assist in drying the lesions, but this preparation should not be continued for long periods. Clinical evidence of secondary infection is usually best treated with an appropriate systemic antibiotic chosen according to bacteriological sensitivity. Routine swabbing for bacteriological examination of clinically clean ulcers is of little value as bacteria will frequently be grown but it will be of very doubtful relevance to the healing of the ulcer.

The skin surrounding the actual ulcer may well be erythematous and irritable with a stasis dermatitis reaction. While this is often responsive to topical steroid preparations, they must be used with caution in this situation and kept away from the ulcer base otherwise they will delay healing. They should not be used constantly on the skin around the ulcer as they will in time cause atrophy and possibly further extension of the ulcer. For this reason the surrounding skin is best protected with a waterproof paste such as plain zinc paste BP, or zinc paste with salicylic acid (Lassar's Paste). The ulcer and surrounding area should be well protected from trauma by padding, and a supporting bandage of the Bisgaard or blue line type. All patients with chronic leg ulcers should be shown exactly how to apply these bandages. Adhesive bandages such as Viscopaste or Ichthopaste are also helpful, particularly for patients who have persistent stasis dermatitis around the ulcer area.

Patients with chronic leg ulcers may develop an allergic contact dermatitis to one of their many medicaments and patch testing to medicaments should be carried out if there is persistent inflammation around the ulcer area. Prevention of allergic contact dermatitis is important and this is one of the reasons why topical antibiotics are not advisable in leg ulcers as the possibility of sensitization is relatively high.

In severe cases resistant to out-patient treatment admission to hospital for pinch grafting may be considered. Although this gives good initial results, there is a high recurrence rate once the patient is ambulant.

ARTERIAL LEG ULCERS

Arterial leg ulcers present with severe pain as a clamant feature. This may be particularly intense on elevating the legs and may interfere with sleep. These ulcers are considerably less common than the venous variety and affect both sexes equally.

In a typical case, the patient has no evidence of varicose veins, but has poor peripheral pulses and multiple small painful ulcers, which have a punched out appearance and are situated in the lower third of the leg (Fig. 8.2). As arterial leg ulcers are frequently associated with generalized arterial pathology, it is important to look for diabetes, atherosclerosis, Buerger's disease, and rheumatoid arthritis.

Diagnosis and treatment

Pain and the site of the lesion may help to differentiate an arterial from a venous ulcer, and further useful pointers are the absence of varicose veins or of a history of deep venous thrombosis.

Treatment is mainly symptomatic. Topical therapy as for venous

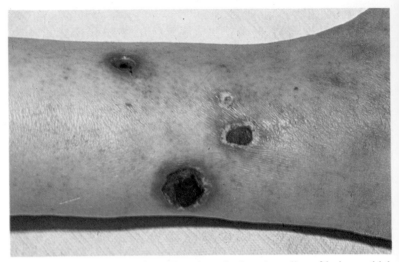

Fig. 8.2. Arterial ulceration. Note 'punched-out' quality of lesions which are multiple and painful.

ulcers (p. 166) should be prescribed, but rest and warmth are of particular importance. Systemic vasodilators may give symptomatic relief in a few cases, but it is debatable whether this is more than a placebo effect. Sympathectomy may be of value and a trial nerve block should be performed to determine whether or not relief of pain can be achieved.

Vasculitis

Definition. A pathological process centred primarily on blood vessel walls (mainly small and medium sized vessels) resulting in purpura, nodules, and ulceration.

Pathology

The classification of vasculitis is confused, and can be based either on clinical or on pathological features. Table 8.1 is based on the pathology and relies on the predominant cell type seen around the damaged vessel. It is crucial in the histological diagnosis of vasculitis to see unequivocal damage to the vessel wall as many conditions are associated with a perivascular cellular infiltrate, but no frank

Table 8.1. The main types of vasculitis classified according to predominant cell type in the infiltrate

Predominant cell type	Clinical conditions
Lymphocyte	Chilblains (lupus pernio) Lupus erythematosus Erythema nodosum Pityriasis lichenoides
Polymorph	Polyarteritis nodosa Allergic vasculitis Henoch–Schoenlein purpura
Granuloma formation	Pyoderma gangrenosum Giant cell arteritis Erythema induratum

damage to the vessel. Even a classification of this type is unsatisfactory, as it is likely that different cell populations will be seen within a lesion at different stages of its development.

Clinical presentations of lymphocytic vasculitis

ERYTHEMA NODOSUM

Definition. A lymphocytic vasculitis seen mainly in women (F:M = 5:1) and predominantly affecting the lower legs.

Clinical features

Erythema nodosum is characterized by painful, palpable, dusky blue-red lesions on the calves and shins, although occasionally the forearms are also affected. General malaise, fever, and joint pains are common. The lesions slowly resolve over a period of 2–4 weeks. At this stage the gradual fading of the lesions has an appearance very similar to simple bruises (Fig. 8.3).

Erythema nodosum is an excellent example of a tissue reaction pattern provoked by a variety of stimuli. The commonest causes identified in Britain at the present time are, in decreasing order of frequency, streptococcal infection, drug ingestion (particularly sulphonamides), sarcoidosis, viral and chlamydial infections, and

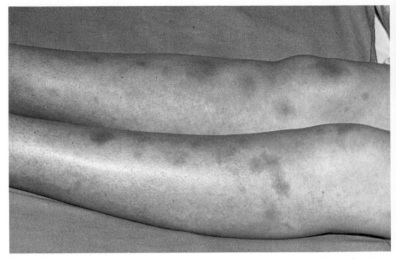

Fig. 8.3. Erythema nodosum. The lesions can be very faint, but are indurated and painful on palpation.

tuberculosis. In other European countries *Yersinia* infection is a relatively common precipitating factor.

Table 8.2 outlines an appropriate plan of investigation for cases of erythema nodosum, but in a high proportion of cases no precipitating factor or underlying cause will be identified.

The clinical picture of an ill patient with painful, non-ulcerating leg nodules is diagnostic. Treatment is mainly symptomatic. If the condition is thought to be drug-induced, the suspected drug should be withdrawn. Bed rest, elevation of the limb, and systemic analgesics should be prescribed. The value of topical preparations is debatable, but 10 per cent ichthyol in water applied twice daily to

Table 8.2.   Investigation plan for erythema nodosum

1 History, including a careful drug history
2 E.S.R.
3 Throat swab, ASO titre
4 Chest X-ray (sarcoid, tuberculosis)
5 Mantoux test (*before* Kveim test)
6 If Mantoux test negative, Kveim test
7 Viral titres, both acute and convalescent

acute lesions is a comfort to some patients. Steroids topically are of no value, and there is little evidence that, given systemically, they change the course of the disease.

PITYRIASIS LICHENOIDES ACUTA

Definition. A purely cutaneous disorder of unknown aetiology characterized by multiple papules and plaques.

Pathology
Histopathologically, there is a lymphocytic vasculitis.

Clinical features
Pityriasis lichenoides acuta presents as multiple pruritic excoriated papules, occurring in crops on the tunk and limbs. Purpuric lesions are occasionally seen. There is rarely any systemic upset, and spontaneous remission is usual after months or years.

Diagnosis and treatment
Diagnosis is based on the clinical appearance and is usually confirmed by biopsy. Insect bites and atypical dermatitis herpetiformis are the most common causes of confusion, but the possibility of the papular form of secondary syphilis should be borne in mind. Syphilitic lesions will commonly affect the palms and soles, whereas those of pityriasis licenoides will only do so rarely.

Treatment is usually based on bland topical preparations such as simple ichthyol 1 per cent in oily calamine lotion. A course of ultraviolet light will benefit some patients.

Clinical presentation of polymorphonuclear vasculitis

POLYARTERITIS NODOSA

Definition. A rare, severe, generalized disease characterized by necrotizing arteritis.

Pathology
Histologically, there is within the blood vessel walls a polymorphonuclear infiltrate and characteristically fragments of disintegrating nuclei from damaged polymorphs ('nuclear dust') will be seen.

Clinical features

The patient generally is ill and febrile. Skin manifestations include subcutaneous nodules, subungual splinter haemorrhages, small purpuric lesions, and occasionally frankly gangrenous lesions. As this is a multisystem disorder, other signs and symptoms result from involvement of the renal, abdominal, cardiovascular, and CNS vasculature (Fig. 8.4).

Diagnosis and treatment

Diagnosis is based on evidence of involvement of multiple vessels and is usually confirmed by biopsy. Treatment with systemic ster-

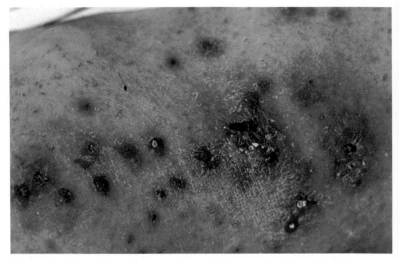

Fig. 8.4. Necrotizing (leucocytoclastic) vasculitis. Palpable lesions are surrounded by purpura and tend to break down easily.

oids and immunosuppressives (e.g. azathioprine) is required, but even so there is a significant mortality.

CUTANEOUS POLYARTERITIS NODOSA (livedo with nodules)

Definition. A mild form of polyarteritis nodosa confined to the skin vasculature.

Clinical features

In this recently described condition, the lesions are found predominantly on the lower legs and consist of livedo reticularis, papable nodules, and, in some cases, neuropathy and myalgia. The prognosis is relatively good and although there is a tendency to chronicity, systemic involvement has not yet been reported.

Treatment

Low doses of systemic steroids (10–20 mg prednisolone on alternate days) may be required to control exacerbations and simple analgesics (e.g. aspirin) to relieve pain. Topical steroid therapy is of little value.

PYODERMA GANGRENOSUM

Definition. A rare dermatological disorder, in which large ulcerating lesions appear suddenly and dramatically.

Pathology

Pyoderma gangrenosum results from underlying thrombosis and vasculitis which may reflect a Schwartzmann type of reaction.

Clinical features

The initial cutaneous lesions resemble indolent boils, but they rapidly expand, break down, and leave large ulcerated painful areas. Systemic upset, with fever and malaise, is frequent. The condition may be associated with the first signs of ulcerative colitis, Crohn's disease, rheumatoid arthritis, and monoclonal gammopathies or frank myeloma (Fig. 8.5).

Diagnosis and treatment

The diagnosis is generally apparent on clinical grounds. Once appropriate investigations to exclude underlying disease have been performed, systemic steroid therapy should be prescribed in a moderately high dose (e.g. 60–100 mg of prednisolone daily) and subsequently reduced as the lesions heal. Topical therapy is symptomatic, Vaseline-impregnated gauze (tulle gras) being the dressing of choice.

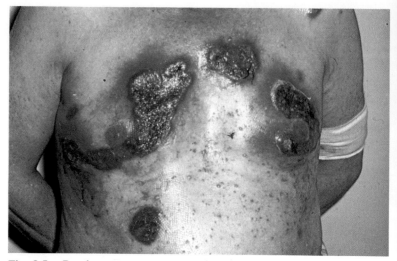

Fig. 8.5. Pyoderma gangrenosum. These large lesions can develop with dramatic rapidity.

Clinical conditions associated with granulomatous vasculitis

TEMPORAL ARTERITIS (giant cell arteritis)

This condition affects the elderly, and causes severe pain, headache, and possibly visual upset. It may be seen dermatologically when tender red nodules appear on the temporal area. Systemic steroids should be commenced without delay as permanent visual damage and even blindness may result.

ERYTHEMA INDURATUM (Bazin's disease)

A condition affecting the lower legs of young women, thought formerly to be a reaction to the tubercle bacillus.

This condition is now relatively rare and presents as painful ulcerating nodules on the back of the lower legs of obese patients, usually female.

The aetiology is unknown.

Treatment is difficult, but weight reduction and avoidance of low temperature environments are both to be encouraged.

URTICARIA

Definition. Recurrent transient cutaneous swellings and erythema due to fluid transfer from the vasculature to the dermis.

This condition is common and varies from minor banal cutaneous lesions to the severe and even life-threatening form called angiooedema affecting the laryngeal area. A local sudden increase in capillary permeability is the common final pathway for a variety of stimuli thought to be aetiological agents. Some of the recognized types of urticaria and their supposed pathogenesis are listed below, but it must be stressed that the majority of cases will fall into the group of unknown aetiology (Fig. 8.6).

The hallmark of urticaria is the rapid appearance of a transient

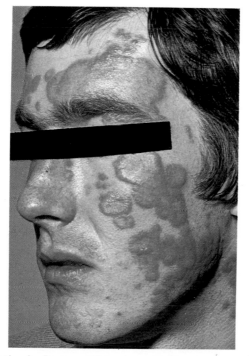

Fig. 8.6. Urticaria. Large erythematous weals are seen on the face.

erythematous, often itchy, raised weal or plaque. Lesions may be multiple and appear with alarming speed. Lesions occurring around the mouth should be regarded as a dermatological emergency, and the patient watched carefully for signs of respiratory obstruction. Many patients have a chronic variety of urticaria, resistant to therapy, which persists for months or years before burning out.

Recognized varieties of urticaria

1 Due to histamine-liberating drugs. Salicylates are the commonest group of drugs in this category and patients with chronic urticaria must be instructed not to use aspirin as a simple analgesic, but an alternative such as paracetamol. Codeine, morphine, and indomethacin are also incriminated as histamine liberators.

2 Due to ingested food additives. The two food additives known to cause or provoke urticaria are the tartrazine group of dyes, found in yellow and orange coloured drinks and sweets, and benzoates, used widely as preservatives.

3 Contact urticaria. Here the lesions develop only on actual sites of contact, e.g. on the site of contact with dog hair or saliva, or on the lips after ingesting some foods. This variety of urticaria is common in atopic patients.

4 Physical urticaria. In a small group of patients pressure, heat, cold, and sunlight may provoke urticarial weals.

5 Urticaria and hereditary angio-oedema. This rare condition is transmitted by autosomal dominant inheritance. The basic biochemical defect is in the complement pathway. The enzyme C_1 esterase inhibitor is lacking in these patients who may present with gross and alarming swellings. They may also present as acute surgical emergencies because of sudden oedema of a part of the small intestine leading to acute pain and obstruction.

6 Related to general medical problems. This is a miscellaneous group. Patients infested with parasites tend to develop urticaria, as do those with chronic bacterial infection in such sites as the nasal sinuses and the urinary tract. Patients with lupus erythematosus, thyrotoxicosis, and lymphomata may also present with urticaria.

7 No known or identifiable causative factor. This comprises by far the largest group of patients.

Diagnosis and treatment

Diagnosis is self-evident and patients frequently do not seek help until they have tried several home remedies. These should be identified and salicylate-containing preparations banned.

The investigation of a case of urticaria can be a time-consuming and expensive exercise, and as the disease is common, a sensible compromise is to investigate only those of 6–9 months' duration or longer who do not obtain relief from systemic antihistamine therapy. A reasonable battery of investigations to be performed as an out-patient is detailed in Table 8.3. A careful history should identify the rare cases of physical urticaria and may be a pointer in cases provoked by food additives. The majority of cases will yield negative results on this screen and must be treated on a symptomatic basis.

Table 8.3. An outline of investigations for cases of chronic persistent urticaria

---

Full blood count (Hb, WBC + eosinophil count, platelets)
Liver function tests
Chest and sinus X-ray
Examination of hot stool for parasites
Examination of urine for bacteria
Complement screen including C_1 esterase inhibitor
Antinuclear antibody

Treatment of acute urticaria may require subcutaneous adrenaline as a life-saving measure. For chronic cases the cornerstone of therapy is systemic antihistamine and often several need to be tried before one is found which combines symptomatic relief with minimal side effects. The anti-H1 group of antihistamines should be used for the management of urticaria. The two antihistamines which are currently particularly widely used are terfenadine (Triludan), 60 mg twice daily, and astemizole (Hismanal), 10 mg daily. Both have significant anti-itch qualities, with minimal sedation. There is little evidence that the addition of an H2 inhibitor, such as cimetidine, is of any value in the management of patients, even with persistent and severe urticaria. Itch and discomfort from individual weals may be relieved by menthol 1–2 per cent in calamine lotion or aqueous cream.

For more persistent cases, the possibility of elimination diets should be considered but these require expert supervision, particularly if provocation tests with the suspected foodstuff is part of the plan.

Systemic steroids should not be prescribed in chronic urticaria, but a short 5–7-day course may be of value in an acute urticarial drug eruption. *Prednisone 40 mg po g day*

Purpuric conditions

Patients presenting with predominantly purpuric eruptions may have a platelet disorder, a disease affecting capillaries, or a more general systematized disease. Common causes of purpura are aging (in which the small blood vessels of the skin lose their normal collagen support), topical or systemic steroid therapy (which similarly increases capillary fragility), vitamin C deficiency, and side effects of drug therapy. Rarer causes include generalized amyloidosis and renal disease. Platelet counts of $60\,000/mm^3$ or more are unlikely to produce purpura and in patients with platelet counts above this level, causes of non-thrombocytopenic purpura should be sought.

HENOCH–SCHOENLEIN PURPURA (anaphylactoid purpura)

Definition. A purpuric eruption due in some cases to an allergic reaction to bacteria or ingested drugs, and associated with fever, malaise, and gastrointestinal and renal involvement.

Pathology
The underlying pathological lesion is a vasculitis affecting small vessels and the degree of systemic involvement is very variable. Children are frequently affected.

Clinical features
Macular or papular purpuric lesions are scattered on the limbs and buttocks. General malaise and fever may be present, as may arthralgia, haematuria, and abdominal pain. The platelet count is normal. In some patients there is a history of a streptococcal throat infection 7–14 days prior to development of purpura, and in others

there is a history of systemic drug ingestion. In most cases, however, no aetiological factor can be identified.

Diagnosis and treatment

Diagnosis is usually straightforward and investigations should be carried out to establish the degree of systemic involvement. The most serious complication is severe renal involvement which can lead to the nephrotic syndrome. The disease is usually self-limiting and there is little evidence that systemic steroids will alter its course. Nevertheless, they are frequently prescribed for patients with severe multisystem involvement. Bed rest and simple analgesics may be required for arthropathy. Regular urinalysis should be performed to look for frank haematuria and developing proteinuria.

GROWTH POINT

Occlusive dressings. In the past few years a wide range of occlusive dressings have become available for wound healing in general and leg ulcer healing in particular. These dressings work on the principle of providing a controlled moist relatively sterile microenvironment in which ulcer healing and re-epitheliasation can take place. The area under the occlusive dressing may look unusually moist, but in fact healing of wounds under these dressings have been shown to be faster than of lesions exposed to the air. At present the majority of these preparations are only available for hospital use, but it is anticipated that they will become more widely available in the near future. Names of some of the more popular ones include Op-site, Granuflex, and Geliperm.

FURTHER READING

Ryan T. J.: 1983 *The Management of Leg Ulcers.* Oxford University Press, Oxford (1983).
An excellent extremely practical short paperback on all aspects of leg ulcer management. Particularly recommended for family doctors and district nurses.
Wolf, K. and Winkleman, R. K.: *Vasculitis.* Blackwell Scientific Publications, Oxford (1980).
Basically, the proceedings of a conference on vasculitis held 5 years ago. A well constructed account with some excellent individual chapters.

NOTES

9

Disorders of the cutaneous melanocytes

The structure and melanin-producing function of the epidermal melanocyte network has already been described (p. 20). The evolutionary function of epidermal melanocytes is considered to have been the production of a protective pigment layer in response to exposure to sunlight as a protection against damaging wavelengths of solar radiation. If this is indeed the case, it is interesting that these cells are normally situated in the basal layer of the epidermis. If they were situated at a higher level within the epidermis additional photoprotection of surrounding keratinocytes might also be achieved.

In biopsies of normal skin, melanocytes are not seen in the dermis and when they are found there in pathological conditions it is considered likely that the reason is an arrest of their normal migration, in foetal life, from the neural crest to the epidermis.

The commonest abnormalities in the distribution, structure, and function of melanocytes with the resulting clinical condition are listed in Table 9.1. All, with the exception of malignant melanoma, are discussed in this chapter.

ALBINISM

Definition. An autosomal recessive disorder, characterized by a lack of pigment production by melanocytes in the epidermis, hair bulb, and eye (Fig. 9.1).

Pathology
The melanocyte either lacks the enzymes necessary for melanin pigment synthesis or these are present in an abnormal non-functional form. In some albinos the enzyme tyrosinase can in fact be demonstrated while in others it is absent. These two distinct varieties

Table 9.1. Melanocyte abnormalities and their clinical manifestations

Generalized non-function of melanocytes	Albinism
Localized loss of melanocytes	Vitiligo
Localized increase in melanogenesis	Freckles (ephelides)
Hormonally-mediated increase in melanogenesis	Chloasma, Addison's disease
Localized increase in numbers of epidermal melanocytes	Junctional and compound naevi
Localized increase in numbers of dermal melanocytes	Mongolian spot, blue naevus, naevus of Ota, naevus of Ito
Localized increase in both epidermal and dermal melanocytes and naevus cells	Giant pigmented hairy naevus
Malignant change in epidermal melanocytes	Malignant melanoma

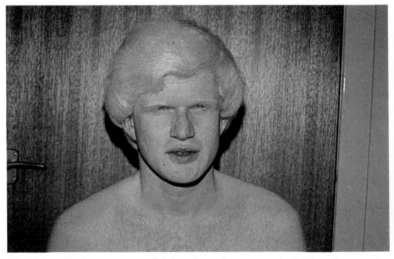

Fig. 9.1. Oculocutaneous albinism (tyrosinase negative). Note the extreme pallor of hair and skin, and photophobia.

of albinism can be differentiated by incubating plucked hair bulbs *in vitro* with tyrosine or DOPA. The hair bulbs with functionally normal tyrosinase will show a black deposit, but in those without the enzyme there will be no pigment deposit.

Light microscopy of albino skin shows poorly formed or apparently absent melanocytes in the basal layer of the epidermis. Electron microscopy, however, shows that they are present, but that they contain very few poorly formed melanosomes.

Clinical features

Lack of normal pigmentation is the striking feature of each of the four recognized genetic variants of albinism. The skin is white or pink, the hair pale blonde, and the iris translucent. Sunlight is very poorly tolerated, and sunburn and photophobia are common symptoms. Nystagmus may also be present. Albinism is very striking in Negroes, and when exposed to tropical or subtropical sunlight their skin ages prematurely and they have a high incidence of malignant skin tumours, mainly squamous carcinoma. In temperate climates, as in the U.K., the presenting features are usually ocular.

Diagnosis and treatment

Diagnosis is straightforward and the biochemical type of oculocutaneous albinism can be established by hair bulb incubation (see above).

Prevention of sun damage is essential. Sun avoidance should be practised and where sunlight exposure is inevitable a sunscreen preparation with a sun protection factor (SPF) of 10 or more should be used (e.g. Coppertone Supershade 15, Roc 10 A + B). Regular clinical surveillance is essential for early diagnosis of skin tumours. Ocular problems require specialist ophthalmological supervision.

VITILIGO

Definition. An area of acquired cutaneous depigmentation due to loss of normal melanocyte function.

Vitiligo affects around 0.4 per cent of the European population, and incidence figures for genetically dark-skinned races suggest that it is commoner among them. A high proportion of affected patients have a positive family history, but the genetic aspects remain obscure. As there is a significant association with autoimmune diseases such as pernicious anaemia, thyroid disease, and Addison's disease, it has been suggested that autoimmune destruction of melanocytes may be involved in the pathogenesis.

Pathology

Special staining techniques show that epidermal melanocytes are lost from the basal layer of the epidermis.

Clinical features

Relative lack of pigmentation is the hallmark. In Caucasians this is obvious only in the summer months, especially when depigmented areas sunburn, while the unaffected skin tans. Vitiligo demonstrates the Koebner (isomorphic) phenomenon as it is activated by minor trauma (Fig. 9.2).

With time, vitiligo generally becomes more extensive, but after some months the lesions become static. In a few cases some degree of spontaneous repigmentation takes place.

Diagnosis and treatment

Diagnosis is usually self-evident, but in coloured skin pityriasis versicolor can be confusing, so scrapings should be taken for mycological examination. Leprosy is a very much rarer possibility, but can worry the patient greatly. However, in leprosy the hypopigmented macules are usually anaesthetic. In cases of doubt a biopsy should be performed.

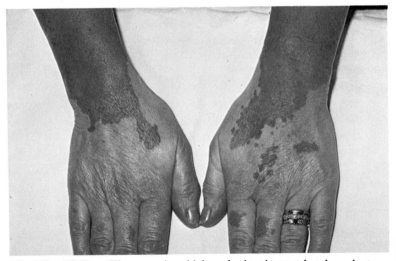

Fig. 9.2. Vitiligo. The areas in which melanin pigment has been lost are particularly prone to sunburn.

Treatment is unsatisfactory. Some patients achieve a reasonable cosmetic result with topical artifical tanning creams containing dihydroxyacetone, but those with a dark skin rarely find these preparations satisfactory. Photochemotherapy (psoralens + UVA = PUVA) is of some value in a proportion of patients, but is time consuming and may carry long-term hazards. There is some evidence that potent topical steroid therapy may promote repigmentation. Patients must be warned that the affected skin is easily sunburned and that they should use a topical sunscreen.

SIMPLE FRECKLES (ephelides)

In freckles, groups of melanocytes produce an abnormally large amount of melanin in response to sunlight. There is no increase in the numbers of melanocytes. Treatment is simple sun avoidance.

CHLOASMA

Definition. A hormonally-stimulated increase in melanogenesis which mainly affects the face, and which is seen in pregnant women and those on the contraceptive pill.

Both oestrogens and progesterone can affect melanogenesis and thereby cause in pregnancy a mask-like increase in facial melanin pigment—*chloasma uterinum.* This is commonest in females with naturally dark colouring and may take months to resolve after parturition. A similar appearance is seen in some women on oral contraception. Sunlight augments the depth of pigmentation. Circulating levels of melanocyte stimulating hormone are normal (Fig. 9.3).

As the condition is self-limiting, treatment, if necessary, consists of cosmetic camouflage and avoidance of natural sunlight.

ADDISON'S DISEASE

In Addison's disease pituitary output of β MSH and ACTH is raised, and both of these stimulate melanogenesis. Melanin deposition is increased mainly in the flexures and in the mucous membranes.

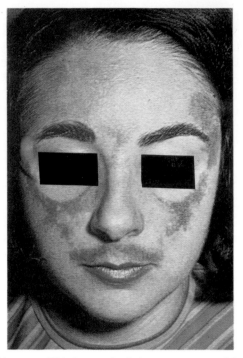

Fig. 9.3. Chloasma. This is seen both in pregnancy and in some users of the oral contraceptive pill. It can persist for some time after parturition or discontinuing the pill.

PIGMENTED NAEVI (Moles)

Pigmented naevi are common. They increase in number during childhood, reach a peak at puberty, and slowly become less numerous throughout adult life. The average young adult has between 10 and 30 melanocytic naevi.

Melanocytic naevi arising from epidermal melanocytes can be divided into three histological groups: junctional, compound, and intradermal naevi (Fig. 9.4).

Junctional naevi are usually small lesions, pale and sandy brown in colour. Histologically, they show increased numbers of melanocytes which maintain contact with the basal layer of the epidermis— an appearance termed 'junctional activity'. Compound naevi are usually larger, darker brown, and frequently palpable. Histologically there are not only increased numbers of melanocytic naevus

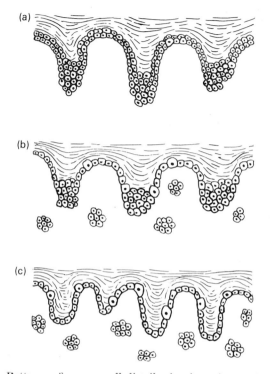

Fig. 9.4. Patterns of naevus cell distribution in melanocytic naevi.
(a) Junctional naevus. All naevus cells are in contact with the dermo-
epidermal junction.
(b) Compound naevus. Naevus cells are seen both in clumps at the dermo-
epidermal junction and lying free in the dermis.
(c) Intradermal naevus. The epidermis is entirely normal, but packets of
mature naevus cells are seen in the dermis.

cells adjacent to the basal layer, but also naevus cells lying in the
underlying dermis. Intradermal naevi commonly consist of a lightly
pigmented skin tag where histology shows only naevus cells in the
dermis, and no associated abnormality of epidermal melanocytes or
naevus cells contiguous with the basal layer of the epidermis. As
most pigmented naevi biopsied in young people are shown to be
junctional or compound, and those in the eldery to be intradermal, it
is thought that, with age, these lesions mature from the junctional
through the compound to the intradermal form.

In a second group of melanocytic pigmented naevi there are
aggregates of melanocytes in the dermis. These cells seem not to be

derived from the epidermis, as is the case in compound and intradermal naevi, but are thought to have failed to complete their migration in foetal life from the neural crest, and are arrested in their migration through the dermis. The most common variety is the *blue naevus*, a palpable blue-black lesion which histologically shows large fusiform or spindle-shaped cells in the dermis, but no overlying epidermal change. Rare variants are the *naevus of Ota*, which occurs over the area served by the trigeminal nerve, and the *naevus of Ito*, over the acromio-deltoid area.

In coloured infants a dark blue-black area is frequently seen over the sacrum. This, the *Mongolian spot*, is also a type of blue naevus.

The congenital *giant hairy pigmented naevus* shows an increase in both epidermal and dermal melanocytes. Reports of the incidence of development of malignant melanoma in these lesions (Fig. 9.5) suggest that the lifetime risk of malignant change is 3 per cent.

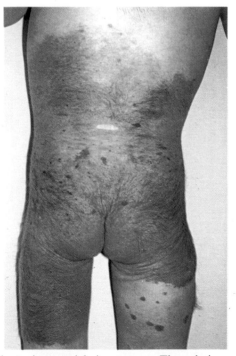

Fig. 9.5.   Giant pigmented hairy naevus. These lesions are also termed bathing-trunk or garment naevi. There is a significant incidence of development of malignant melanoma in this type of lesion.

GROWTH POINTS

'Dysplastic' Naevi. There is currently intense interest in a group of patients who have large numbers of large 'atypical' melanocytic naevi. These naevi are over 1 cm in diameter, are irregularly pigmented brown and black, and have an irregular lateral edge. The importance of these naevi is that they appear to be a valuable cutaneous marker of a patient group who are at significantly increased risk of developing cutaneous malignant melanoma (Ch. 15). Both sporadic and familial forms of the condition are reported. Familial dysplastic naevi are also known as the BK mole syndrome or the FAMMM syndrome (Familial Atypical Mole Malignant Melanoma Syndrome). The accurate incidence of this syndrome and the true risk of malignancy in affected families is not yet fully established. Patients with the condition require regular supervision, photography of any unusual naevi and local excision of any such naevi which show growth or any other change.

FURTHER READING

Greene M. H. *et al.*: Acquired precursors of cutaneous malignant melenoma: the familial dysplastic naevus syndrome. *New England Journal of Medicine* **312,** 91–8 (1985).
A very useful article, illustrated in colour.
Ortonne J. P., Mosher J. B., and Fitzpatrick T. B.: *Vitiligo and other hypomelanoses of the hair and skin.* Plenum Publishing Co., New York (1983).

NOTES

10

Disorders of the hair, nails, and sweat glands

Although hair and nails in man are relatively vestigial, abnormality in either can cause apparently disproportionate concern. Obtrusive sweat production is socially unacceptable and can cause considerable distress.

Disorders of the hair and scalp

The normal structure and growth cycle of hair are detailed on p. 27. When dealing with alopecia, however, it is helpful to bear in mind that normally 85 per cent of scalp hairs are in the anagen phase and 15 per cent in catagen or telogen, and that new follicles cannot be formed in the adult, so that a scarred scalp with irreversible damage to hair follicles will have permanent alopecia.

Hair loss on the scalp may be diffuse or patchy, and the commoner causes are listed in Tables 10.1 and 10.2. Patients rarely complain of hair loss from other sites although it does occur, both in isolation and in association with scalp disorders.

The commonest cause of localized or patchy hair loss is alopecia areata (p. 196). The other causes form two groups: those which do not damage hair follicles and can therefore resolve completely, and those which destroy the follicle and lead to *scarring alopecia* with permanent loss of hair.

MALE PATTERN BALDNESS (androgenic alopecia)

Androgen-dependent loss of scalp hair is extremely common in men and increases with age. There is a genetic component determining the age of onset and severity of the process. A small proportion of post-menopausal women are similarly affected. The main area of

Table 10.1.   Common causes of diffuse hair loss

Male pattern baldness (androgen-dependent baldness)
Telogen effluvium (post-partum, fever, 'stress')
Syphilis
Systemic lupus erythematosus
Endocrine causes: hypothyroidism, hypopituitarism
Nutritional (iron deficiency)
Drug-induced (cytotoxics, anticoagulants, vitamin A and analogues) (see Table 10.3)
Hair shaft defects (pili torti and monilethrix)
Trichotillomania
Alopecia areata (may be diffuse or localized)

Table 10.2.   Common causes of localized patchy hair loss

Alopecia areata
Naevoid abnormalities
Fungal infections, including kerion
Chronic discoid lupus erythematosus
Follicular lichen planus
Traction ('ponytail' hair styles, the use of harsh setting implements)

---

loss in men is the crown, with some frontal recession, whereas in women there is fronto-vertical thinning but retention of the frontal hair margin.

In otherwise healthy young men, one can only reassure that there is no underlying disease. Patent remedies and hair tonics are of no proven value, and patients should be told of this.

When women are concerned by androgenic alopecia, a wig may well be justified once endocrine, drug-induced, and iron deficiency alopecia have been excluded (see below). In the U.K., however, there are clear-cut regulations governing the prescription on the National Health Service of either human or synthetic hair wigs. Artificial hair wigs are relatively inexpensive and, unlike those made of human hair, they can be easily washed at home.

TELOGEN EFFLUVIUM

Under certain conditions, notably during pregnancy when blood oestrogen is raised, the percentage of hair follicles in anagen rises. As a result, there is a luxuriant head of hair, but after parturition the follicles held in anagen all enter telogen, and these hairs are therefore shed. This can give rise to significant hair thinning, commonly seen 4–9 months after delivery, but the situation is self-limiting. Possibly, the diffuse loss of hair which follows high fever, severe illness, or 'stress' results from a similar disturbance of the hair cycle. No specific treatment is required, and after 3–4 months hair follicles resume their normal synchronization.

SYPHILIS

Some patients with secondary syphilis present with a diffuse 'moth-eaten' pattern of hair loss, but its relationship to the other signs and symptoms at this stage is unclear. Serology is positive. Hair regrowth follows adequate antibiotic therapy (p. 138).

SYSTEMIC LUPUS ERYTHEMATOSUS

Patients with active, usually severe, systemic lupus erythematosus and multisystem involvement may have diffuse generalized hair loss. Unlike the patchy alopecia seen in chronic discoid LE, it is temporary and good regrowth will follow successful systemic therapy.

ENDOCRINE ALOPECIA

Hair loss can accompany hypofunction of the thyroid and pituitary glands. In hypothyroidism hair growth is poor, and the hair shaft is coarse and wire-like. In hypopituitarism total loss of scalp, eyebrow, and secondary sexual hair is frequently seen. This type of alopecia does not always recover after adequate endocrine replacement.

NUTRITIONAL ALOPECIA

Chronic iron deficiency anaemia is associated with thin fragile scalp hair (Fig. 10.1). Severe generalized malnutrition also causes hair loss and premature greying of remaining hair.

DRUG-INDUCED ALOPECIA

Certain cytotoxic drugs commonly give rise to alopecia and those responsible are listed in Table 10.3. Patients tolerate this form of

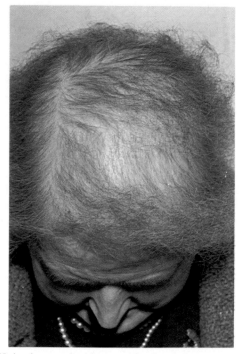

Fig. 10.1.   Hair loss coincident with hypochromic anaemia. Good regrowth was achieved after correction of the iron deficiency.

iatrogenic alopecia much more readily if they are warned beforehand of its inevitability. A well-made wig will greatly improve morale. Heparin and warfarin occasionally cause hair loss, and large

Table 10.3.   Drugs which commonly cause alopecia

Cytotoxic drugs	Cyclophosphamide
	Mercaptopurine derivatives
	Colchicine
	Adriamycin
Anticoagulants	Heparin
	Coumarins
Antithyroid drugs	Thiouracil
	Carbimazole
Antituberculous drug	Ethionamide
Excess vitamin A and synthetic retinoids	

doses of vitamin A and the newer synthetic retinoids cause generalized diffuse alopecia.

Topical applications have, as far as is known, only a placebo effect in the above disorders. All patients presenting with generalized hair loss should be investigated for a remediable cause. In a small proportion, usually female, no obvious cause is found and the condition fits no recognized pattern. In these cases, the label 'idiopathic diffuse hair loss' is applied.

HAIR SHAFT DEFECTS

A variety of congenital abnormalities of the hair shaft causing undue fragility have been described. Patients present with short broken hair and patchy alopecia. The most common are *monilethrix* (beaded hair) and *pili torti* (twisted hair) (Fig. 10.2). Both of these, and also rarer abnormalities, can be diagnosed on light microscopy of the hair. No topical treatment is available, but gentle handling and a short hair style can be of some value.

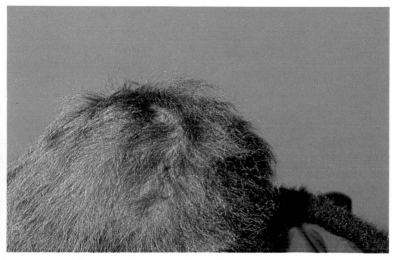

Fig. 10.2. Pili torti. Note the 'spangled' appearance and dry, brittle hair.

TRICHOTILLOMANIA

Definition. A compulsive desire to pull, twist, and tug at scalp hair.

Extreme forms may be seen in inmates of homes for the mentally subnormal and bizarre patterns of hair loss, often unilateral, with clearly visible broken hairs, will suggest the diagnosis.

ALOPECIA AREATA

Definition. A condition characterized by either generalized or localized sudden hair loss from the scalp or other body sites.

In some patients there appears to be an underlying genetic predisposition. Certain sub-groups are recognized, including one associated with atopy and one with 'autoimmune' disorders (e.g. thyroid disorders, vitiligo, diabetes). The condition is commoner in children with Down's syndrome.

Alopecia areata is common and accounts for approximately 2 per cent of new cases seen as dermatological out-patients. Most cases are in children or young adults, and the commonest initial sign is one or more well demarcated, completely bald areas. The affected scalp is normal with no sign of inflammation, scaling, or scarring, but hairs plucked from the margin of the area are often 'club hairs', i.e. in telogen, and broken hairs in this area resembling exclamation marks (!) are diagnostic (Fig. 10.3).

Complete loss of scalp hair is referred to as *alopecia totalis*, and when all body hair also is lost, the term *alopecia universalis* is applied.

It is not unusual in alopecia areata for the nails to be pitted and ridged.

Sponatenous regrowth takes place after an interval of 2–6 months in the majority of cases, but repeated episodes of hair loss are by no means uncommon. Features suggesting that the prognosis must be guarded include associated atopy, loss of eyebrows and lashes, nail change, and multiple lesions at the scalp margins—the so-called ophiasic type.

Diagnosis and treatment

The diagnosis is usually evident on clinical examination but a typical or scaly lesions require mycological examination of scrapings and hair samples to exclude a fungal infection. The use of Wood's light (p. 7) will exclude fungal infection due to most *Microsporum* species and to *Trichophyton schoenleinii*, but not to other species of fungi.

Fig. 10.3. Alopecia areata. Regular circular lesions appear rapidly. The underlying scalp appears smooth and healthy.

Scalp biopsy is rarely necessary, although the histology is characteristic. There is no loss of hair follicles, but the bulbs lie high in the dermis, are surrounded by lymphoid cells, and produce imperfectly keratinized hair.

As most cases of alopecia areata are self-limiting, the best plan is to reassure the patient and to encourage patience. Sometimes a placebo, such as a course of ultraviolet light (UVB), is justified and helpful. Corticosteroids (e.g. triamcinolone) intralesionally may stimulate the regrowth of a tuft of hair adjacent to the needle track, but the cosmetic result is no improvement on the pre-existing alopecia. In severe and extensive cases prescription of a wig is indicated.

Regrowth of hair may be achieved with systemic steroid administration, but as in many cases it is sustained only by continuing the steroid therapy, these drugs are not recommended, particularly for children.

NAEVOID ABNORMALITIES

Infants and very young children are occasionally seen with a well-demarcated patch of complete alopecia, and with neither scaling nor fragility of the surrounding hair. This may be due to naevoid abnormalities such as *aplasia cutis*, but histological confirmation of this diagnosis is needed.

FUNGAL SCALP INFECTIONS

The patient is usually a child with patchy scaly alopecia and siblings may also be affected. All suspected cases and contacts should be examined under Wood's light (long UV wavelength 365 nm). However, only lesions due to *Microsporum canis* or *M. audouini* will show bright blue-green flurescence. Other fungi which commonly cause tinea capitis, such as *Trichophyton verrucosum* and *T. tonsurans*, will not fluoresce in this manner. Scalp scrapings and hairs should be examined microscopically, and cultured to demonstrate the fungus.

Sometimes the fungus stimulates an intense inflammatory reaction which forms a large boggy lesion with hair loss and a purulent discharge from the follicles. This constitutes a *kerion* and is usually due to *T. verrucosum* or *T. mentagrophytes* (animal ringworm).

Proven scalp ringworm is treated with full doses of griseofulvin by mouth (p. 130). Hair regrows normally except when lesions such as a kerion leave scarring.

CHRONIC DISCOID LUPUS ERYTHEMATOSUS

Patients with facial lesions of CDLE may have similar lesions on the scalp. The alpecia resulting from these lesions is patchy and scaly, and has follicles plugged by scales and an erythematous advancing margin. As it is a scarring process, permanent alopecia will result. Treatment of early lesions and attempts to prevent new lesions developing are discussed on p. 149.

LICHEN PLANUS

Occasionally, lichen planus affects the scalp and causes permanent scarring alopecia.

TRACTION ALOPECIA

Localized hair loss and broken hairs, particularly round the hair margin, may be caused mechanically by tight hair styles (e.g. 'ponytails') or the use of harsh hair setting equipment.

EXCESSIVE GROWTH OF HAIR

Two terms are applied to excessive hair growth. *Hirsuties* refers to excess growth of androgen-dependent hair in a male pattern, whereas *hypertrichosis* is an excess growth of hair in a non-androgenic pattern. Hypertrichosis is seen in both sexes, but hirsuties is restricted to females, for although men are quick to seek help for baldness, they do not complain of excessive growth of hair in a normal distribution.

HIRSUTISM

Fine vellus hair covers much of the body in both sexes and can be induced by androgens to transform into coarse terminal hair. The causes of hirsutism can be grouped under general headings as in Table 10.4.

Women with hirsutism complain of hair growth in the beard area

Table 10.4. Causes of hirsutism

---

1 Adrenal: Cushing's syndrome, virilizing tumours, congenital adrenal hyperplasia
2 Pituitary: acromegaly
3 Ovarian: polycystic ovaries, virilizing tumours, gonadal dysgenesis
4 Turner's syndrome
5 Iatrogenic: due to androgenic drugs
6 Idiopathic: target or end-organ hypersensitivity

(Fig. 10.4), around the nipples, and in a male pattern on the abdomen. They are more likely to be dark-haired and the problem appears to be commoner in certain racial groups, e.g. those of Mediterranean origin. Hirsutism can cause remarkable distress to a healthy woman and psychological disturbance with depression is common in younger women, even those in whom the condition is relatively mild.

Investigation and treatment

The aim in investigating the hirsute patient is to exclude an underlying remediable endocrine cause. Although many tests of adrenal, ovarian, and pituitary function are available, the young

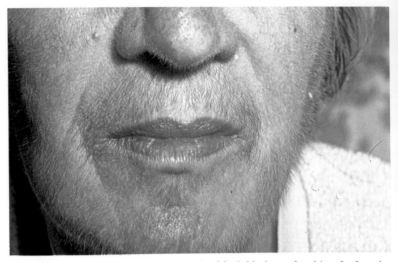

Fig. 10.4.   Hirsuties. Excessive growth of facial hair on the chin of a female.

woman who is menstruating regularly and has had one or more successful pregnancies, probably requires little in the way of endocrine assessment and is likely to fall into the idiopathic group, in which to date only marginally elevated levels of plasma testosterone have been found. It would appear that the fault in this group, by far the largest, lies in the hypersensitivity of the hair follicle as an end-organ of androgen stimulation.

Full endocrine assessment is however essential in patients with amenorrhoea, scanty, irregular periods, or other signs of excess androgen stimulation.

Therapy for those with no demonstrable remediable cause consists of physical methods of hair removal. Shaving, bleaching, and depilatory creams are all used, but the most satisfactory method is waxing as it also removes a large part of the hair shaft lying under the skin surface. Most patients find a professional demonstration of the technique helpful.

HYPERTRICHOSIS

Hypertrichosis may be either congenital or acquired.

Congenital varieties are frequently associated with melanocytic naevi, while lumbosacral hypertrichosis ('faun tail') should alert the paediatrician or obstetrician to the possibility of spina bifida occulta.

Acquired hypertrichosis is most commonly drug-induced, 201 although porphyria (p. 248) and endocrine disorders (thyroid dysfunction and anorexia nervosa) are recognized causes. Drugs in current use which can cause hypertrichosis include diazoxide, diphenylhydantoin, penicillamine, and the psoralens. If the offending drug is withdrawn, the excessive hair growth will cease.

PITYRIASIS CAPITIS

Excessive scaling of the scalp is frequently associated with mild degrees of seborrhoeic dermatitis (p. 97). It can be controlled by regularly applying a weak salicylic acid preparation, such as 2–10 per cent salicylic acid in aqueous cream, for 6–8 hours before shampooing.

Disorders of the nails

The normal anatomy of the nail is described on p. 30. Factors controlling nail growth are poorly understood but the average time taken for a finger nail to grow out is 6–12 months and for a toe nail 18–24 months. These figures increase with age and there is seasonal variation, with some acceleration in the summer months. Individual nails also vary in their growth rates, with the thumb nail growing relatively rapidly.

Although nail biopsy through both nail and nail bed is feasible it is more traumatic than a routine skin biopsy, so fewer histological specimens from nail disorders than from other sites have been studied. Diagnosis is therefore commonly based on clinical appearances.

Nail involvement is common in many skin diseases: for example, onycholysis and pitting in psoriasis, discoloration and crumbling in fungal infections, pitting and ridging in chronic dermatitis, and a more severe dystrophy in lichen planus. These are all discussed with the relevant diseases.

Nail disorders can however occur in isolation and can be either congenital or acquired.

Congenital nail disorders

THE NAIL-PATELLA SYNDROME

This condition is transmitted by autosomal dominant inheritance. The patellae and some of the nails are rudimentary or absent. The thumb nails are usually involved.

PACHYONYCHIA CONGENITA

Misshapen, hypertrophic nails are present from birth and there may also be associated mucous membrane abnormalities. The condition is inherited by autosomal dominant transmission (Fig. 10.5).

Acquired nail defects

BEAU'S LINES

Definition. Transverse ridges on the nails due to temporary interference with nail formation.

These lines are commonly seen during convalescence from a variety of severe disease states, e.g. pneumonia and other conditions causing prolonged fever.

The condition is self-limiting.

KOILONYCHIA

Definition. Loss of the normal nail contour resulting in a flat or even depressed surface.

Nails of this shape are commonly slow-growing and brittle. They are most commonly associated with hypochromic anaemia and correction of iron deficiency may be followed by return to normal growth of the nails.

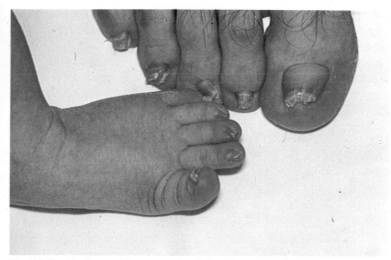

Fig. 10.5. Pachyonychia congenita. Note the gross abnormality of all toe nails in both father and son. Finger nails were similarly affected.

FINGER CLUBBING

Definition. An exaggeration of the normal nail curve associated with loss of the normal angle between nail and posterior nail fold.

In adults this appearance is commonly seen in those with pulmonary pathology. If of slow onset, chronic respiratory infection and bronchiectasis is a likely cause, and if of more rapid onset, the possibility of carcinoma of the lung must be considered. In young people clubbing and nail changes may be seen in association with cyanotic congenital heart disease.

The mechanisms giving rise to these conformational changes of the finger tips are not understood. The resultant lesions may be both disfiguring and painful.

PARONYCHIA

Acute paronychia is commonly due to staphylococcal infection and consists of an acutely inflamed posterior nail fold with a purulent discharge. There is frequently a history of trauma. Response to an appropriate systemic antibiotic is prompt.

Chronic paronychia is more persistent and troublesome. Usually, several nails arc affected and show striking loss of the cuticle with tender bolstered posterior nail folds. If bacterial in origin the likely organisms are *Pseudomonas pyocyanea* and *Proteus vulgaris*, but frequently the cause is *Candida*, usually *C. albicans*. Persistent immersion of the hands in water is a common predisposing factor, so that housewives and barmaids are particularly at risk.

Treatment should be directed at organisms identified on culture. *Candida albicans* usually responds well to nystatin suspension or amphotericin B lotion. A useful paint is freshly prepared sulphacetamide 15 per cent in 50 per cent ethanol applied four times daily. Griseofulvin is not of value in these cases.

If the paronychia is shown to be due to *Candida* and does not respond to topical therapy a 2–4 week course of ketoconazole (Nizoral) 200 mg/day in justified. The day must not be given to pregnant women and liver function must be monitored.

If wet work must be done, cotton gloves under rubber gloves must be worn and changed frequently.

HERPETIC WHITLOW

Acute paronychia due to herpes simplex is an occupational hazard in doctors and nurses. It is discussed on p. 118.

PARONYCHIAL TUMOURS

Warts are frequently found around the nails and may be extremely painful due to pressure on the nail bed. They respond slowly to conventional therapy (p. 114).

Malignant tumours may also occur in this site, the most serious being a malignant melanoma. Any patient with a bleeding or pigmented nodule in the region of a nail should be referred without delay for a diagnostic biopsy and definitive treatment.

IATROGENIC NAIL ABNORMALITIES

Systemic drug therapy can cause a variety of nail changes. Tetracycline-induced photosensitivity can lead to nail loss and long-term ingestion of tetracyclines may cause yellow nails. Antimalarial drugs cause blue and blue-black discoloration of the nail beds.

Disorders of the sweat glands

The sweat glands are of two sorts. The *eccrine glands* are concerned with thermoregulation and are distributed over the entire body surface. The *apocrine glands*, found chiefly in the axillae and groins, have no apparent function in man, but appear to be stimulated by emotional stress and contribute to axillary odour.

Eccrine gland disorders

MILIARIA (prickly heat)

In the U.K. miliaria is a rarity, except in a heat wave or the tropical environment of a neonatal nursery. In subtropical or tropical climates, it is common, especially in new arrivals who have not yet acclimatized. Sweat duct obstruction due to high humidity is the cause.

Clinically, there is an acute papulo-vesicular eruption, usually on the trunk. It is itchy, and scratching often leads to crusting and secondary infection.

Treatment is palliative, unless the humidity can be adequately reduced. This is feasible, desirable, and effective in the nursery. Residents in the tropics with no adequate air conditioning may find that wearing a thin layer of cellular cotton clothing next to the skin facilitates evaporation of sweat and decreases humidity of the epidermal horny layer. A shake lotion such as calamine lotion BP can be soothing.

HYPERHIDROSIS

Over-production of eccrine sweat can be due to heat or to emotional stimuli, but is rarely due to endocrinological or neurological disorders. The nature of the stimulus determines whether the hyperhidrosis is localized or generalized. When localized, the palms, soles, and axillae are the usual sites. Malodour of the feet and axillae due to bacterial overgrowth is common and distressing. Hyperhidrosis of the palms can incapacitate those whose work involves writing and handling of paper.

In generalized hyperhidrosis it is important first to exclude underlying systemic disease, then prescribe glycopyrronium bromide 2–8 mg/day, propantheline bromide 15–30 mg/day, or propranolol 20–40 mg t.i.d. Anticholinergic side effects may limit the value of the first two preparations.

For localized hyperhidrosis, topical preparations are generally more effective, but may require supplementation with systemic therapy. A paint consisting of 20 per cent aluminium chloride hexahydrate made up in 70 per cent alcohol applied overnight to clean, dry palms, soles, and axillae is effective, mainly in the axillae. If the axillae only are affected surgical excision of ellipses of skin 2–4 inches long from the vault of the axilla can be dramatically effective. The areas of maximum sweat production should be removed and they can be identified prior to surgery by starch-iodine application. This entire procedure can be done as an out-patient under local anaesthesia.

Other surgical procedures such as sympathectomy are rarely helpful.

Apocrine gland disorder

HIDRADENITIS SUPPURATIVA

Definition. Deep-seated inflammatory lesions chiefly in the axillae and groins (Fig. 10.6).

A functional and structural abnormality of apocrine sweat glands is postulated as the cause of this disorder. Patients present with multiple deeply-situated pustules and abscesses which in time damage the dermis and lead to deep scarring. Deep cord-like fibrotic lesions may restrict movement.

Long-term systemic antibiotic therapy given for a minimum of 3–6 months may give temporary relief, but relapse when the antibiotics are stopped is the usual course of events. In some patients hidradenitis suppurativa is associated with severe acne. In patients with this combination the use of oral 13-*cis*-retinoic acid (Ro-accutane) given

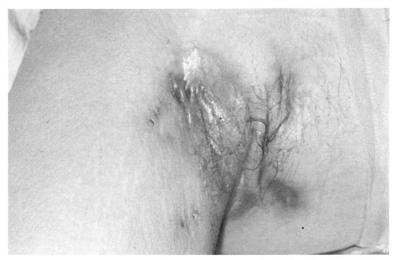

Fig. 10.6. Hidradenitis suppurativa. Recurrent infection in the apocrine glands causes development of fibrotic scar tissue.

orally in a dose of 1 mg/kg/day for 3 months may be of therapeutic value. In women of childbearing age adequate contraception is essential.

Surgical excision of the affected area with skin grafting if required tends to be the most useful method of permanently erradicating this difficult problem.

GROWTH POINTS

The use of topical irritants and vasodilators in the treatment of alopecia areata. There has over the last few years been a large number of publications claiming successful regrowth of hair in patches of alopecia areata following application of topical sensitizing agents such as Dinitrochlorobenzene, Primula leaf, Diphencyprone, and also of the use of the vasodilator Minoxidil topically. Reports of this nature have reached the popular press and patients may well ask for such therapy. The few double blind controlled trials which have been done comparing any of the above agents with placebo have shown little statistically significant benefit of the use of these agents. The problem here is that we are dealing with conditions which are self limiting and spontaneous regrowth is to be expected.

FURTHER READING

Baran, R. and Dawber, R. P. R.: *Diseases of the Nails and their Management*. Blackwell Scientific Publications, Oxford (1984).
An excellent account of all known abnormalities of the nail.
Rooke, A. J. and Dawber, R. P. R.: *Disorders of the Hair and Scalp*. Blackwell Scientific Publications, Oxford (1983).
A comprehensive account of abnormalities of the hair follicle.

NOTES

11

Blistering diseases

Blisters may develop in the course of a large number of dermatological disorders, but in adults there is a smaller group of diseases in which blisters appear early and are the predominant feature. The three principal diseases in this category are *pemphigus vulgaris, bullous pemphigoid,* and *dermatitis herpetiformis,* and they all usually present in adult life. Children develop blisters more easily, and in a wider range of diseases which are discussed in Chapter 14.

The word 'blister' is used here to describe an elevated cutaneous lesion filled with clear fluid. Other terms in current usage for such lesions are *bulla* and *vesicle,* which is an alternative term for a blister smaller than 3–5 mm in diameter.

As will be seen below, a biopsy of a blistering eruption is frequently required to confirm a clinical diagnosis. In such cases, both paraffin wax-embedded material and frozen material will be required, the first for conventional microscopic examination, and the second for immunopathological studies. In such cases it is important to biopsy a lesion that will yield accurate information, and ideally a small blister should be excised intact. If the blister is older than 24 hours, early epidermal regeneration may make histological diagnosis difficult. In general it is better to perform two small biopsies, submitting an intact blister for paraffin wax embedding, and a biopsy from a second site for instant freezing and subsequent immunopathological studies. In pemphigus vulgaris and bullous pemphigoid, this second specimen may be a second small blister, whereas in dermatitis herpetiformis the skin adjacent to a blister will yield more useful information. It is usual to compromise and remove a small blister together with a reasonable amount of normal skin on the long axis of the skin ellipse. While punch biopsies may be acceptable for the study of perilesional skin, scalpel biopsies will give very much better orientation in the study of blistering skin.

PEMPHIGUS

Definition. A group of disorders characterized by the formation of a blister within the epidermis.

There are four varieties of pemphigus: pemphigus vulgaris, pemphigus vegetans, pemphigus foliaceus, and pemphigus erythematosus. The latter three varieties are rare and will not be discussed further in this chapter.

Pemphigus vulgaris affects both sexes equally and is found more frequently in the Jewish race. Immunological studies in the past decade have provided considerable circumstantial evidence that pemphigus vulgaris is an autoimmune disease. An antibody has been demonstrated which has specificity for the intercullular substances of the epidermis. This is found both in the skin and circulating in the peripheral blood. Circulating levels of this antibody correlate with disease activity in the individual patient. Passive transfer of this antibody has led to the development of histological changes of pemphigus in animal models, and similar findings have been recorded when pemphigus antibody is added to short-term organ cultures of human skin.

Pathology

The striking and diagnostic histological feature in pemphigus is loss of cohesion of the epidermal cells. This results in *acantholysis*, in which individual keratinocytes lose their normal intercellular bridges and round off. They may be seen floating freely in the resultant blister. In pemphigus vulgaris this blister usually lies just above the basal layer, which remains adherent to the basal lamina and is said to resemble a row of tombstones.

Immunopathology

If frozen sections of pemphigus skin are cut at 4–6 μm, and treated with fluorescein-conjugated immunoglobulin directed against IgG and complement components, deposits of both will be observed in the intercellular spaces, giving a 'crazy-paving' effect. This is the *direct* test. The *indirect* test for circulating antibody requires a suitable substrate tissue which may be mucous membrane or skin from a variety of species, e.g. primate oesophagus, guinea-pig lip, or human vaginal mucosa. The patient's serum is layered on 4–6 µm frozen sections of this tissue, washed off, and fluorescein-labelled antibody to IgG and complement applied. As in the direct test, bright apple-green fluorescence of the intercellular spaces will be seen (Fig. 11.1). This test can be quantified in that the serum can be diluted until no reaction is obtained. In active cases serum dilutions greater than 1/1000 will still give a positive result. As the disease responds to treatment the level of circulating antibody falls, so sequential estimations of circulating antibody level are a useful guide to efficacy of therapy and the patient's response.

Clinical features

Pemphigus vulgaris frequently begins insidiously with the slow development of raw areas and shallow erosions on the mucous membranes (Fig. 11.2). Involvement of the skin tends to come later (Fig. 11.3). The patient may therefore complain first of mouth ulcers or genital discomfort. The lesions do not itch, but can be very painful. Blisters may develop on both mucous membrane and skin, but they are quickly denuded by friction or pressure, leaving a raw surface. This feature reflects the thin blister roof of the intraepider-

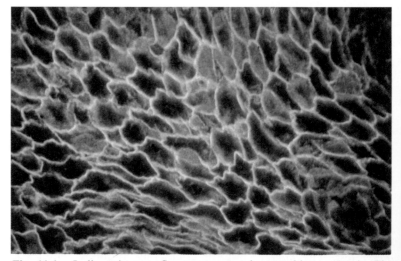

Fig. 11.1.   Indirect immunofluorescence test in pemphigus vulgaris. The patient's serum has been layered on mucous membrane substrate and subsequently treated with fluorescein-conjugated antihuman IgG. Specific staining of the intercellular substance is observed.

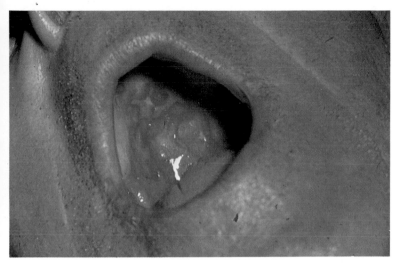

Fig. 11.2. Oral lesions in a case of early pemphigus vulgaris.

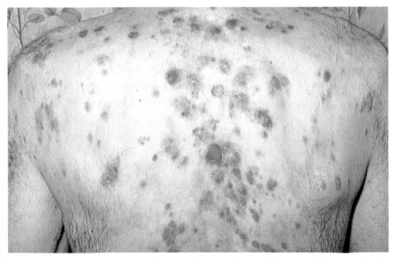

Fig. 11.3. Lesions on the back of a patient with pemphigus vulgaris. Shallow erosions are seen, and healing lesions show some increase in pigmentation.

mal blister in pemphigus in contrast to the greater resilience of the subepidermal blister in bullous pemphigoid and dermatitis herpetiformis. Clinically normal skin may display the *Nikolsky sign*—if lateral pressure is put on the skin surface with the thumb the epidermis appears to slide over the underlying dermis.

Secondary infection and disturbance of fluid and electrolyte balance are common complications of untreated pemphigus which, prior to the introduction of corticosteroid therapy, was regularly fatal.

Diagnosis and treatment

Shallow erosions and blisters on the skin and mucous membranes suggest the diagnosis. Skin biopsy will show an *intraepidermal* blister and, if available, direct immunofluorescence will confirm the presence of tissue-fixed intercellular antibody in the epidermis. A serum sample will demonstrate the presence of circulating intercellular antibody. Table 11.1 lists conditions which may cause diagnostic confusion.

The diagnosis should be confirmed and treatment started without delay. Systemic steroids should be administered. The exact dose depends on the patient's size and disease severity, but the range is from 60–100 mg of prednisolone or equivalent per day. Once control has been achieved and no fresh blisters are developing, the dose can be slowly reduced by 20–30 mg/week. A maintenance dose is usually necessary, possibly for life to prevent recurrence. This should be kept as low as possible, preferably using an alternate day regime to minimize steroid side-effects. In some patients the addition of an immunosuppressive agent, such as azathioprine or cyclophospha214 mide, will allow further reduction of the steroid dose. Plasmapheresis is occasionally needed in severe cases.

Topical therapy is mainly symptomatic, and aimed at protecting the raw areas and decreasing the incidence of secondary infection. Vaseline-impregnated gauze dressings are kind to the patient and the lesions should be managed in the same way as burns. In severe cases a ripple bed, burns hammock, or net bed may be valuable.

Although the disease is usually controllable, it has little tendency to remit spontaneously. Consequently, the patient will probably have to remain on systemic steroids for life and will therefore require careful surveillance for steroid-induced side effects.

	Site	History	Histology	Immunology	Other tests
Pemphigus	Mucous membranes, and trunk	Insidious onset	Intraepidermal blister	Direct IgG C$_3$ Circulating IgG,	
Pemphigoid	Upper arms and thighs	Blisters on eczematous base	Subepidermal blister	Fixed Ig and C$_3$ at dermo-epidermal junction. Circulating IgG	
Dermatitis herpetiformis	Scalp, scapular area, elbows, buttocks	Pruritus + + +	Subepidermal blister	IgA in papillary dermis	Subtotal villous atrophy on jejunal biopsy
Erythema multiforme	Hands and feet	Target lesions	Subepidermal blister	Negative	Occasionally drug or viral history
Mechanical blisters	Site of trauma	Friction, e.g. marching, poorly fitting clothes	Subepidermal blister	Negative	
Atypical herpes simplex	Variable	Prodromal pain and tingling	Balloon degeneration within the epidermis	Rising specific antibody titre	Electron microscopy to demonstrate virus particles
Herpes zoster	Linear dermatome distribution	Pain and tingling: may be severe	Intraepidermal balloon degeneration	Rising specific antibody titre	
Porphyria cutanea tarda	Sun-exposed sites	Sun exposure, minor friction, and trauma	Subepidermal blister	Autofluorescence of porphyrins	Raised uroporphyrin levels

BULLOUS PEMPHIGOID

Definition. A chronic blistering disorder characterized by large, tense blisters on an erythematous base.

As its name implies, this disease was formerly confused with pemphigus and it was not until 1953 that the distinctive histological features of the disease were identified. Any paper written on 'pemphigus' before this time is likely therefore to relate to a mixture of the two disorders.

Bullous pemphigoid in the U.K. is a commoner disease than pemphigus, and there is no racial prevalence. Patients are usually elderly and present in the sixth decade or later. There is some debate about a possible association between bullous pemphigoid and 216 malignancy. This is further discussed on p. 262.

Pathology

The blister is *subepidermal*, formed between the dermis and epidermis. As the entire thickness of the epidermis forms the roof of the blisters, they are relatively resilient and may remain intact for several days.

As with pemphigus, tissue-fixed and circulating autoantibodies have been demonstrated, suggesting that the disease may have an autoimmune pathogenesis. In bullous pemphigoid, immunoglobulin and complement are found at the dermo-epidermal junction in a linear band (Fig. 11.4), and there is a circulating antibody specific to this site. Passive transfer studies have not yet reproduced pemphigoid lesions and the titre of pemphigoid antibody does not correlate as well with disease activity as does pemphigus antibody.

Clinical features

Patients present with large tense blisters, mainly on the upper arms and thighs (Fig. 11.5). These arise on an eczematous base and there is itch rather than pain. Some spontaneous haemorrhage into the blisters is not uncommon. Oral lesions are less frequent than in pemphigus but should be sought.

Treatment

Systemic steroid therapy is necessary, but unlike pemphigus, it may be possible to discontinue this after two to three years. A starting

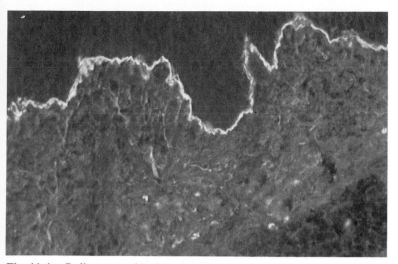

Fig. 11.4. Bullous pemphigoid. Direct immunofluorescence test. A piece of skin from the edge of a blister has been treated with FITC conjugated antihuman C₃. A linear band of fluorescence is seen at the dermo-epidermal junction.

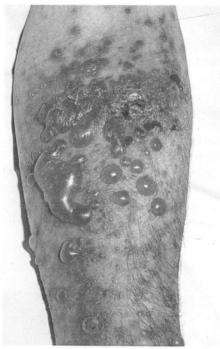

Fig. 11.5. Blisters of bullous pemphigoid. Large, tense, raised lesions are seen on an erythematous eczematized base.

dose of 60–100 mg prednisolone or equivalent should be gradually reduced to the minimum which will control the disease. Further dose reduction may be possible if immunosuppressive agents are added to the regimen.

DERMATITIS HERPETIFORMIS

Definition. An intensely itchy blistering condition associated with a gluten-sensitive enteropathy.

Dermatitis herpetiformis (DH) affects a younger age group than the other two blistering disorders. Patients present in the third and fourth decade and males are more commonly affected.

Pathology

The blisters are subepidermal and are small by comparison with the larger lesions in bullous pemphigoid. There are frequently aggregates of leukocytes in so-called 'microabscesses' at tips of the dermal papillae flanking the blister.

No circulating antibody has yet been consistently found in DH patients, but direct immunofluorescence of the skin around lesions will reveal the presence of IgA and sometimes complement in the dermal papillae (Fig. 11.6).

Clinical features

Patients complain of an intense burning itch on the affected sites, commonly the scalp, scapular area, buttocks, and elbows (Fig. 11.7). Very small blisters may be found, but as they are quickly excoriated, raw papules may be the only lesions seen.

Most patients will have no overt signs or symptoms of malabsorption but, even so, a jejunal biopsy should be performed, for subtotal villous atrophy, if present, should be treated with a gluten-free diet. Some dermatologists believe that gluten intolerance is an invariable accompaniment of dermatitis herpetiformis and manage all patients on a gluten-free diet.

Treatment

Dermatitis herpetiformis does not respond to steroids. Itch will be controlled by dapsone in doses of 100–400 mg/day, but careful haematological monitoring is necessary, as a haemolytic anaemia

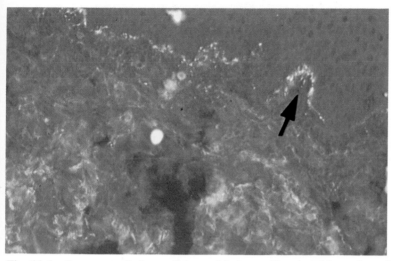

Fig. 11.6. Immunopathology of dermatitis herpetiformis. This section of perilesional skin has been treated with FITC-labelled antihuman IgA. Note fluorescence marked with arrow in dermal papilla.

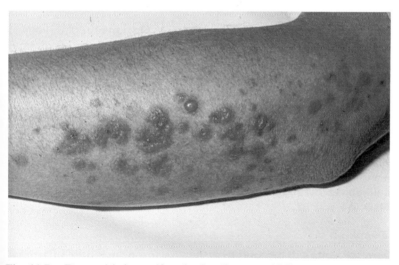

Fig. 11.7. Dermatitis herpetiformis. Small grouped blisters are seen.

may develop. Sulphapyridine by mouth is also useful, the dose being 0.5–1.0 g/day. Other newer sulphonamides arc less effective. Topical steroid-antibiotic combinations (e.g. vioform-hydrocortisone, β-methasone 17-valerate with chinoform, or aureomycin) are useful supplements to systemic therapy.

There is some evidence that strict adherence to a gluten-free diet will benefit the skin as well as the gut, but this may not be apparent until after many months or even years of diet.

As this is a chronic disease, treatment may need to be life-long.

LINEAR IgA DISEASE

Definition. A pruritic blistering eruption, clinically resembling dermatitis herpetiformis and bullous pemphigoid.

Until the late 1970s, this condition was considered a variant of dermatitis herpetiformis. Recent studies have demonstrated a different immunopathology, different immunogenetic association, and a varying response to therapy appropriate for dermatitis herpetiformis. It is now therefore considered to be an entity in its own right.

Pathology and immunopathology

Small subepidermal blisters are present. On immunopathological testing, a fine continuous band of IgA is seen at the dermo-epidermal junction, in contrast to the coarse clumps of IgA seen in the dermal papillae in dermatitis herpetiformis.

Clinical features

Affected patients have blisters mainly on the extremities. A common pattern of blister development is an erythematous central area, with small vesicles or blisters on the periphery.

Affected individuals do not have any gastrointestinal pathology and unlike dermatitis herpetiformis there is no association with HLA A1 and B8.

Treatment

Some patients will respond to systemic dapsone in a dose of around 100 mg daily. Others will require low doses of systemic steroids (prednisolone 10–20 mg daily or equivalent).

ERYTHEMA MULTIFORME

Definition. An erythematous disorder characterized by annular target lesions which may develop into frank blisters.

Erythema multiforme (EM) is a cutaneous reaction pattern which may be provoked by viral infection, commonly herpes simplex, by bacterial infection, by drug ingestion, and many other stimuli. In many cases, however, no aetiological or precipitating factor can be identified. In the bullous lesions of EM, the blister forms at the dermo-epidermal junction, and there is necrosis and destruction of the overlying epidermis.

The lesions are most commonly seen on the hands and feet and initially present as raised erythematous plaques which expand laterally to give the classic 'iris lesion' or 'target lesion' appearance. Severe involvement of the eyes and mucosal surfaces is termed the *Stevens–Johnson syndrome.*

Mild cases will remit spontaneously and require only topical therapy to prevent secondary infection. In severe cases a 7–10-day course of systemic steroid therapy may be necessary.

The differential diagnosis of blistering disorders

In adults the differential diagnosis of blistering disorders includes the three major immuno-bullous disorders discussed in this chapter, and also occasionally mechano-bullous blistering disorders initiated by friction. Onset of these disorders is, however, rare in adult life. Herpes zoster and herpes simplex may present as blistering conditions, as may porphyria cutanea tarda. Viral diseases are discussed on p. 118 and porphyria on p. 248. Erythema multiforme may present as blisters in the centre of target lesions predominantly on the hands and feet (see above).

Toxic epidermal necrolysis (TEN) may present either as blisters or as grossly denuded areas of skin resembling a second-degree burn (Fig. 11.8). Some cases of this condition are the result of adverse reactions to systemic drugs but others are of unknown aetiology. The pathological lesion in TEN is very similar to that in erythema multiforme and many workers consider TEN to be a severe variant of erythema multiforme.

The *staphylococcal scalded skin syndrome* may also present as fragile, quickly-ruptured blisters. The lesion here is situated high in the epidermis and is caused by an epidermolytic toxin of certain phage types of *Staph. aureus* (Fig. 11.9). The condition is commoner in children than in adults.

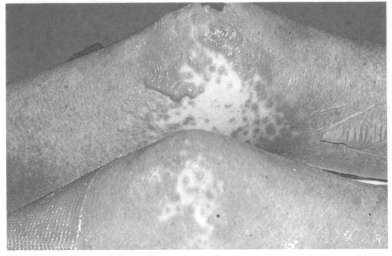

Fig. 11.8.   Toxic epidermal necrolysis. Note extensive erythema and early development of blisters and raw areas on the legs.

General points concerning the investigation of patients with blisters

A careful history, and examination of the skin and mucous membranes of a patient presenting with a blistering disease will usually give a lead as to the disease process responsible. A skin biopsy is frequently required for confirmation, and wherever possible skin should be taken for both pathological and immunopathological studies. A serum sample should also be taken for assay of circulating antibodies. If a viral cause is suspected, electron microscopy of a thick smear of exudate from the lesion will confirm the presence of virus particles, and an acute and convalescent serum sample will confirm the presence of a rising antibody titre to the suspected virus.

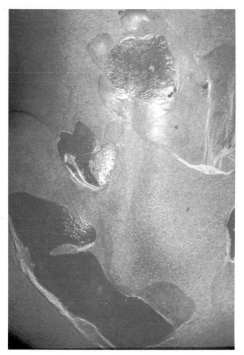

Fig. 11.9. Staphylococcal scalded skin syndrome. Note the shearing of the epidermis, and the lack of inflammation of the surrounding skin.

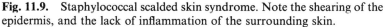

It is frequently necessary to start treatment of a patient with extensive blisters before the results of all investigations are available, as this group of disorders is one of the few areas in which there is still a significantly mortality. Early introduction of systemic steroid therapy can be a life-saving measure.

GROWTH POINTS

Isolation and characterization of pemphigus antigen. Over the years the number of workers have attempted to demonstrate the antigen against which pemphigus antibody is directed. Initially, this was thought to be the desmosomes which run between one keratinocyte and another, but early work clearly proved that pemphigus antibody is not the same as antidesmosome antibody. Recent work carried out by Stanley and his colleagues has suggested that pemphigus antigen may be a high molecular weight protein of around 130 000 daltons. If this is confirmed it may mean that in the future we move from the immunofluorescent type of identification of pemphigus antibody to a rather more sophisticated and easily mechanised radio-immuno assay.

FURTHER READING

Sams, W. M. and Gammon W. R.: Mechanism of lesion production in pemphigus and pemphigoid. *Journal of the American Academy of Dermatology* **6,** 431–46 (1982).

It is obvious that more than the presence of pemphigus or pemphigoid antibody is necessary to produce the actual lesions characterizing the disease as the antibody can be demonstrated in what is clinically normal skin. This excellent and scientific review explains the other features which are involved in the actual production of blisters in these conditions.

NOTES

12

Drug eruptions

The commonest request for a dermatologist to visit in-patients in other hospital wards is to advise on suspected adverse reactions to systemically administered drugs. It is therefore essential that all hospital doctors have some understanding of cutaneous drug reactions. This applies equally to family doctors as they take on a greater share of after-care. Topical therapy may also give rise to undesirable side effects, as is the case with relatively potent topical steroid preparations.

THE MECHANISM OF CUTANEOUS DRUG REACTIONS

The majority of skin rashes induced by systemic medication are the result of immunological sensitization to the medicament. Ideally, it should be possible to classify them under Gell and Coombs' classic types of immunological reaction, namely:

Type I   Anaphylactic reactions
Type II   Cytotoxic reactions
Type III Arthus or immune complex mediated reactions
Type IV   Delayed hypersensitivity or cell-mediated reactions

In practice many adverse reactions are probably admixtures of two or more of these mechanisms.

History

The most important factor in establishing the likely precipitating agent in a suspected drug rash is a good history. However, the patient's notion of a 'drug' may be surprisingly variable, and laxatives, hypnotics, and simple analgesics are often regarded as part of a normal diet. Similarly any medicament taken for a long period of time (e.g. a diuretic for the past year) seems scarcely to merit mention as patients tend to be keen to incriminate a newly added item. The most useful approach is to ask the patient to bring samples of *all* his or her pills and potions for inspection. A relative will often be invaluable in presenting a complete collection. A list from the family doctor is frequently incomplete for he may not be aware of patent medicines and other over-the-counter preparations.

Patients with rheumatological disorders seem relatively susceptible to adverse drug reactions, probably due either to the nature of the medicaments or to inherently enhanced immunological responses. It should also be remembered that patients on multiple medication for general medical disorders may well have quite unrelated dermatological disorders, and that scabies and asteatotic eczema may first make their appearance after hospital admission at a time when systemic medication is being considerably modified.

Clinical features

A common pattern of drug eruption is that of a toxic erythema (Fig. 12.1). This is a widespread erythematous and morbilliform eruption which tends to affect the trunk more than the extremities. It appears 5–10 days after first introduction of the causative drug, but only 2–3 days after introduction if the drug has been given previously. Malaise fever and lymphadenopathy are common. Although it can be said that 'any drug can cause any eruption', commoner causes of various types of eruption are outlined in Tables 12.1 and 12.2. Antibiotics, the sulphonamides, barbiturates, and antirheumatic agents are all commonly incriminated in drug eruptions, but this may be more related to their widespread use than to any inherent tendency to trigger immune reactions.

Other cutaneous reaction patterns associated with adverse drug reactions are erythema multiforme and its more severe form the Stevens–Johnson syndrome (Fig. 12.2), erythema nodosum, vasculitic lesions and purpura, hair loss, pigmentation, exfoliative dermatitis, lichen planus-like eruptions, and urticaria (Figs 12.3–12.6).

Once a drug is strongly suspected it should be discontinued. If it has been the cause, the reaction can be expected to subside within the following 4–7 days. Confirmation by laboratory tests is not yet feasible as available *in vitro* immunological tests will yield both false-positive and false-negative results. No safe or satisfactory provocation test is available and challenge tests based on reintroduction of the drug are *not* recommended. Indeed, patients should be warned

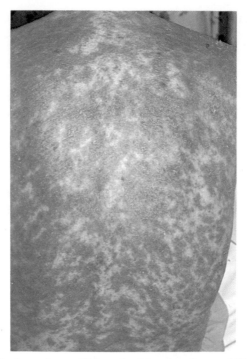

Fig. 12.1.   Toxic erythema. This patient developed a morbilliform eruption 10 days after commencing a course of phenylbutazone.

Table 12.1.   Medicaments which are relatively common causes of drug eruptions

Medicament	Pattern of eruption
Sulphonamides, penicillins	Morbilliform eruption, erythema multiforme, systemic lupus erythematosus
Phenylbutazone	Purpuric eruption
β-blockers	Psoriasiform
Barbiturates and tranquillizer overdosage	Blistering eruption of lower limbs
Penicillamine	Pemphigus-like eruption
Phenothiazines	Light-sensitive dermatosis
Antimalarials	Lichen planus-like eruption
Iodides and bromides	Acneiform eruption
Salicylates	Urticaria, angio-oedema

Table 12.2. Cutaneous reaction patterns which may be due to drug reactions

Reaction pattern	Likely drugs
Toxic erythema	Antibiotics (ampicillin), sulphonamides, barbiturates, antirheumatics
Erythema multiforme and Stevens–Johnson syndrome	Sulphonamides, antibiotics, antirheumatic drugs
Erythema nodosum	Sulphonamides, contraceptive pill
Erythroderma	Antibiotics and antirheumatic drugs
Vasculitic and purpuric eruptions	Carbromal, phenytoin, indomethacin
Psoriasiform eruptions or aggravation of psoriasis	β-blockers, lithium
Very severe blistering eruption (toxic epidermal necrolysis)	Sulphonamides, allopurinol, phenylbutazone
Photosensitivity	Tetracyclines, phenothiazines
Alopecia	Coumarin anticoagulants, cytotoxics, antithyroid drugs
Acne, gingival hyperplasia	Phenytoin
SLE-like syndrome	Classically hydralazine. Also penicillin, sulphonamides, and rarely, many others
Exfoliative dermatitis	Gold, isoniazid, phenylbutazone

about the drugs incriminated and relevant notes made in case sheets or practice notes as subsequent exposure is likely to provoke more severe reactions. The one exception to this rule is the morbilliform rash produced by ampicillin in patients with infectious mononucleosis (Fig. 12.7). For reasons which are not understood, this is a time limited hypersensitivity and once the infectious mononucleosis has resolved, the patient is unlikely to show an adverse reaction to ampicillin.

Dermatologists were first to recognize the important and serious adverse drug reaction to β-blocker drugs, particularly practolol (Fig. 12.8). This gave rise to the *oculomucocutaneous syndrome* characterized by keratoconjunctivitis sicca, a psoriasiform or eczematous rash, and more serious problems such as pericarditis and sclerosing peritonitis. Practolol was not introduced to North America and has been withdrawn from the European market. Other β-blocker drugs

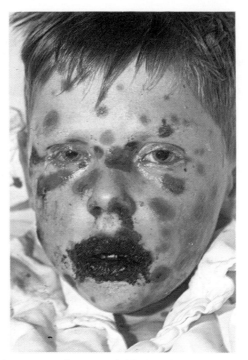

Fig. 12.2.   Mucous membrane and skin involvement in a child with drug-induced Stevens–Johnson syndrome.

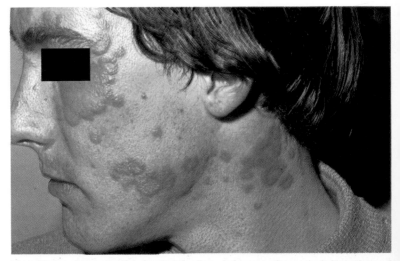

Fig. 12.3.   Acute urticaria developing 4 hours after administration of systemic penicillin.

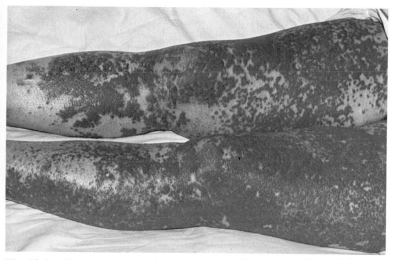

Fig. 12.4. Purpuric lesions developing eight days after initial administration of oxyphenbutazone. The platelet count was normal.

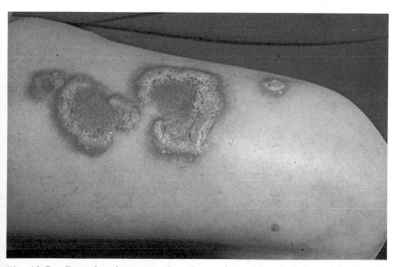

Fig. 12.5. Pustular drug eruption due to bromide administration. Acneiform lesions are also seen.

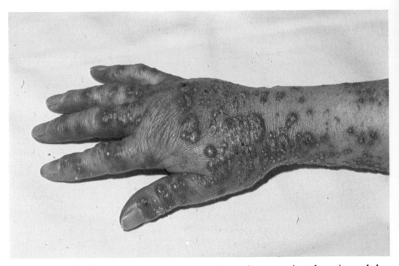

Fig. 12.6.   Vesiculo-pustular drug eruption due to trimethoprim-sulpha-methoxazole.

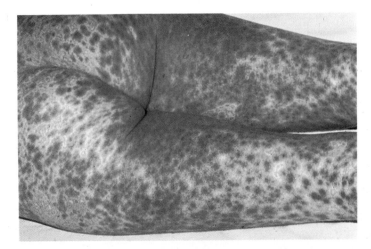

Fig. 12.7.   Morbilliform eruption caused by administration of ampicillin to a patient with infectious mononucleosis.

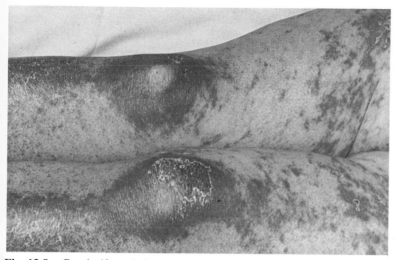

Fig. 12.8. Psoriasiform lesions developing for the first time 3 months after commencement of β-blocker therapy.

do not cause such serious complications, but several will provoke a psoriasiform eruption.

Penicillamine is of current interest. It is used as a chelating agent and as an antirheumatic, and in a proportion of patients it causes a blistering eruption which is clinically, histologically, and immunologically identical to pemphigus vulgaris. The blistering eruption does not always subside after withdrawal of penicillamine.

TREATMENT

Withdrawal of the offending medicament is frequently all that is required, followed by careful instructions to the patient concerning future avoidance. In very severe anaphylactic reactions emergency administration of subcutaneous adrenaline (0.5 ml of 1 in 1000 solution given slowly over 2–3 minutes) may be life-saving. Systemic antihistamines will relieve itch but there is little evidence that they accelerate spontaneous clearance of drug-induced lesions. Systemic corticosteroid administration may be of value, particularly in severe exfoliative dermatitis or the Stevens–Johnson syndrome. An initial dose of parenteral hydrocortisone may be followed by oral prednisolone and withdrawn over a period of 7–10 days. Soothing topical therapy, such as simple calamine lotion or 1–2 per cent menthol in calamine cream, may also be helpful.

ADVERSE REACTIONS TO TOPICAL APPLICATIONS

Adverse reactions to topical applications are relatively common, especially to those containing antihistamines, anaesthetics, and antibiotics. Adverse reactions to topical steroid preparations are, however, probably the commonest current problem of this nature.

Antihistamines, if required, should only be given systemically as they are potent sensitizers when administered topically. The same applies to topical anaesthetics, and certain antibiotics, notably neomycin and sulphonamides, are equally troublesome. An added reason for avoiding their use topically is that, once sensitized, these patients will react subsequently to systemic as well as topical administration of the causative drug.

ADVERSE EFFECTS OF TOPICAL CORTICOSTEROIDS

Sensibly used, topical steroids represent the most important advance in dermatological therapy in the past 20 years. However, as with any potent and effective form of therapy, they must be prescribed with care and commonsense, bearing in mind that percutaneous absorption, particularly through inflamed and excoriated skin, can be significant. If large quantities of a potent steroid are applied continuously to damaged skin, all the classic side effects associated with systemic steroid administration can occur, particularly in children. Much commoner, however, are the adverse effects on the skin itself. These are frequent and include a thin and fragile skin, spontaneous bruising, striae, and telangiectasia (Figs 12.9 and 12.10). The skin thinning which is due to loss of dermal collagen, is reversible on withdrawal of the steroid, but striae and telangiectasia are permanent.

The speed of onset of such changes will depend on the site of application, the frequency of use, and the potency of the preparation. They develop rapidly in the warm humid microclimate of the body flexures and were frequently seen when the occlusion of steroid-treated areas with polythene film was a common method of therapy.

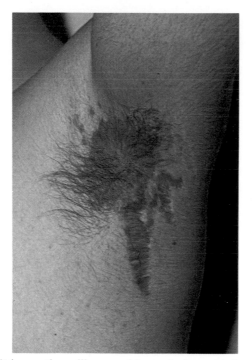

Fig. 12.9. Striae on the axilla caused by topical steroid therapy.

This is now restricted to small areas (e.g. palms and soles) and to brief periods of time.

Other complications of topical steroid therapy include *tinea incognito*, a term used to describe an atypical presentation of fungal infection on the skin due to unchecked growth of fungi on the steroid-treated skin, and *perioral dermatitis* (p. 70), a condition aggravated and possibly initiated by steroid therapy to the face. If simple scabies is not diagnosed or incorrectly treated with steroids the presentation may be confusing and atypical.

Topical steroid preparations are now very widely available and a small proportion of patients may become addicted to their use, insofar as withdrawal of the preparation, even with a detailed explanation of the reason for withdrawal, will lead to the patient seeking a supply elsewhere. A common problem of this type is when patients with facial dermatoses, including rosacea and perioral

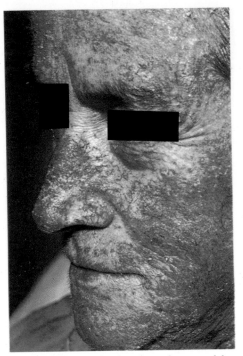

Fig. 12.10.   Facial erythema and telangiectasia caused by application of potent topical steroid preparations.

dermatitis, refuse to accept that potent steroids aggravate their condition. Given time, perseverance, and support, however, these patients can usually be slowly weaned off such preparations.

The sensible approach to topical steroid usage is to prescribe the weakest effective preparation for as brief a spell as possible, and to review the patient regularly. This is particularly important in paediatric practice.

The choice of topical steroid preparation requires care. In the past it was considered that in topical steroids halogenation (usually fluorination) of a side chain was synonymous with potency and possible side effects, and non-halogenated preparations were relatively 'safer'. However, as new base formulations designed to promote absorption become available, and additives such as urea are introduced, it has been recognized that the problem is rather more complex. Table 12.3 divides a representative list of topical

Table 12.3. Relative strengths of some topical steroid preparations

Very strong	Medium
Beclomethasone dipropionate 0.5% (Propaderm forte) *Diprolene*	*Desoximetasone 0.25% (Topicort)* Hydrocortisone 17 butyrate 0.1% (Locoid)
Clobetasol propionate 0.05% (Dermovate Removate) *Temovate*	*Amcinonide 1% (Cyclocort)* Clobetasone butyrate 0.05% (Eumovate)
Fluocinolone acetonide 0.2% (Synalar forte, Synalar HP) *Lidex*	*Fluocinolone 0.025% (Synalar)* Flurandrenolone 0.0125% (Haelan)
Strong	*Triamcinolone (Kenalog) 0.1%* **Mild**
Betamethasone 17-valerate 0.1% (Betnovate) *(Valisone)*	Hydrocortisone 0.1% 1.0%, 2.5% (Efcortelan) *(Westcort)*
Beclomethasone dipropionate 0.025% (Propaderm)	Fluocinolone acetonide 0.01% (Synandone)
Difluocortolone valerate 0.1% (Nerisone)	

steroid preparations into very strong, strong, medium, and mild categories (a very much fuller list can be obtained in any current prescribers' manual.)

It is good practice only to prescribe preparations in the mild category for the face and flexures, and to avoid using the very strong preparations in children. It is possible to weaken a strong steroid by dilution, but the correct diluent must be used, otherwise all potency may be lost through the molecular change in the steroid molecule.

GROWTH POINTS

1 *Cutaneous side effects of Amiodarone.* The drug Amiodarone is being increasingly used by cardiologists for control of cardiac dysrhythmias. A large proportion of patients treated with this drug develop a photosensitivity eruption on light exposed skin, predominantly the face. Patients with this problem develop a bluish-grey tinge to their light exposed skin after sun exposure. The mechanisms underlying this eruption are currently in the process of investigation.

The problem can be avoided by use of one of the new extremely effective topical sunscreen preparations with a sun protective factor (SPF) of 10 or more.

2 *Side effects of systemic retinoids.* Until recently, adverse drug reactions have commonly been associated with systemic effects from drugs given for systemic diseases. Now that systemic retinoids are available and effective in the management of common skin diseases such as psoriasis and acne a relatively new problem has developed in this area. This is the fact that drugs used for control of cutaneous disease may have both undesirable cutaneous side effects and also systemic problems. The risk/benefit ratio must be worked out for each individual patient and their circumstances. It is likely in the future that dermatologists will be faced with similar problems of this type as new potent drugs become available which in addition to the desired effect may have a number of potentially serious side effects. Side effects associated with the retinoids include topical problems such as cheilitis with severe dryness and cracking of the lips, nose bleeds, and a dry, dermatitis-like eruption. Some patients receiving retinoids, particularly 13-*cis*-retinoic acid, develop pyogenic granuloma-like lesions, mainly on the trunk. These appear to be self limiting lesions even if the drug is continued.

Systemic side effects related to retinoid administration include the elevation of serum lipids, a problem which appears at present to be rapidly reversible once the drugs are discontinued, and also the development of bony exostoses in patients given 13-*cis*-retinoic acid, even for short periods of time. The pathological significance of these lesions is not as yet fully understood.

FURTHER READING

Bruinsma W.: *A Guide to Drug Eruptions* (2nd edn). De Zwaluw, P.O. Box 21, Oosthuizen, The Netherlands (1982).
A useful pocket-sized paperback cataloguing the clinical varieties of drug reactions and giving exhaustive lists of individual reactions seen with specific drugs. A free looseleaf update of such reports is sent annually to purchasers of this book. Strongly recommended.

NOTES

13

Cutaneous medicine

In many systemic diseases the first signs are in the skin and thus they may alert the physician to a developing and possibly life-threatening condition. These diseases come under the general term of 'cutaneous medicine', an important 'link area' between dermatology and other specialties in which an alert dermatologist can, by careful history and examination, play Sherlock Holmes in an impressive and valuable manner.

Certain important diseases, such as SLE, which are unequivocal examples of cutaneous medicine have already been discussed. Tables 13.1–13.3 list some of the commoner or more important diseases covered in this chapter. Inevitably, this is not exhaustive and the reader is referred to larger textbooks for a more comprehensive account.

Cutaneous manifestations of endocrine disease

DIABETES

Diabetes is a prime example of a generalized disease associated with a wide range of dermatological manifestations. These include pruritus vulvae, which should never be dismissed as psychogenic without first looking for glycosuria. More specifically but not exclusively related to diabetes is *necrobiosis lipoidica* (Fig. 13.1), which generally appears on the shins and may predate frank development of diabetes by several years. The individual lesions are shiny, atrophic, red or yellowish plaques with marked telangiectasia over their surface and a tendency to ulcerate. These ulcers may be very slow to heal. The severity of necrobiosis lipoidica is not directly related to the severity of the diabetes, nor does it improve with careful diabetic control.

Treatment is unsatisfactory, but protection from trauma and

Table 13.1. Cutaneous manifestations of endocrine disease

Diabetes	Necrobiosis lipoidica (diabeticorum) Pruritus Fungal and bacterial skin infections ?Granuloma annulare Atherosclerosis and diabetic ischaemia
Hypothyroidism	Diffuse hair loss, coarse hair, broken hair Puffy oedema, xeroderma, pruritus
Hyperthyroidism	Hyperhidrosis Fine hair + hair loss, pruritus Pretibial myxoedema (usually associated with exophthalmos)
Cushing's syndrome	Acne vulgaris, hirsutism Cutaneous striae 'Buffalo hump' obesity
Acromegaly	Soft tissue hypertrophy Seborrhoea
Addison's disease	Increased cutaneous pigmentation, especially intraoral

Table 13.2. Commoner dermatological associations with gastrointestinal disease

Dermatitis herpetiformis	Gluten-sensitive enteropathy
Flexural eczematous eruptions	Malabsorption Mild zinc deficiency states
Acrodermatitis enteropathica	Defective zinc absorption
Peutz-Jeghers syndrome	Polyps of small intestine
Gardner's syndrome	Polyps of large intestine
Pyoderma gangrenosum	Ulcerative colitis, Crohn's disease, rheumatoid arthritis
Perineal ulceration and skin tags; sinus formation	Crohn's disease

resultant skin damage are important. Intralesional injections of a steroid such as triamcinolone acetonide may be initially beneficial in some cases.

The lesions of *granuloma annulare* are considered by some derma-

Table 13.3.   Cutaneous manifestations of systemic disease

Porphyria	Photosensitivity
	Skin fragility, blister formation
	Hypertrichosis, pigmentation
Sarcoidosis	Blue-red subcutaneous nodules
	Lupus pernio
	'Scar' sarcoid
Hyperlipidaemias	Xanthomata—tendinous, tuberous, and eruptive
	Xanthelasma
Neurofibromatosis	Multiple cutaneous neurofibromata
	Freckling and *café au lait* spots
Tuberous sclerosis	'Adenoma sebaceum' (perifollicular fibromata)
	Periungual fibromata
	Shagreen patches
Pellagra (nicotinic acid deficiency)	'Diarrhoea, dermatitis, and dementia'
	Erythema after sunlight exposure
Scurvy (vitamin C deficiency)	Bleeding gums, purpura, poor wound healing

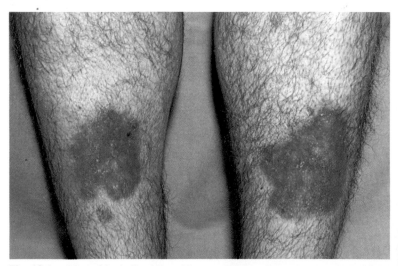

Fig. 13.1.   Necrobiosis lipoidica. Firm, reddish-yellow plaques are seen on the shins.

tologists to be associated with diabetes although this is not well established (Fig. 13.2). The condition is commoner in children than in adults, and it would appear to be more frequently associated with diabetes when it occurs in adults. The lesions are erythematous and circular with a well-marked, raised, palpable lateral border. The hands and feet are most commonly affected. The lesions are frequently multiple and tend to clear spontaneously after 3–6 months or longer. Occasionally, trauma, such as a diagnostic biopsy, appears to stimulate spontaneous clearance in the remainder of the lesion.

Secondary trophic change from diabetic ischaemia and atherosclerosis is a less specific, but accepted association, and if these changes are present diabetic gangrene is a very real hazard of inexpert chiropody of minor trauma. Diabetics are also susceptible to bacterial and fungal infections which must be treated promptly and aggressively.

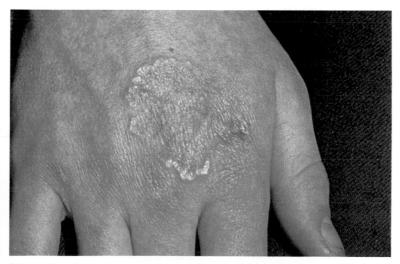

Fig. 13.2. Granuloma annulare on a typical site, the dorsum of the hand.

THYROID DYSFUNCTION

Abnormal hair growth is common in thyroid disease. Classically, in *myxoedema* the scalp hair is sparse, coarse, and brittle and the outer part of the eyebrows is lost, while in *hyperthyroidism* there is fine scalp hair, and sometimes associated alopecia.

Pretibial myxoedema is seen mainly after successful treatment of hyperthyroidism, especially when there are also ophthalmological complications. Clinically, there are asymptomatic, raised, red nodules and, although the name suggests that they are found chiefly on the shins (Fig. 13.3), they are also seen around the ankle and on the dorsum of the foot. Histological examination shows oedema and mucin.

Topical corticosteroid preparations *may* be of some benefit but in general these lesions tend to persist.

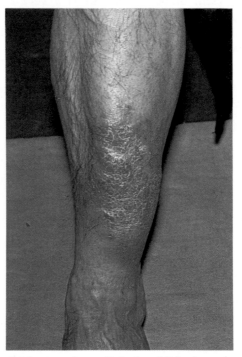

Fig. 13.3. Pretibial myxoedema. Raised, reddish plaques and nodules are seen on the shins.

ADRENAL CORTICAL HYPERFUNCTION

This may present with acne vulgaris, seborrhoea, and hirsutism.

Cutaneous striae may develop with great rapidity and be associated with 'buffalo hump' type of obesity.

ADRENAL CORTICAL HYPOFUNCTION

Adrenal cortical hypofunction may be associated with a striking increase in melanin pigmentation, particularly on mucous membranes and sites of friction (Fig. 13.4). This is a result of melanocyte stimulation by raised circulating levels of ACTH.

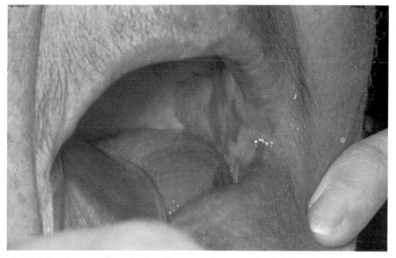

Fig. 13.4. Intraoral melanin pigmentation seen in Addison's disease.

ACROMEGALY

This condition is associated with acne, seborrhoea, and soft tissue hypertrophy (Fig. 13.5, p. 246).

Cutaneous associations of gastrointestinal disease

GLUTEN-SENSITIVE ENTEROPATHY

Gluten-sensitive enteropathy is common in dermatitis herpetiformis and has already been discussed (p. 218).

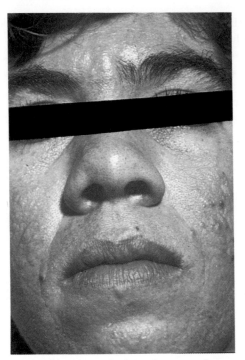

Fig. 13.5.   Acromegaly. Note soft tissue hypertrophy, acne, and seborr-hoea.

MALABSORPTION SYNDROMES

These may lead to a secondary dermatosis in which there are moist, eczematous skin lesions chiefly in the flexures. These may have a psoriasiform appearance and a small proportion of patients may have deficiencies of trace metals, such as zinc.

ACRODERMATITIS ENTEROPATHICA

Acrodermatitis enteropathica is a genetically determined disorder recently shown to be due to grossly defective zinc absorption. It is frequently first seen when the infant is being weaned off breast milk and presents as erythematous, raw, and pustular areas around the mouth, anus, fingers, and toes. Severe diarrhoea is common, and if the condition is not recognized and treated, hair and nails will be shed. Oral zinc supplements bring about dramatic and rapid improvement, and must be continued for many years, possibly for life.

A similar condition is seen in patients receiving total parenteral nutrition or elemental diets in which zinc is lacking. Onset can be very rapid, but once the diagnosis is made and zinc supplements administered, the lesions clear equally rapidly.

PYODERMA GANGRENOSUM

Pyoderma gangrenosum (p. 173) may precede the development of frank gastrointestinal symptoms in both ulcerative colitis and Crohn's disease. Patients with the latter condition also tend to have multiple perianal skin tags, ulcers and fistulae, and occasionally severe oral ulceration. Pyoderme gangrenosum is also associated with rheumatoid arthritis and Still's disease.

PEUTZ–JEGHERS SYNDROME

The Peutz–Jeghers syndrome consists of freckle-like pigmentation on and around the lips, and polyposis of the gastrointestinal tract, particularly the small bowel. Intussusception may develop, but the polyps are rarely premalignant (Fig. 13.6).

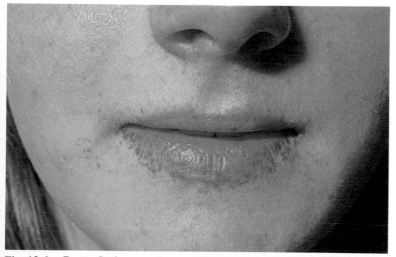

Fig. 13.6. Peutz–Jeghers syndrome. Macular melanin pigmentation is seen on and around the lips.

GARDNER'S SYNDROME

In Gardner's syndrome, an autosomal dominant disorder, there are polyposis coli, multiple sebaceous cysts of the face and neck, and bony cysts in the mandible. Malignant change in those polyps is reported (p. 262).

Other disorders

PORPHYRIA

The porphyrias frequently present with cutaneous signs and symptoms. *Porphyria cutanea tarda* is most likely to present to the dermatologist, and is characterized by photosensitivity, skin fragility, subepidermal blister formation, and hyperpigmentation and hypertrichosis of sun-exposed skin (Fig. 13.7). There is usually a history of underlying liver damage due most commonly to excessive alcohol intake. The diagnosis can be confirmed by demonstrating grossly elevated levels of urinary uroporphyrins. Elevated levels of serum iron are a feature and venesection to reduce this will alleviate symptoms. A variety of drugs aggravate the condition and the patient should be given written instructions on avoidance of these.

Other much rarer forms of porphyria may present to dermatologists. In *erythropoietic protoporphyria* very brief exposure to sunlight may cause itch, pain, and oedema. Pitted scars tend to develop on facial skin. Elevated erythrocyte and plasma protoporphyrin levels confirm the diagnosis. Topical sun-screen preparations will give symptomatic relief.

SARCOIDOSIS

Sarcoidosis frequently presents with cutaneous lesions. The basic pathological process is non-caseating granuloma formation in a variety of sites. The aetiology is not yet established, but it may be significant that sarcoidosis is much commoner in countries where tuberculosis has been well controlled. The commonest dermatological presentation of sarcoidosis is *erythema nodosum* and an appearance on chest X-ray of hilar lymphadenopathy.

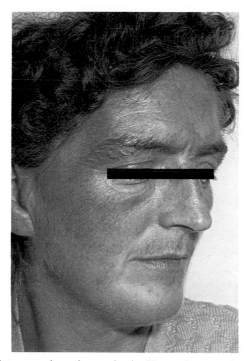

Fig. 13.7. Cutaneous hepatic porphyria. Hyperpigmentation and hypertrichosis are present.

Other cutaneous manifestations of sarcoid are *lupus pernio* (Fig. 13.8)—blue-red nodules on the nose, face, and hands and *scar sarcoid* —the development of sarcoid granulomas in scars.

The *Kveim test* is used to confirm the diagnosis. Kveim antigen is injected intradermally, and 6 weeks later the site is biopsied and examined carefully for evidence of granuloma formation. Practical details are important if a valid result of this test is to be obtained: the antigen must be injected intradermally, not subcutaneously, the syringe used should be glass, not disposable plastic which may be lubricated with a granuloma-producing material and the injection site must be marked accurately with reference to bony land-marks. Reference to moles or freckles can cause great confusion if the patient returns six weeks later having spent some time sun-bathing!

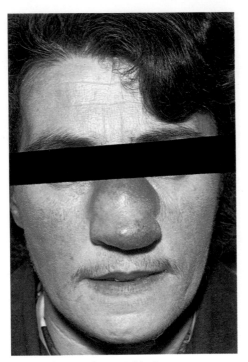

Fig. 13.8.   Lupus pernio seen in sarcoidosis.

HYPERLIPAEMIAS

The hyperlipaemias may present or be associated with *xanthelasmata* and *xanthomata*. Xanthelasmata are white or yellow plaques of lipid deposited in the periorbital skin. The majority of these are not associated with hyperlipaemic states and are of cosmetic importance only, but in 10–20 per cent of cases fasting lipids will be elevated. An arcus senilis may also be seen. Simple xanthelasma should be treated, if necessary, by excision or destruction with trichloracetic acid.

Most *cutaneous xanthomata* are eruptive, tendinous, or tuberous (Fig. 13.9). The rare variant of *plane xanthoma* may resemble plane warts and may be associated with paraproteinemia. Eruptive lesions occur on any body site and have an inflammatory halo. Tendinous lesions are most commonly seen over the Achilles tendon or on the dorsa of the hands, and tuberous lesions, which may be very large

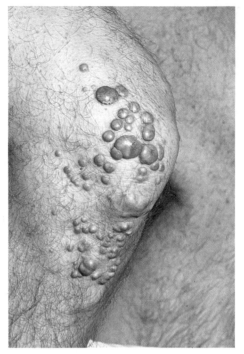

Fig. 13.9. Tuberous xanthomata. This patient had a normal lipoprotein profile.

and bizarre in shape, tend to be prominent around knees and elbows. Xanthomata may be a pointer either to a primary hyprlipae-mic state due to a genetic abnormality or to a secondary hyperlipae-mic state due to renal, hepatic, endocrine, or pancreatic disease. The hyperlipaemias are classified according to relative proportions on serum electrophoresis of α-lipoprotein, pre-β-lipoprotein, β-lipopro-tein, and chylomicrons. Treatment will vary according to which of the five currently recognized types of hyperlipoproteinemia is identi-fied, and may include dietary restriction of fat and carbohydrate, possibly with additional systemic therapy.

MULTIPLE NEUROFIBROMATOSIS (von Recklinghausen's disease)

This genodermatosis is inherited as an autosomal dominant trait, so a positive family history is usually present. The cutaneous features include macular hyperpigmentation (*café au lait* patches), neurofibromata, and multiple skin tags (*molluscum fibrosum*). These are soft, sessile, pink lesions which may be extremely numerous and disfiguring (Fig. 13.10). The pigmentary changes may be relatively mild, but the presence of even a few macular pigmented lesions in the axillary vaults is regarded by some workers as pathognomonic. Forty per cent of sufferers may develop neurological complications such as acoustic neuroma or optic nerve glioma and careful neurological examination at presentation, and thereafter is therefore important. Sarcomatous change within such a tumour is reported.

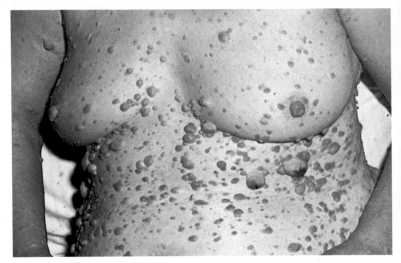

Fig. 13.10.   Multiple molluscum fibrosum of von Recklinghausen's disease.

BEHÇET'S SYNDROME

The cardinal features of this condition are severe and persistent oral and genital ulceration, iritis, and arthropathy (Fig. 13.11). A viral aetiology is postulated. Involvement of the central nervous system may result in a pattern very similar to disseminated sclerosis. An interesting dermatological feature is 'hyperergy', i.e. the tendency of sterile blisters to develop at venepuncture sites.

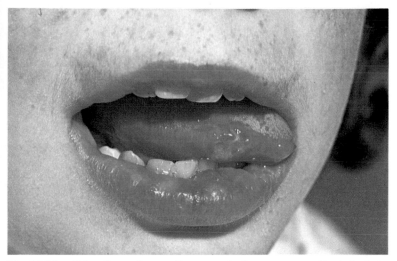

Fig. 13.11.   Behçet's syndrome. Severe oral ulcers are seen. Genital ulcers and iritis were also present.

TUBEROUS SCLEROSIS (epiloia, Bournville's disease)

Tuberous sclerosis is inherited by autosomal dominant transmission, but may not first present until puberty or later. It comprises the triad of cutaneous abnormalities, mental retardation, and seizures. There are four main types of skin lesions: (1) *Periungual fibromata*: multiple hypertrophic nodules around the nails which may look rather like viral warts; (2) *Shagreen patches*: normal-coloured plaques on the trunk which have a firmer texture than normal skin; (3) *adenoma sebaceum*: this term is pathologically incorrect as these lesions are in fact *perivascular fibromata* and are raised, red papules on the face, mainly around the nose (Fig. 13.12); and (4) *ash-leaf hypopigmentation*: this is well demonstrated under Wood's light as multiple oval areas of hypopigmentation and may be the earliest cutaneous sign of the disorder.

The individual prognosis varies with the degree of mental retardation and neurological involvement. Treatment of the perivascular fibromata with diathermy or surgery will produce a considerable cosmetic improvement.

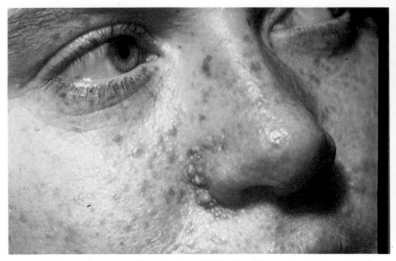

Fig. 13.12.   Adenoma sebaceum (perifollicular fibroma) of tuberous sclerosis.

NUTRITIONAL DEFICIENCY DISORDERS

A variety of relative nutritional disorders may present with cutaneous lesions in the absence of frank malnutrition.

Hypovitaminosis C, even frank scurvy, is seen in elderly people on a self-imposed 'tea and toast' diet. Their bleeding gums, easy bruising, and even frank purpura may all be dismissed as 'age changes'. In such cases low levels of leucocyte ascorbic acid will confirm the diagnosis and oral vitamin C supplements will effect a rapid cure.

Nicotinic acid deficiency may produce pellagra, which presents classically with the 'three Ds triad' of *dermatitis, diarrhoea*, and *dementia*. The dermatitis affects sun-exposed sites and consists of scaly erythema with a clear-cut, raised lateral margin, and subsequent hyperpigmentation. The antituberculous drug INAH can elicit the same syndrome. Nicotinic acid replacement is rapidly curative.

In *kwashiorkor* (protein malnutrition) the affected infant's skin is dry, with a glazed erythematous eruption, and the hair is dry, brittle, and hypopigmented. Oedema and ascites may also be present.

DERMATITIS ARTEFACTA (factitial dermatitis)

Definition. Bizarre lesions on any body site deliberately initiated or aggravated by the patient.

Incidence and aetiology

This condition is rare, but commoner in women than in men. The aetiology is poorly understood. In some cases 'dermatological malingering' or self-induced aggravation of pre-existing lesions may be related to claims for industrial compensation, but in the majority no such tangible motive is identified. Many patients are withdrawn, solitary individuals and consultation with medical attendants is one of their few social contacts. Clearly complicated psychological motives and at times frank psychoses are involved in the aetiology of this group of disorders, but recognition of this and appropriate referral is not always accompanied by disappearance of lesions.

Clinical features

These are varied and diverse. The condition should be considered in any bizarre skin lesion, particularly if it is on an exposed site and is an unusual angular or geometric shape. Application of caustic liquids to the skin will cause erythema to develop on the site of drips or splashes from the applicator (Fig. 13.13). Material may be injected into the skin, and finger nails and hair may be damaged or even removed. Important pointers are an inappropriate interest in the lesions with relative lack of real concern, and persistence or extension of the lesions if treated as an out-patient. In contrast, hospital admission is often accompanied by rapid healing of the lesions.

Treatment

This is difficult and delicate. Direct confrontation of the patient with one's suspicions will generally result in angry denial and failure to keep return appointments. A complicated degree of collusion may exist between the patient and the patient's relatives so that they too may react in this manner to a direct statement that the lesions are self-provoked. Similarly, referral for psychiatric consultation may be the signal for the patient to remove him/herself to the care of another dematologist. In general, treatment and, on occasion, cessation of self-mutilation becomes possible when the dermatol-

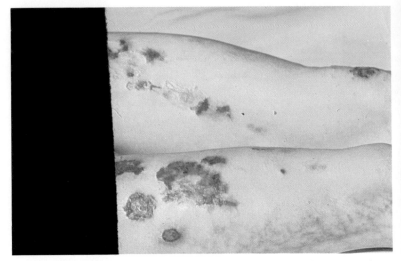

Fig. 13.13. Dermatitis artefacta. The lesions on the thighs had been produced with a caustic liquid.

ogist establishes a degree of rapport with the patient and it is understood, but not frankly stated that both parties know how the lesions are produced. Collaborative treatment with a sympathetic psychiatrist may be beneficial, but much can be achieved by emotional support. The lesions will clear speedily if occlusive dressings and bandaging are used, but tend to recur on other body sites.

The investigation of pruritus

A number of systemic disease states may be associated with persistent and severe pruritus of clinically normal skin. This may be a presenting feature of the systemic condition. Patients are usually elderly and may complain bitterly of sleep loss due to clamant itch. However great the temptation to dismiss the condition as 'simple pruritus' or even 'neurotic excoriation', it is important to take a careful history and carry out appropriate investigations to exclude both simple remediable exogenous causes and more serious precipitating factors.

History-taking must include details of occupational exposure to possible causative agents (e.g. fibreglass), and also details of recreational and domestic agents. Take a careful family and contact history, and remember that scabies in those with high standards of hygiene can be very atypical. A careful history of topical and systemic drug ingestion may also be relevant and should be sought. Well-demarcated localized pruritus may be exogenous, but generalized itch is more likely to be due to a systemic cause.

A list of the commoner systemic associations of severe generalized pruritus is given in Table 13.4. Currently diabetes, primary biliary cirrhosis, and polycythaemia are frequent associations.

After obtaining a full history, appropriate investigations should be initiated. Initial screening tests should include a full blood count, chest X-ray, serum urea, electrolytes and cholesterol, serum iron and TIBC levels, liver enzymes, thyroid function studies, and an autoantibody screen. More specialized subsequent investigation will depend on the history and results of this screening procedure. If all results are negative, a diagnosis of idiopathic or 'senile' pruritus may be justified. Relief from pruritus in this condition may be obtained by vigorously treating the dry skin (xerosis, *eczema craquelé*) which is frequently present. The prescription of lubricant bath oils and substitution of emulsifying ointment BP in place of soap may be soothing. A proportion of these patients are bed-ridden inmates of geriatric or psychogeriatric units and in these cases careful removal

Table 13.4. Some of the commoner systemic disease associations with cutaneous pruritus

---

Diabetes mellitus
Thyroid dysfunction (hypo- and hyperthyroidism)
Hepatic disease
Primary biliary cirrhosis
Chronic renal failure: itch may be present despite regular dialysis and
    normal blood urea
Polycythaemia
Haemochromatosis
Lymphoma
Hodgkin's disease
Neurological disorders, e.g. tabes dorsalis
Parasitosis
Drug addiction and abuse

---

of all soap, if used, after blanket baths, is important. While systemic antihistamines may give some relief they may also cause confusion in the elderly and should therefore be used with caution. The specific problems of *pruritus ani* and *pruritus vulvae* are relatively common. It is important in these cases to exclude easily remediable infections such as candidosis, trichomonal vaginitis, and threadworms. Women should be examined carefully for the presence of lichen sclerosis et atrophicus (p. 155), although here both itch and pain are the usual symptoms. The urine should be tested for sugar to exclude occult diabetes. In a high proportion, however, no obvious precipitating cause will be identified. Many of these patients are relatively obsessional, rather tense individuals whose symptoms flare at times of domestic or occupational stress. Both psychosomatic and psychosexual explanations have been offered for their symptoms.

Therapy should include advice on the avoidance of proprietary local anaesthetic preparations which can cause allergic contact dermatitis. Weak topical steroid/antibiotic combinations may offer some relief. Systemic antihistamines and antidepressants may be of some value, but the condition tends to recur.

Cutaneous graft versus host disease

A graft versus host reaction is stimulated when foreign immunocompetent lymphoid cells encounter new antigens in a recipient incapable of rejecting these cells. This results in graft versus host disease which may be seen in patients with congenital immunodeficiencies given blood transfusions, but is currently much more commonly in patients with malignancies who receive transplantations of allogeneic bone marrow.

Although there is some overlap, graft versus host disease has two relatively distinct clinical presentations. These are early onset graft versus host disease appearing within 100 days of marrow transplant, and late or chronic graft versus host disease appearing after the 100-day period.

ACUTE GRAFT VERSUS HOST DISEASE

Affected patients usually have the triad of fever, diarrhoea and a skin rash. This is commonly seen 7–10 days after the marrow graft at a time when the patient has been on multiple drug therapy. Consequently, the rash which may be transient may very easily be confused with a drug eruption. The rash of graft versus host disease at this stage is maculopapular and tends to involve the trunk, the palms, the soles, and the oral mucous membranes. These latter three sites may be of some value in differentiating the rash from a drug eruption. A skin biopsy taken at this point in time will show a lichenoid tissue reaction in the skin with liquefaction degeneration of the basement membrane and will frequently show the histological sign of 'satellite cell necrosis'. This describes the pattern within the epidermis of a lymphocyte in contact with an apparently necrotic keratinocyte. It is not totally specific for graft versus host disease, but its presence will add weight to the diagnosis.

CHRONIC GRAFT VERSUS HOST DISEASE

The onset of this form of graft versus host disease is usually more insidious. Patients may first notice a darkening of their normal skin colour, followed by a tightening and sclerosis of the skin causing immobility and contractures. Hair and nails may be shed, and the overall picture resembles that of systemic sclerosis. A skin biopsy taken from this type of graft versus host disease will show very gross thickening of the dermal collagen.

Treatment

Treatment of either type of graft versus host disease is difficult, but the acute phase may respond to high dose oral steroid therapy. At present strenuous attempts are being made to prevent graft versus host disease using a cocktail of monoclonal antibodies directed against T lymphocyte subsets to treat the marrow prior to introducing it into the recipient. Early results suggest that this approach is of value.

Cutaneous manifestations of systemic malignancy

An interesting group of cutaneous lesions are those associated with internal malignancy. This group of lesions may indeed be the pointer to a systemic neoplasm which has not yet been recognized, and is therefore an important area of collaboration between the dermatologist and the general physician or internist. The list of skin conditions in this category can be very long indeed and only those whose association is relatively well proven will be included in this section.

ACANTHOSIS NIGRICANS

The form of this rare condition which is associated with malignancy develops in the absence of gross obesity, and is characterized by hyperpigmentation and hyperkeratosis, most marked in the body flexures. The commonest association is with gastrointestinal malignancies (Fig. 13.14).

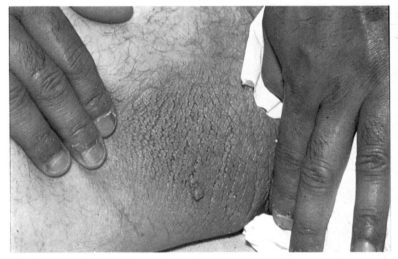

Fig. 13.14. Acanthosis nigricans of the inner thigh. This patient had a carcinoma of stomach.

DERMATOMYOSITIS

This condition has already been discussed (p. 156). Ten to twenty-five per cent of adult-onset dermatomyositis is associated with an occult malignancy involving any body site. The dermatomyositis may precede the development of the malignancy by months or even years. Removal of the tumour may result in clearance of the dermatomyositis.

GLUCAGONOMA (necrolytic migratory erythema)

These patients present with a raw, painful tongue, and superficial erosions and blisters on the face, buttocks, thighs, and abdomen. Diabetes is present and the malignancy is generally a glucagon-secreting tumour of the pancreatic islet cells. Removal of the tumour will result in dramatic clearance of the skin lesions.

ACQUIRED ICHTHYOSIS

The development of excessively dry and scaly skin in elderly patients may herald the development of Hodgkin's disease, non-Hodgkin's lymphoma, or a solid tumour.

BOWEN'S DISEASE

A small proportion of patients with Bowen's carcinoma in situ of the skin (p. 289) will also have an unrelated systemic neoplasm. It may be that the common factor in the aetiology of the two malignancies is prior ingestion of arsenic in 'tonics' or other medicaments.

COWDEN'S DISEASE (multiple hamartoma syndrome)

This condition is a marker for breast and thyroid malignancies. Although rare, it is important, as the association with malignancy is so strong. Patients develop multiple papules and papillomata on the face, hands, and forearms and also have papules and a cobblestone appearance on the mucous membranes. Neural abnormalities may also be present.

PARANEOPLASTIC ACROKERATOSIS (Bazex syndrome)

Patients with this rare condition develop psoriasiform plaques on the hands, feet, and face. There is thickening of the palmar and plantar skin, and the nails may become dystrophic and break easily. All reported cases of the condition to date have had a malignancy of the pharynx or larynx.

GARDNER'S SYNDROME

This syndrome is characterized by sebaceous and epidermal cysts, skeletal abnormalities, and polyposis coli. The polyps, which may be asymptomatic, mainly involve the large bowel and malignant change in these polyps is recorded in about one-third of cases.

Other rare associations between cutaneous lesions and systemic malignancy include severe herpes zoster, erythema gyratum repens (a pattern of cutaneous erythema resembling wood grain which rapidly changes shape on the skin), and the sudden appearance of profuse growth of lanugo hair or of multiple basal cell papillomata. Individual case reports associate severe bullous pemphigoid with concomitant systemic malignancy, but this may be a chance association of two conditions both commoner in elderly people.

GROWTH POINT

Changes in the vasculature in diabetics. As is described at the beginning of this chapter there are a large number of cutaneous associations with the diabetic state. A recent well controlled study has clearly demonstrated that the cutaneous vasculature is abnormal, with significant reduction in the luminal area in diabetes, and even greater luminal reduction in those with vascular complication which may involve other organs outwith the skin such as the kidneys. It is therefore quite possible that, in future, a small skin biopsy with quantitative assessment of the vasculature in the skin biopsy may have significant value in predicting complications for diabetic state and thus possibly introducing appropriate therapy at an earlier date than is currently possible.

FURTHER READING

Ajjam S. J.: Quantitative Evaluation of the Dermal Vasculature of Diabetics. *Quarterly Journal of Medicine* **215**, 229–39 (1985).
   A well conducted study on 51 diabetic patients, indicating that cutaneous changes may be of prognostic value.
Huntley, A. C.: Cutaneous manifestations of diabetes mellitus. *Journal of American Academy of Dematitis* **7**, 427–5 (1982).
   An extensive account of the many cutaneous problems which may affect the diabetic patient. 188 references.

Lehner T. and Barnes C. G. (eds): *Behcets Syndrome. Clinical and Immuno-logical Features.* Academic Press, London and New York (1979).
A useful monograph on this poorly understood condition.
Powell F. C. *et al.*: Pyoderma Gangrenosum. A Review of 86 Patients. *Quarterly Journal of Medicine* **55,** 173–86 (1985).
This article gives the Mayo Clinic experience over 13 years.
Saurat J. H.: Graft versus Host Disease. In *Current Perspectives in Immuno-dermatology* (ed. Rona M. MacKie). Churchill Livingstone. Edinburgh (1984).
An excellent of cutaneous aspects of graft versus host disease. 58 well selected references.

NOTES

14

Paediatric dermatology

The incidence of certain common dermatological conditions differs in an adult and in a child population. For example, psoriasis is relatively uncommon in the prepubertal child, whereas atopic dermatitis is extremely common in children, particularly in those under 5 years of age. In addition, a variety of relatively rare but important conditions, including genodermatoses, are found predominantly in childhood. Early recognition and diagnosis is important in many of these, as genetic counselling and antenatal screening may be required for the more serious disorders. This chapter deals with several conditions frequently or exclusively encountered in infants and children, and not covered elsewhere in this book.

INFANTILE SEBORRHOEIC DERMATITIS

Definition. An acute self-limiting inflammatory dermatosis of early infancy.

Seborrhoeic dermatitis affects young infants and usually presents in those under the age of 3 months. It is a less likely diagnosis in the older infant in whom atopic dermatitis is commoner.

The early signs are coarse yellow scales on the scalp, sometimes also on the eyebrows and face, with erythema and scaling in the 265 body flexures (Figs 14.1 and 14.2, p. 266). Despite a florid eruption, the infant is well, feeds normally, and is in no apparent discomfort. This contrasts with the atopic infant, who is irritable, is obviously distressed by itch, feeds poorly, and sleeps badly.

The family history is usually negative. There is moreover, no convincing evidence that infantile and adult seborrhoeic dermatitis are related. The cause of both conditions is unknown. Secondary infection with *Candida albicans* and bacteria is common in the infantile form.

Fig. 14.1. Infantile seborrhoeic dermatitis. Severe scalp involvement with large yellow adherent scales.

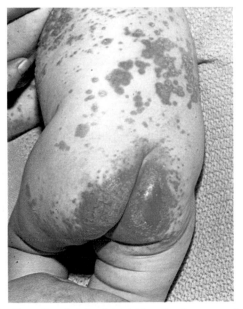

Fig. 14.2. Infantile seborrhoeic dermatitis. Erythema and scaling are present, but there is no apparent pruritus.

The most effective form of treatment is to prevent secondary infection and to accelerate remission by topical application of a weak steroid-antibiotic mixture, such as vioform-hydrocortisone. Scalp scales can be removed by a weak salicylic acid preparations (e.g. 2 per cent salicylic acid in aqueous cream).

ATOPIC DERMATITIS (Fig. 14.3)

Atopic dermatitis in infancy and childhood has been discussed in detail (p. 78). In young infants it may be difficult to distinguish atopic dermatitis from seborrhoeic dermatitis, and in such cases it is wise to delay for 2–3 months until the situation is clearer before labelling the condition and explaining the prognosis to the parents. Pointers towards a diagnosis of atopy are a positive family history of either cutaneous or respiratory atopy, obvious pruritus, and associated bronchospasm. It is important in infants and young children to keep the use of strong topical steroids down to a minimum, as their large surface area facilitates percutaneous absorption and subsequent side effects. Topical steroid reduction can be made very much easier by the liberal use of emollients.

NAPKIN DERMATITIS (Fig. 14.4)

Definition. A simple irritant dermatitis due to prolonged skin contact with urine or faeces.

Most cases of this extremely common condition are managed by parents and are referred for specialist care only when severe, and resistant to home remedies. Clinically, there is a glazed erythema, with papules and sometimes large erosions. The flexures are relatively spared (Fig. 14.4).

A fundamental point in management is to ban the use of occlusive plastic pants. Ideally, the infant should be nursed without napkins, in a warm room on an absorbent sheet which is changed regularly. Resolution is hastened by the temporary use of a mild steroid preparation, but this should on no account become the regular 'nappy cream'.

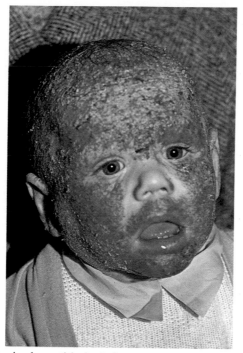

Fig. 14.3. Atopic dermatitis in infancy. The face and scalp are often affected in young children, and relative sparing of the perioral and nasal region is common as seen here.

CANDIDA ALBICANS INFECTION

Candida albicans is a normal commensal in the gastrointestinal tract but in the young, the old, and the metabolically or immunologically compromised host it may become a pathogen. Primary infection with *C. albicans* in an otherwise healthy infant is rare, but secondary colonization of pre-existing seborrhoeic, atopic, or napkin dermatitis is common.

The signs of infection are erythema, scaling, and satellite lesions beyond the active margin. These can be quickly controlled by a candicidal agent such as nystatin or one of the newer broadspectrum preparations (clotrimazole, miconazole). As the reservoir of infec-

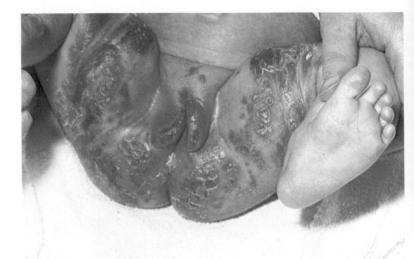

Fig. 14.4. Napkin dermatitis. Severe involvement with relative sparing of skin flexures.

tion is in the gastrointestinal tract, it is good practice to prescribe a 7-day course of nystatin drops or oral suspension.

Oral thrush is also seen in infants and may be precipitated by a systemic antibiotic. There is a curd-like white deposit on the cheek or tongue and when it is scraped off, a bleeding area remains. This also should be treated with nystatin drops or oral suspension.

VASCULAR NAEVI

About one child in ten develops cutaneous angiomata during the first month of life. They are not usually apparent at birth. These are the port wine stains and superficial and deep angiomas or strawberry marks.

The *port wine stain* (naevus flammeus) is usually found on the face and is a pale pink to deep red flat vascular stain like lesion (Fig. 14.5). A lesion of this type is common on the nape of the neck ('stork mark') and disappears spontaneously in early life. If biopsied these lesions show iregular dilitation of capillaries in the upper dermis.

With the exception of the nape of the neck lesions there is little or no tendency for these lesions to improve with age, and indeed with the larger variants there is a tendency for the lesions to become more rugose and develop central nodules in adult life. The very large lesions are occasionally associated with neurological or opthalmological developmental defects and any child with a lesion of this type which covers a large proportion of the face should be fully assessed in infancy.

Until recently, cosmetic cover has been the most useful therapy for these lesions. Preparations such as Covermark (U.K.) or Dermablend (U.S.) are acceptable for both sexes and the British Red Cross runs an excellent cosmetic camouflage advisory service in many parts of the U.K.

At present there is considerable interest in the use of laser

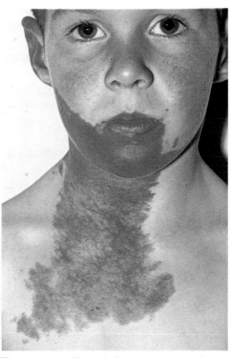

Fig. 14.5. Capillary naevus. These lesions tend to persist with little change throughout life.

technology to treat these lesions. The technique is still new, but it would appear that darker raised lesions in adults respond best to laser therapy and the flatter paler lesions in children do not respond so well. The technique is at the developmental stage and is extremely time consuming.

The *superficial angioma* usually appears during the first week of life as a bright red raised area most commonly on the skin of the head and neck. These are the results of proliferation of superficial capillaries in the dermis. They tend to grow with the child the first year of life, and then gradually become paler and involute for the next 4–5 years. Bleeding from superficial ulceration due to trauma is easily stopped by gentle pressure. Bleeding episodes seem to hasten spontaneous resolution (Figs 14.6 and 14.7). Because of this natural history, treatment should be conservative and surgical intervention delayed until all spontaneous resolution has ceased. Parents need reassurance that this approach is the best one for their child and a series of sequential photographs of previous cases resolving spontaneously is of value. Once resolution is complete, surgical removal of the redundant skin may be required.

The *deep cavernous angioma* has all the features described for the superficial cavernous angioma, but in addition there appears to be a proliferation of vessels in the deeper capillary plexus. These do not shrink spontaneously as completely as the superficial vessels, and resolution is usually less complete.

Rare variants of cavernous angiomata can be associated with systemic abnormalities, such as thrombocytopenic purpura, and any infant who has a very large lesion or with a family history of angiomata should be appropriately investigated.

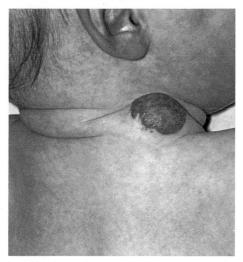

Fig. 14.6. (top)   Mixed, predominantly cavernous angioma. Child is 3 months old.

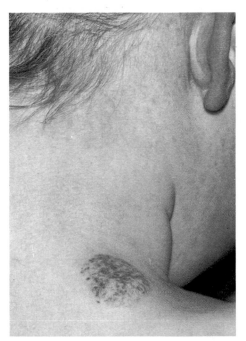

Fig. 14.7. (bottom)   The same child aged 3 years, to demonstrate spontaneous resolution. Further improvement can confidently be expected.

ICHTHYOSIS

Definition. A disorder of keratinization characterized by excessively dry and scaly skin.

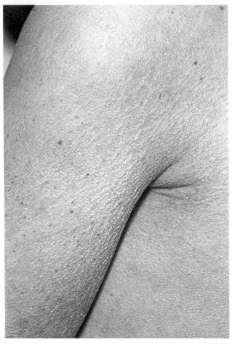

Fig. 14.8. Autosomal dominant ichthyosis. Fine, white scales are most profuse on the upper arms.

The majority of patients with ichthyosis present in infancy and childhood. The remainder acquire the condition in adolescence or adult life. A proportion of patients with adult-onset ichthyosis may have an underlying neoplasm.

Two main forms of ichthyosis account for most paediatric cases. These are autosomal dominant ichthyosis vulgaris (Fig. 14.8) and the rarer sex-linked recessive variety (Fig. 14.9). In addition, there are several very much rarer ichthyotic conditions.

AUTOSOMAL DOMINANT ICHTHYOSIS VULGARIS

In the U.K. autosomal dominant ichthyosis is common, having an incidence of 1 in 250 to 1 in 300. There is an underlying disorder of

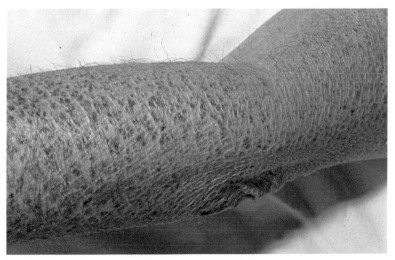

Fig. 14.9. Ichthyosis nigricans (sex-linked ichthyosis vulgaris). The scales are large, greasy, and yellowish in colour.

keratinization seen on light microscopy as an absent epidermal granular layer.

Affected children present in early childhood with a rough, dry skin, most marked on the extensor surfaces of the hands and worst in winter. The scales are fine and white. Many children have rough, horny papules, seen best on the extensor surfaces of the upper arms, thought to be due to faulty keratinization around hair follicle openings.

Frequently, the skin of atopic children is dry, but the relationship of this xerosis (dry skin) to true ichthyosis is uncertain. Dominant ichthyosis vulgaris tends to improve slowly during childhood and puberty, but may also persist into adult life.

Treatment depends on the use of lubricants and emulsifying preparations. Excessive use of soap should be discouraged, and emulsifying ointment BP substituted. Water-soluble oils should be added to bath-water or used after bathing. Preparations containing urea in a water-miscible base may help to maintain adequate hydration of the stratum corneum, but some patients complain of intense stinging for a few minutes after their application. Topical steroids should not be used routinely, but reserved for those patients who have associated atopic dermatitis.

SEX-LINKED ICHTHYOSIS VULGARIS (ichthyosis nigricans)

This is very much rarer than the autosomal dominant variety, and although the fully developed disease is seen in males only, female heterozygotes may have mild degrees of the condition, mainly on the lower legs. An associated abnormality is a deficiency of the enzyme steroid sulphatase seen in both affected children and carrier mothers. This enzyme deficiency can be detected in the placenta, but does not appear to be associated with any increased incidence of perinatal problems.

Its histological differentiation from ichthyosis vulgaris is easy as there is, in contrast, a striking increase in the granular layer with a thickened overlying stratum corneum. Clinically too, the distinction is clear-cut, as there are large, greasy, polygonal, yellow or brown scales mainly on the trunk. There is little tendency for the condition to improve with time. Therapy is unsatisfactory, but some patients can obtain cosmetic benefit by removing the scales with an abrasive pad (e.g. Buf-Puf) and then applying emulsifying ointment.

Other very rare ichthyotic conditions include ichthyosiform erythroderma and Refsum's syndrome. The latter is due to a specific defect in phytanic acid metabolism and is characterized by ichthyosis, retinitis pigmentosa, and neurological defects.

PAPULAR URTICARIA (bites)

Although papular urticaria is frequently seen in paediatric skin clinics, a high proportion of affected children are managed either by parents or the family doctor.

Characteristically, the lesion are grouped and occur in crops (Fig. 14.10). Morphologically, they are tender, erythematous papules or small blisters. They are quickly scratched and subsequently become secondarily infected.

In a high proportion of cases fleas or mites are to blame, but tact must be used when persuading parents that this is so. There is some evidence that a proportion of these may be allergic reactions to dyestuffs (tartrazine) in brightly coloured aerated drinks and sweets.

Suitable treatment of established lesions is a topical antipruritic such as crotamiton or 2 per cent menthol in calamine cream. Prevention of further crops is difficult and depends on eliminating the causative factor. the child's bedding and family pets should be

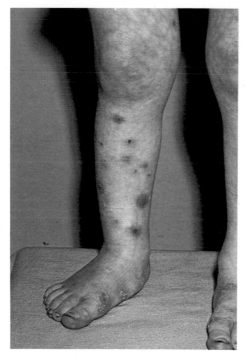

Fig. 14.10. Papular urticaria. Crops of papules are seen most commonly on the lower legs.

treated with an insecticidal dusting powder. If this is not successful, removal of tartrazine-containing preparations from the diet may be of value.

URTICARIA PIGMENTOSA

Definition. An eruption due to focal aggregation of mast cells in the dermis, seen usually in infancy.

Although both children and adults are affected, urticaria pigmentosa is most often seen in infancy. The lesions are multiple erythematous weals which may blister and are provoked by minor trauma or a warm bath. The lesions resolve, leaving some melanin pigmentation (Fig. 14.11). Biopsy will reveal foci of mast cells: these degranulate on trauma, releasing vasoactive substances which elicit the lesion.

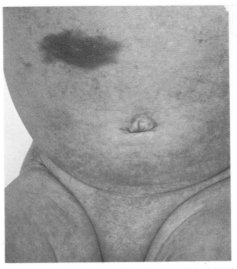

Fig. 14.11.   Urticaria pigmentosa. This 2-year-old child had three lesions which urticated on pressure and left surrounding pigmentation as seen here.

Spontaneous improvement throughout infancy and childhood is usual. Treatment consists of avoiding trauma until remission occurs. Antihistamines are not indicated.

In severe cases of urticaria pigmentosa, a trial of oral sodium cromoglycate (Nalcrom) is justified as there are reports of a good response, presumably due to mast cell stabilization.

Epidermolysis bullosa

Although rare, epidermolysis bullosa is of great importance in neonatal paediatrics as affected infants may present at or shortly after birth with severe blisters. Several different forms of the disorder exist, and as each is inherited differently and has a very different prognosis, it is important to have some understanding of the group as a whole.

The main varieties are:

1 Epidermolysis bullosa simplex   Autosomal dominant
2 Junctional epidermolysis bul-   Autosomal recessive
   losa (Epidermolysis bullosa
   letalis)
3 Dystrophic epidermolysis bul-   Two types: one autosomal domi-
   losa   nant, one autosomal recessive

A tentative diagnosis can be made on the basis of a family history, clinical examination, and light microscopic examination of a skin biopsy, but a definitive diagnosis is essential for genetic counselling and for this electron microscopy is required to locate the site of the damage at ultrastructural level.

EPIDERMOLYSIS BULLOSA SIMPLEX

The pathological damage in this variety lies within the epidermis and consists of a split through the cytoplasm of the basal cells. Thus, there is true cell *lysis* whereas in the other types of the disease the term *epidermolysis* is a misnomer.

    The first signs of epidermolysis bullosa simplex appear when the child starts to walk or crawl, and develops mild blistering and desquamation on knees, hands, feet, and other sites of friction (Fig. 14.12). These blisters quickly rupture and heal with no subsequent

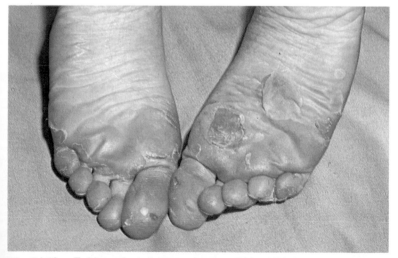

Fig. 14.12.   Epidermolysis bullosa simplex. This child develops blisters on sites of friction only. Healing is rapid without scarring.

scarring. Other ectodermal structures (hair, teeth, and nails) are unaffected and mucous membranes, although occasionally involved, do not show gross changes. There is little tendency to remission in later childhood or adult life.

JUNCTIONAL EPIDERMOLYSIS BULLOSA
(Herlitz type, formerly epidermolysis bullosa letalis)

This disease is inherited by autosomal recessive transmission and the basic abnormality appears to lie in the connections between the basal cell and the basal lamina. This results in the development of a split at the level of the lamina lucida. The overlying epidermis appears normal and there is no obvious loss of cohesion between the cells. The base of the blister is formed by an intact basal lamina still firmly adherent to the dermis.

Clinical abnormality may be present at birth either as blisters, often around the nails, or raw denuded areas, with little tendency to heal. Mucous membranes may be severely involved, and the teeth are commonly abnormal. A high proportion of these children die in infancy.

DYSTROPHIC EPIDERMOLYSIS BULLOSA
(autosomal dominant type)

The abnormality consists of defective anchoring fibrils connecting the basal lamina to the dermis and a subepidermal blister results. In later infancy or early childhood bullae form on friction sites and heal with scarring. Milia may be seen in these scars, which tend to become keloidal or hyperplastic. Hair and teeth develop normally.

DYSTROPHIC EPIDERMOLYSIS BULLOSA
(autosomal recessive type)

As with the dominant variety, there is a defect of anchoring fibrils, but a total increase in cutaneous collagenase activity has also been reported. Large bullae are present at birth, and they heal with scarring which is associated with the formation of webs between fingers and eventually a useless fist (Fig. 14.13). Mucous membranes, hair, nails, and teeth may all be abnormal, and there are reports of the development of squamous carcinoma on the scar sites.

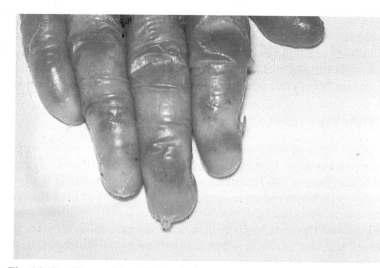

Fig. 14.13.   Dystrophic epidermolysis bullosa. Note the loss of finger nails. This 5-year-old child already has web formation between the digits.

TREATMENT AND PRENATAL DIAGNOSIS OF EPIDERMOLYSIS BULLOSA

Once an accurate histological diagnosis has been established by electron microscopy, simple protective measures should be taken in all cases to prevent friction bullae. Thereafter, a trial of systemic steroids may be justifed in the junctional and dystrophic varieties. Occupational therapy may delay the development of contractures or webs in the autosomal recessive dystrophic variety, but the prognosis for both survival and the ability to lead an independent adult life must be guarded in these varieties of the disorder.

It is important that genetic counselling be offered to parents of children with epidermolysis bullosa. This entails making an accurate diagnosis, and constructing a full and accurate family tree going back at least two generations. Parents can then be given a reliable estimate of the risks of producing another affected child, and informed that prenatal diagnosis is possible by amniocentesis.

The technique of foetal skin biopsy to diagnose epidermolysis bullosa in mothers who are at risk is now relatively well established. A skin biopsy is taken at 14–18 weeks gestation through a foetoscope. In the affected foetus the abnormalities can be clearly seen when the skin is examined in the electron microscope and it is likely in the future a number of antibodies directed against the basement membrane components will also be used in this situation. If the test is positive for one of the more severe types of epidermolysis bullosa the parents can decide whether or not the pregnancy should proceed.

GROWTH POINTS

Kawasaki disease. In 1974 an entity called the mucocutaneous lymph node syndrome or Kawasaki disease was first described in Japan. Since that time 50 000 Japanese cases have been recorded. It is also a relatively common pediatric dermatological problem in both Europe and North America. The symptoms are, however, relatively non-specific and this may explain its recent recognition. Alternatively, this may be due to the fact that it is caused by an infectious agent which has only recently become more virulent.

Three-quarters of affected children are under the age of 4 years. They present with fever, conjunctivitis, a bright red 'strawberry tongue' lymphadenopathy, and striking brick red erythema and peeling of the palms and soles. The disease frequently occurs in small epidemics. The importance of the condition lies in the fact that in the acute phase 20 per cent of children have dilatation of the coronary arteries, and this may progress to frank coronary aneurysms and death. Angiography is essential to monitor these children. Treatment at present is with oral salicylates and the condition subsides in 2–3 weeks. Long-term follow-up is essential in any child with cardiac problems.

2 *The use of phenytoin in the therapy of autosomal recessive epidermolysis bullosa.* The increase in collagenase activity in children with this disorder can be partly corrected in some cases by the use of oral phenytoin. Plasma levels of phenytoin of at least 8 μg/ml appear to be required and a reduction in the number of blisters forming will be seen in some cases.

FURTHER READING

Cooper T. W. and Bauer, E. A.: Therapeutic efficacy of phenytoin in recessive dystrophic epidermolysis bullosa. *Archives of Dermatology* **120**, 490–5 (1984).

A useful report of 22 children with this rare disorder treated with phenytoin.

Rowe, R. D. and Rose, V.: Kawasaki disease. *Canadian Medical Association Journal* **132,** 25–8 (1985).

A good review of the interesting and topical problem of Kawasaki Disease.

Verbov, J. and Morley, W. N.: *An Atlas of Paediatric Dermatology.* MTP Press, Lancaster (1983).

A well selected collection of illustration of both rare and common skin diseases seen in children.

NOTES

15

Skin tumours

INTRODUCTION

The range of cell types found within both the epidermis and the dermis results in a wide variety of benign and malignant cutaneous tumours. The benign tumours tend to present as isolated skin nodules, whereas the malignant lesions form a complete spectrum from aggressive, rapidly gowing and metastasizing lesions to slowly growing tumours which tend to invade only locally.

Table 15.1 gives a comprehensive list of malignant epidermal tumours and the cells types from which each is thought to arise. Tumours of the dermis may arise from any of its cellular components such as the blood vessels, nerve cells, fibroblasts, and smooth muscle. They tend to be non-specific cutaneous nodules and their origin has to be determined by histological examination. Metastasis to the skin from other organs is a relatively rare event, but here again the final diagnosis depends on histological study.

Table 15.1.   Cutaneous malignancies

Type of malignancy	Cell of origin
Squamous carcinoma	Keratinocyte
Malignant melanoma	Melanocyte
Basal cell carcinoma	?Hair follicle epithelium
Tumours of skin appendages	Skin appendage structures
Histiocytosis X	Langerhans cell
'Trabecular cell' carcinoma	Merkel cell
In situ local malignancies of the epidermis	
Bowen's disease	Keratinocytes
Actinic carcinoma *in situ* (actinic keratosis)	Keratinocytes—apparently sparing periappendageal keratinocytes

The epidermis has been used extensively in the past as an experimental model for a detailed study of chemical carcinogenesis, although currently more emphasis is being placed on the role of ultraviolet irradiation in the induction of cutaneous malignancies. Clinicians have identified known carcinogens in cutting oils used in industrial processes and in tars. The classic example of the action of a carcinogen on the skin is the report of Percival Potts who observed scrotal cancer in young chimney sweeps due to prolonged contact with soot.

Prolonged exposure to ultraviolet light in the UVB (280–320 nm) part of the spectrum is established as a carcinogenic factor in man, and a clear quantitative relationship exists between UVB exposure of Caucasian skin and the incidence of squamous carcinoma. The evidence for sunlight in general and UVB in particular influencing the incidence of cutaneous malignant melanoma is also strong, but the relationship here is not so clear-cut as with squamous carcinoma. Despite this, there is a clear increase in incidence of melanoma in the south of Norway by comparison with the north and the highest incidence of melanoma recorded in the world is among the white population of Queensland, Australia. Genetic factors may also be at work here, however, as many present-day inhabitants of Queensland are of Scottish or Irish descent and have a history of poor tanning, and a tendency to sunburn and develop cutaneous malignancies even in a temperate climate.

Incidence figures for both malignant melanoma and squamous carcinoma in black and white-skinned populations in the same geographic area show a very much lower figure for cutaneous malignancies for the black populations, suggesting that melanin pigment does play a significant role in protecting against ultraviolet-induced carcinogenesis.

Cumulative exposure to ultraviolet light over a life-time results in the easily recognized age changes in the skin. In Europeans who are not avid sun worshippers, these changes are not visible until the fifth to sixth decades, but in beach dwellers of Australia or the west coast of North America they may be observed much earlier, particularly in fair-skinned, blue-eyed individuals. The skin gradually becomes coarse and lined, and irregular macular hyperpigmentation is seen. These changes predominantly affect the face, neck, and hands, and are clearly demonstrated when the skin on these sites is compared with the normally covered skin of the buttocks. The current enthusiasm for sun-tanning and decrease in body sites regarded as 'normally covered' will almost certainly result in a higher incidence of ultraviolet-induced skin changes and their appearance at a younger age than formerly.

Other factors predisposing to the development of cutaneous malignancies may be either genetically determined or environmental. The autosomal dominant condition, *Gorlin's syndrome*, predisposes to multiple basal cell carcinoma (p. 300). A second rare, genetically determined condition, which predisposes to the development of several types of cutaneous malignancy, is *xeroderma pigmentosum*. This is transmitted by an autosomal recessive gene, and is of interest in that the majority of sufferers are unable to carry out unscheduled DNA repair in fibroblasts and lymphocytes after exposure to ultraviolet irradiation. Affected individuals show very early 'age changes' in the skin with freckling and atrophy before the age of 5 years. Thereafter, basal cell carcinoma, squamous carcinoma, or malignant melanoma may develop (Fig. 15.1).

Complete avoidance of sunlight and the use of chemical and physical sunscreens will delay the onset of these changes.

Exposure to ionizing radiation is an environmental factor which predisposes to cutaneous malignancy. After excessive X-irradiation,

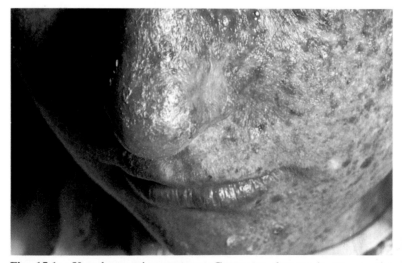

Fig. 15.1. Xeroderma pigmentosum. Gross sun damage is seen on the facial skin of this 12-year-old girl.

patients develop atrophy and telangiectasia. This stage is termed radiodermatitis. Subsequently, cutaneous malignancy may develop on these lesions.

Premalignant lesions

Ultraviolet light can induce premalignant changes in the epidermis which are recognizable both clinically and histologically and termed *actinic keratoses* or *senile keratoses*. Clinically, these are scaly, hyperpigmented lesions, sometimes ulcerated, which develop on exposed skin (Fig. 15.2). The striking histological changes in the epidermis are a loss of the normal keratinocyte maturation pattern, with some epidermal cells showing individual cell keratinization, and the appearance in the dermis of a dense area of 'elastic' tissue replacing the collagen of the papillary dermis—the so-called senile or actinic elastosis. This type of change was formerly called 'farmer's skin' or 'seaman's skin' as it was seen mainly on agricultural workers, fishermen, and others with outdoor occupations. Nowadays, however, recreational rather than occupational sun exposure is likely to be an important factor. Genetic factors are also important,

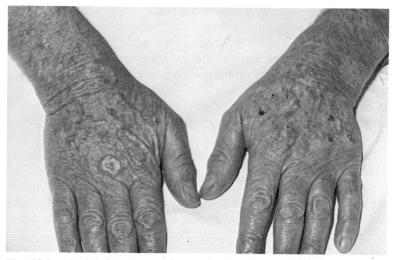

Fig. 15.2. Actinic keratoses. The hands of a 60-year-old farmer from the Scottish islands.

and the fair- or red-haired, blue-eyed, freckled individual who tans poorly and burns easily is particularly at risk.

A striking histological feature of these lesions will be seen if an area adjacent to a hair follicle is examined. It will be observed that while the keratinocytes of the epidermis show the loss of normal maturation pattern described above and demonstrate the formation of abnormal parakeratotic keratin, the more deeply situated keratinocytes within the hair follicle produce normal orthokeratin, resulting in alternating areas of normal and abnormal keratin in these lesions. In more advanced lesions the keratinocytes may lose their normal adhesive properties and round up, causing acantholysis.

Actinic keratoses have the potential for transformation into metastasizing squamous carcinoma, but in practice the time interval between development of an actinic keratosis and transformation to frank malignant change is relatively long, and as many patients have in the past been elderly there has been a tendency to be relatively unconcerned about these lesions as the patient is likely to die of other unrelated causes. This relaxed attitude may well have to change as younger people present with these lesions and patients should be cautioned about further excessive UV exposure. Appropriate sun-screening creams should be used. These should have a sun protective factor (SPF) of 10 or more. Preparations such as Spectraban 15, RoC 10 A & B and Coppertone Supershade 15 are all appropriate. Existing lesions can be treated with cryotherapy, or the topical application of the cytotoxic preparation 5-fluorouracil (Efudix). This preparation has the interesting property of 'seeking out' and stimulating an inflammatory response in 'preactinic' lesions which are not yet clinically visible. It is applied topically to the affected areas daily, carefully avoiding the eyes. After 2–3 weeks a brisk inflammatory reaction develops and the skin looks temporarily very much worse. After this, the lesions slowly clear and the end-result is cosmetically most acceptable. Careful dermatological supervision, occasionally as an in-patient, is necessary during this procedure. Histological monitoring of the changes induced by 5-fluorouracil show a remarkable return to normality of actinically damaged skin, although treatment of other deeper lesions (e.g. basal cell carcinoma) may result in residual nests of tumour cells in the dermis.

Local excision is also a useful method of dealing with large or disfiguring lesions, but as the problem tends to be a multifocal one, it is not always feasible.

Malignant lesions

BOWEN'S CARCINOMA *IN SITU* (Bowen's disease)

Definition. A form of intraepidermal carcinoma *in situ* which on rare occasions progresses to invasive squamous carcinoma.

In the past, a high proportion of patients with Bowen's disease have had a history of arsenic ingestion, formerly an ingredient of 'tonics' and 'appetite stimulants'. Such preparations are no longer generally available and it will be of interest to see whether or not the incidence of Bowen's disease falls over the next two decades. Some dermatologists have found that patients with Bowen's disease have a higher than expected incidence of unrelated internal malignancy, but others have not confirmed these findings. In the face of this controversy it is wise to take a careful general history in patients with Bowen's disease and order ancillary tests as indicated.

Clinically, Bowen's disease presents as an isolated, scaling, erythematous plaque, generally on the trunk (Fig. 15.3). It may be remarkably similar to an isolated patch of psoriasis and is frequently initially treated as such. If untreated, the lesions slowly expand laterally over a period of years and a very small proportion develop into metastasizing squamous carcinomas.

The histological features include thickening of the epidermis (acanthosis), and lack of normal organization and maturation within the epidermis. Individual cell keratinization is seen as isolated eosinophilic cells and the hallmark of the condition is the presence of huge Bowen's cells—very large keratinocytes with large nuclei, many of which contain aberrant mitotic figures. A few actinic keratoses show a histological picture similar to that seen in classic Bowen's disease but their very different clinical appearance and distribution on sun-exposed rather than covered skin will enable the two conditions to be differentiated. Surgical excision is recommended as this allows for the best possible specimen preservation for

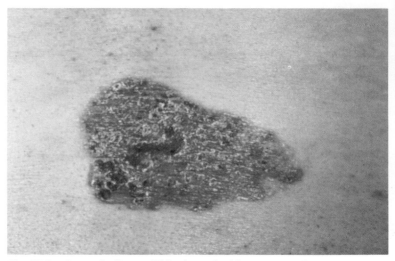

Fig. 15.3. Bowen's disease. This plaque had been present for 5 years on the sacral area.

histology. Cryotherapy or cautery are not as acceptable in this respect.

SQUAMOUS CELL CARCINOMA

Definition. A malignant tumour derived from keratinocytes.

A high proportion of squamous carcinomas arise on sun-damaged skin. Others may develop in scar tissue, such as the scars of previously treated lupus vulgaris. It is not clear in this situation whether the previous skin condition or the therapy with which it was treated is the important predisposing factor.

Clinically, the lesions present as hyperkeratotic, ulcerated, rapidly expanding nodules (Fig. 15.4). Metastatic spread to the local draining lymph nodes and beyond will occur in the lesion is not treated promptly.

The striking histological features are gross disorganization of the epidermis with invasion of tongues of epidermal tissue and isolated discrete foci of neoplastic keratinocytes within the dermis. Mitotic figures, both normal and abnormal, are frequent, and the loss of the

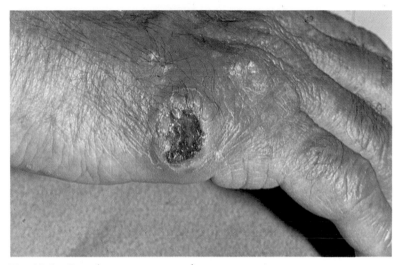

Fig. 15.4. Invasive squamous carcinoma.

normal keratinization pattern is reflected in hyperkeratosis and parakeratosis.

Once a histological diagnosis has been established by biopsy, the recommended method of treatment is surgical excision. Wide excision and grafting may be needed. An alternative surgical technique gaining widespread acceptance in North America is Mohs' chemosurgical technique. This method entails removal of the affected tissues in single cell layers by applying a zinc chloride paste. These layers are then examined microscopically and the procedure continued until no further malignant cells are seen. This method, although expensive in time and expertise, is economical in sparing normal tissue and therefore useful in areas such as the periorbital skin where wide excision may result in technical problems. Radiotherapy can also be used for squamous carcinoma.

CUTANEOUS MALIGNANT MELANOMA

Definition. A malignant tumour of epidermal melanocytes.

The incidence of malignant melanoma of the skin is rising rapidly in all parts of the world for which accurate records are available.

Norway shows a doubling in incidence over a 10-year-period. The reasons for this rapid rise are not yet fully understood, but appear to reflect a true increase in incidence rather than improved recognition or registration of the tumour. Increasing sun exposure, both in terms of body area exposed and numbers of hours spent in pursuit of a sun-tan, almost certainly play an important part in this increase, but there is not a straightforward linear relationship between the incidence of melanoma and cumulative life-time sun exposure except in the case of lentigo maligna melanoma. Current work suggests that short sharp episodes of sun exposure resulting in burning are more common in the melanoma population.

In the U.K., the female/male incidence of melanoma is two to one, but in other parts of the world it is equal. Over 50 per cent of female melanomas are on the lower leg, while in males the trunk is the commonest site.

There are four main clinicopathological varieties of malignant melanoma: lentigo maligna melanoma, superficial spreading melanoma, nodular melanoma and acral lentiginous melanoma. Further work is needed to determine if different aetiological factors are at work in these four varieties.

Superficial spreading melanoma is the commonest type in both sexes. It is an irregular brown, black, or bluish-black lesion with frequently some intermingled inflammation. The phenomenon of central tumour regression and concomitant peripheral extension is seen, and may result in bizarre horseshoe-shaped or crescentic lesions. The development of raised and ulcerated nodules within the lesion is a bad prognostic sign, suggesting active vertical invasion of tumour cells into the dermis. Figures 15.5 and 15.6 illustrate this type.

Lentigo maligna melanoma arises on the sun-exposed skin, usually the face, of the elderly. It is preceded by a lesion termed *lentigo maligna,* which is the lateral growth phase or *in situ* stage of tumour development (Fig. 15.7). This early lesion is a macular, dull brown or black lesion with a very irregular lateral margin. It may undergo partial central regression at the same time as lateral extension of the tumour is continuing. This *in situ* phase may continue for years or even decades, but the development of raised nodules within the lesion suggests that vertical invasion of the tumour cells into the dermis is now taking place and the term *lentigo maligna melanoma* is

✱ Hutchison's freckle

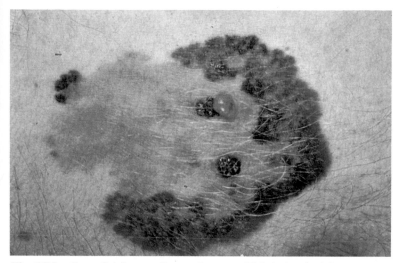

Fig. 15.5. Superficial spreading melanoma. This lesion had been present on the trunk for 9 months.

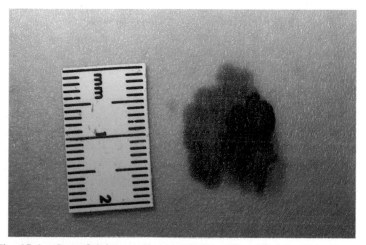

Fig. 15.6. Superficial spreading melanoma. Note that the lesion is larger than 1 cm in diameter, has a very irregular edge, and has irregular pigmentation in the centre.

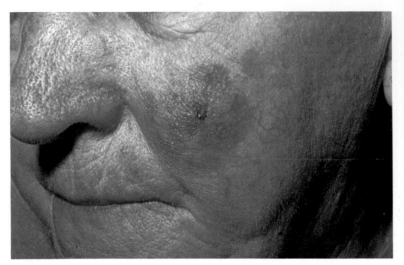

Fig. 15.7.   Lentigo maligna. A slowly expanding, flat, brown-black lesion is present on exposed skin, most commonly the cheek.

now justified (Fig. 15.8). Although metastasis to lymph nodes does occur, it is less common in this variety of melanoma than in the other two varieties.

Nodular melanoma is the most rapidly growing and aggressive clinicopathological variant. It arises on apparently normal skin and may contain relatively little melanin pigment (Fig. 15.9). It commonly has a rich blood supply and may therefore be mistaken for a vascular lesion. Ulceration of these lesions is frequent.

Acral lentiginous melanoma is seen mainly on the sole of the foot and occasionally on the palm of the hand. It is a raised dark area surrounded by a paler macular (lentiginous) area which may extend for several centimetres around the raised area (Fig. 15.10).

Periungual melanoma is commonly regarded as a variant of acral lentiginous melanoma. The importance of melanomas in the periungual area lies in the fact that they are frequently misdiagnosed and initially inappropriately treated as ingrowing toenails or as periungual warts. Always examine with care a pigmented lesion in the region of the nail bed and remember that periungual or plantar warts are rare in those over 40 years of age. The presence of brown pigmentation (Hutchinson's sign) on the nail fold is a very import-

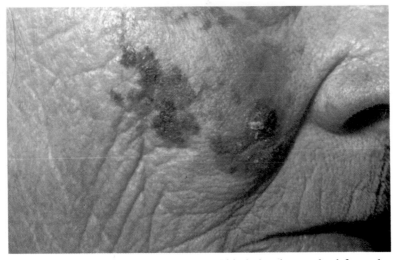

Fig. 15.8. Lentigo maligna melanoma. This lesion has evolved from the phase depicted in Fig. 15.7 to invasive melanocarcinoma. Note the raised dark nodule.

ant marker suggesting that the lesion is almost certainly malignant melanoma.

Prognostic features in malignant melanoma

In the past 10 years it has become very clear that the prognosis for patients with malignant melanoma varies very widely according to the thickness of the primary melanoma tissue measured in millimetres from the overlying granular layer of the epidermis to the deepest easily identifiable tumour cells (Fig. 15.11). This measurement of the primary malignant melanoma is known as the tumour thickness or Breslow thickness. The Breslow thickness in millimetres is inversely proportional to the 5-year survival rate. At the present time it is common practice to divide melanomas arbitrarily into good prognosis lesions with a Breslow thickness of 1 mm or less (5-year survival figure 90 per cent), intermediate prognosis lesions with a Breslow thickness of 1–3 mm (5-year survival around 70 per cent) and poor prognosis lesions with a Breslow thickness of 3–3.5 mm or greater (5-year survival figure around 40 per cent). It will be seen from these figures that the patient's prognosis varies very widely

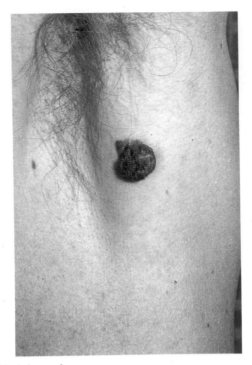

Fig. 15.9.   Nodular melanoma.

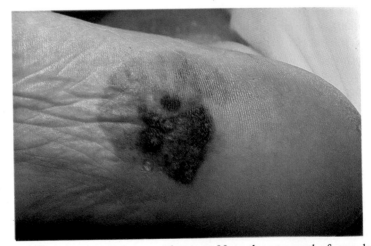

Fig. 15.10.   Acral lentiginous melanoma. Note the surround of macular brown pigmentation expanding beyond the densely pigmented area.

MALIGNANT MELANOMA THICKNESS MEASUREMENT (Breslow)

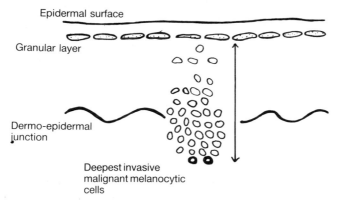

Fig. 15.11. Diagrammatic representation of tumour thickness measured by the Breslow method. The distance between the granular layer and the deepest tumour cell (arrowed) is the Breslow thickness in millimetres.

according to this Breslow thickness measurement. This is a figure which all dermatologists should request from the pathologist reporting a melanoma and is a figure which all family doctors should be aware of as it is of vital importance in determining the outlook for the individual patient.

Treatment of malignant melanoma

Treatment for all types of malignant melanoma is best performed by surgical excision. In the past, excision of very wide margins of apparently normal skin around the lesion has been advocated, but current practice is to encourage an *excision* biopsy and histological examination of a suspected malignant melanoma.

Once the tumour thickness is known, appropriate therapy can be planned. Thin melanomas—those under 1.0 mm thick—have a good prognosis, and local excision and direct closure may be adequate. Thick tumours—over 3.5 mm thick—are poor-risk tumours, and wide excision and grafting, followed by adjuvant chemotherapy, may be needed. Melanoma does not respond well in general to cytotoxic drugs, but imidazole carboxamide (DTIC) and vindesine are currently the most commonly used anti-tumour agents. Superficial spreading melanoma and nodular melanoma are not radiosensitive, but some workers report good results with radiotherapy for lentigo maligna melanoma.

There is controversy over the value of prophylactic lymph node dissection in thick malignant melanomas. It is common practice at the present time for prophylactic node dissection to be performed fairly routinely in the U.S., but only rarely in the U.K. An alternative approach to management of patient with either recurrent melanoma on a limb or with a poor prognosis primary tumour on a limb is the technique of limb perfusion in which arterial perfusion of the affected limb is carried out with a cytotoxic drug such as Melphalan. This technique is currently practised in a limited number of centres.

The relationship between benign pigmented melanocytic naevi (moles) and melanoma

Pigmented melanocytic naevi can be divided broadly into those present at birth, and those acquired during the second and third decade of life. Congenital naevi vary in size from the very small up to the giant garment or bathing trunk variety. It is established by careful long-term follow-up that the life-time risk of malignant melanoma developing in the giant congenital naevus is 3 per cent. There are no accurate data on the risk of melanoma developing in the smaller congenital naevi, but on the basis of the data for the larger lesions it has been assumed that such a risk may be present in the smaller lesions and that prophylactic local excision of small congenital naevi is recommended where this is feasible.

The commoner acquired melanocytic naevus has a very much lower risk of malignant change. Although histological evidence of a pre-existing acquired melanocytic naevus is found in association with around 30 per cent of all melanomas, it must be remembered that the average normal young adult has 20–30 benign acquired melanocytic naevi and that only six individuals in every 100 000 annually develop malignant melanoma in the U.K. There is thus no rationale for large scale prophylactic removal of all acquired melanocytic naevi.

The recently recognized dysplastic naevi are, however, an important marker of a population at increased risk of melanoma.

The dysplastic naevus syndrome (familial atypical multiple moles-malignant melanoma syndrome, BK mole syndrome)

This condition has only recently been recognized. The initial descriptions were of malignant melanoma occurring in multiple members of one family with in many cases more than one primary tumour in each affected patient. It was observed that in addition to multiple melanomas, members of these families had very large numbers of atypical melanocytic naevi. These naevi were described as large (over 7 mm in diameter), irregularly pigmented, and with an irregular lateral margin (Fig. 15.12). Affected family members frequently had 30 or more of such moles. Following the descriptions of these

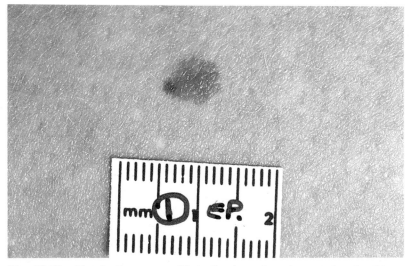

Fig. 15.12. Dysplastic naevus. Note the irregular pigmentation in this lesion. This patient has a positive family history of malignant melanoma.

affected families, it was recognized that a sporadic form of this condition also existed. At the present time work on the true frequency and significance of the dysplastic naevus syndrome is in progress. It would appear that patients with this abnormal mole pattern are at significantly increased risk of developing malignant melanoma. Any patient with malignant melanoma who also has this abnormal mole pattern should be persuaded to have his first degree relatives examined to determine whether or not there is a familial disorder so that appropriate advice about sun avoidance and excision of any growing or changing pigmented lesion can be given.

BASAL CELL CARCINOMA (rodent ulcer)

Definition. A common, slowly growing and locally destructive neoplasm.

This tumour is by far the commonest form of cutaneous malignancy, but attracts less attention than squamous carcinoma or malignant melanoma.

Despite the term 'basal cell carcinoma', the cell type from which this tumour is derived has yet to be established. A suggested site is from the hair follicle epithelium.

Basal cell carcinomas are seen predominantly on exposed sites, commonly around the nose and the inner canthus. Initially, the lesion is a reddish, dome-shaped nodule with a translucent surface and visible dilated surface capillaries. As it expands the central area may show necrosis and ulceration, leaving the characteristic rolled edge (Fig. 15.13). The lesion has frequently been growing for 1–2 years before the patient seeks advice and further slow growth will continue if the lesion is not treated. Although these lesions do not metastasize, they may cause extensive and distressing local destruction of soft tissue, cartilage, and even bone (Fig. 15.14).

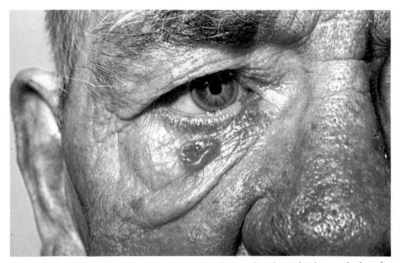

Fig. 15.13.   Early basal cell carcinoma. Note classic, raised, pearly border and central ulceration.

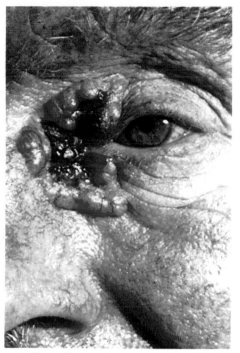

Fig. 15.14.   Basal cell carcinoma. Later stage than Fig. 15.13 to illustrate local destruction.

The classic histological picture is composed of well-demarcated islands of cells with a clear-cut lateral margin of basophilic cells arranged in palisade form around the tumour mass. Mitotic figures are plentiful but the turnover time is slow.

Basal cell carcinoma can be treated either by surgery or by radiotherapy. In frail and elderly patients, curettage or cryotherapy may be acceptable therapy but follow-up is essential. The prognosis is excellent and follow-up should be aimed at early detection of local recurrence, more common in certain sites, such as the naso-labial fold, and with certain morphoeic histological variants. In the very rare instances when a basal cell carcinoma is thought to metastasize the histology should be reviewed as the lesion may have been a tumour arising from one of the skin appendages.

A rare, genetically determined condition, *Gorlin's syndrome,* is characterized by the appearance of multiple basal cell carcinomas, jaw cysts, palmoplantar cutaneous pits, and skeletal abnormalities. Inheritance is by an autosomal dominant gene and lesions are first seen in childhood. The basal cell carcinomas in this condition should be treated by surgery and not by radiotherapy as further new tumours may develop in the irradiated field.

SKIN APPENDAGE TUMOURS

A wide range of tumours can arise from the cells which comprise the pilosebaceous follicle, the eccrine and the apocrine glands. Clinically these lesions present as isolated cutaneous nodules and accurate classification depends on specialized histological examination. In general, local recurrence is relatively common, but metastasis is rare. They are best treated by surgical excision.

Cutaneous lymphoma

A small number of lymphomas may actually arise in the skin or preferentially involve it. Most of these are demonstrated by membrane marker studies to originate from T lymphocytes.

MYCOSIS FUNGOIDES

Definition. A slowly evolving T cell lymphoma initially involving the skin.

Many workers consider mycosis fungoides to be a malignant lymphoma *ab initio*, but the natural history of the condition suggests that, at least in some cases, the condition is a reaction to chronic antigenic stimulation and that development of a true malignant lymphoma is a later event.

The condition is seen mainly in middle-aged or elderly individuals who present with pruritic cutaneous plaques (Fig. 15.15). They may involve spontaneously, remain relatively unchanged, or progress to frank nodules and ulceration (Fig. 15.16). A small number of patients present with nodular lesions from the start and others present with poikiloderma (dappled skin)—a macular pigmentary change with alternating increased and decreased pigmentation.

The lesions are usually associated with severe and persistent

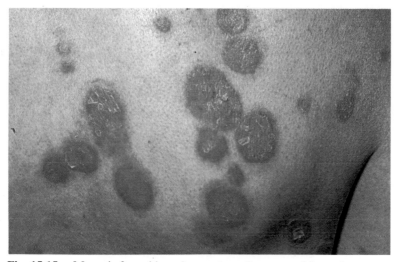

Fig. 15.15. Mycosis fungoides: plaque stage. Large pruritic erythematous plaques are seen mainly on the trunk.

pruritus, and the salient histological feature is the presence of a lymphoid infiltrate in the papillary dermis and epidermis which is shown to be composed predominantly of T lymphocytes. A small proportion of patients show progression of the disease to involvement of the lymph nodes and distant organs. This picture appears to be more common in patients with mycosis fungoides in North America than in Europe.

Treatment is generally aimed at control rather than cure of the disease. Topical steroids, conventional ultraviolet light (UVB), and photochemotherapy (PUVA) all improve symptoms; the latter may cause dramatic regression of lesions, but maintenance therapy is generally required. A course of electron beam therapy or low-penetration superficial X-rays may alleviate symptoms for long periods of time and are useful methods of therapy if the patient is unable to attend a centre for maintenance therapy. In general, mycosis fungoides responds poorly to systemic chemotherapy, but the regular use of topical nitrogen mustard is of value.

Selection of the appropriate therapy for the individual patient depends on availability of the various methods of treatment described and on local expertise. If available, PUVA is currently

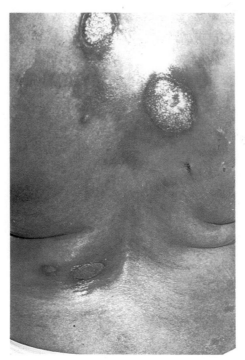

Fig. 15.16. Mycosis fungoides: tumour stage. Plaques such as those depicted in Fig. 15.15 have progressed to ulcerating nodular lesions.

popular, but the possibility of long-term side effects makes careful follow-up mandatory.

Benign cutaneous tumours

The differential diagnosis of a malignant cutaneous lesion will include a variety of benign skin tumours. In general, these are very much commoner than the malignant lesions and it is therefore important to be able to recognize these lesions.

BASAL CELL PAPILLOMA (seborrhoeic keratosis, seborrhoeic wart)

Definition. A benign proliferation of epidermal cells.

Basal cell papillomas become commoner with increasing age. Clinically, they present as raised, frequently multiple lesions, mainly on covered body sites. Many are brown due to benign and incidental melanocytic activity within the lesion, and may therefore be mistaken for malignant melanoma. The very superficial 'stuck on' appearance is a helpful differential point, but when doubt exists excision biopsy and histological examination must be carried out (Fig. 15.17).

In lesions in which the diagnosis of basal cell papilloma is clear cut and removal requested, curettage and diathermy is acceptable treatment.

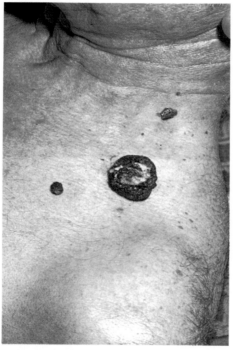

Fig. 15.17. Basal cell papilloma. Although deeply pigmented, these are entirely benign epidermal tumours.

PYOGENIC GRANULOMA

Definition. A rapidly growing, benign tumour arising from the cutaneous vasculature.

Classically, these lesions develop after trauma, commonly on the fingers of keen gardeners after pruning roses (Fig. 15.18). Over a period of 2–3 weeks a raised, wet, pedunculated lesion develops and frequently becomes secondarily infected. The rapidity of growth may give rise to concern about a malignant lesion, but the natural history is of spontaneous regression over a period of weeks or months. The histological appearance is of a network of capillaries embedded in an oedematous stroma.

Surgical excision or diathermy is recommended as the lesions can be painful and inconvenient.

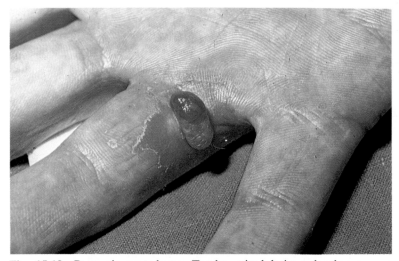

Fig. 15.18 Pyogenic granuloma. Tender raised lesions develop over a period of 1–2 weeks.

HISTIOCYTOMA (dermatofibroma, sclerosing angioma)

This lesion appears most commonly as a firm, elevated nodule on the leg (Fig. 15.19). In some cases there is a history of trauma such as an insect bite to the site. The nodule is often brown and this pigmentation together with a history of fairly rapid enlargement may suggest that the lesion is a malignant melanoma. In fact, however, the pigment is chiefly iron rather than melanin and the lesion is quite benign.

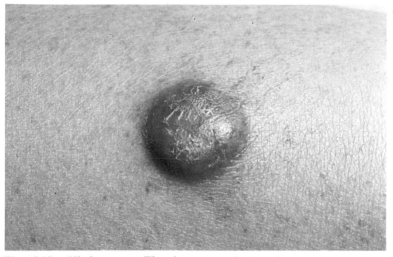

Fig. 15.19. Histiocytoma. The pigment seen in these benign lesions is both iron and melanin.

Surgical removal is generally performed to obtain histological confirmation of the diagnosis.

KERATOACANTHOMA

Definition. A rapidly growing and spontaneously resolving epidermal tumour.

The aetiology of this lesion has not yet been established.

This benign, self-limiting lesion commonly occurs on exposed skin, most often the face and hands. Initially, there is a small erythematous nodule which grows rapidly over 3–4 weeks to reach a final size of up to 2–3 cm in diameter. Central ulceration is common, the crater being encircled by a heaped-up shoulder (Fig. 15.20). Subsequently, this dramatic lesion involutes over 2–3 months if untreated and finally leaves an ugly, irregular, pitted scar.

The pathological features of this rapidly growing lesion are important as the clinician is frequently worried over the possibility of a developing malignancy. It is important that an adequately deep biopsy transects the lesion as the salient points in differentiating a keratoacanthoma from a squamous carcinoma are the raised, rolled

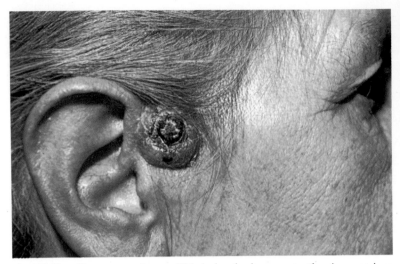

Fig. 15.20. Keratoacanthoma. This lesion had grown to the size seen in a period of 3–4 weeks.

shoulder around the lesion and the absence of any rapidly dividing neoplastic keratinocytes below the level of the deepest skin append-ages. No individual infiltrating cells are seen in the deeper parts of this lesion.

Treatment should be by excision biopsy to provide the entire lesion for histological study. This procedure will result in a cosmeti-cally more acceptable end result than that observed by allowing spontaneous regression.

Prevention of cutaneous malignancy

At the present time, cutaneous cancer is the commonest of all malignancies on a world scale. Moreover, it is likely that the numbers of affected patients will increase with an ageing population and even greater sun exposure. This trend should be able to be partially prevented or reversed by education of the paler skinned races of the world concerning the undesirable effects of excessive sun exposure leading initially to premature aging and then to premalig-nant and malignant skin lesions. Commonsense about sun exposure, avoiding strong tropical mid-day sun and use of the newer and extremely effective topical sun-screening creams will all be of value. These new sun-screens all have a number known as a sun protective factor (SPF) as a measure of efficacy. Preparations with an SPF of 10 or greater are to be recommended as they will prevent burning of the skin in a significant proportion of patients.

GROWTH POINTS

1 *Oncogenes and skin cancer.* In the past 3 years there has been a great deal of interest in the role of fragments of genetic material known as oncogenes in the development of various types of malignancy. Activated oncogenes are found in unusual amounts or in unusual situations in individual chromosomes in a number of human malignancies. To date about 20 of these oncogenes have been identified and many are similar to growth factors which control growth in normal cells. So far the only skin cancer which has been studied is malignant melanoma, and in samples of this tumour the 'ras' oncogene has been identified. In the next 5 years the true significance of oncogene detection in malignancies should be established, and the presence or absence of similar fragments in malignant and, more importantly, premalignant skin tumours will be known.

2 *Viruses and cutaneous lymphoma.* The human T cell leukaemia lymphoma virus 1 (HTLV 1) has been identified in a small percentage of patients with cutaneous lymphoma. These are mainly patients with a particularly aggressive form of cutaneous lymphoma. The patients affected have, to date, been mainly negroes from the Caribbean area and also a small number of patients with an aggressive T cell lymphoma found in an isolated geographic region of Japan. Careful studies have not yet identified the presence of this virus in the majority of patients with the commoner T cell lymphoma of the mycosis fungoides type. Work is in progress, however, to determine whether or not a new and as yet unnamed member of the retrovirus family of viruses may be involved in the development of mycosis fungoides.

FURTHER READING

Burg, G. and Braun-Falco, O.: *Cutaneous Lymphomas.* Springer-Verlag, Berlin (1983).

A beautifully illustrated textbook covering clinical and pathological aspects of rare skin lymphomas.

Epstein, J. H.: Photocarcinogenesis, skin cancer and ageing. *Journal of the American Academy of Dermatology* **9**, 487–502 (1983).

An excellent background review to the problems of skin cancer prevention.

MacKie, R. M. (ed.) *Malignant Melanoma*, Pigment Cell Series, Vol. 6. S. Karger, Basel (1983).

A monograph gathering together advances in the past decade.

NOTES

Appendix 1

Brief notes on topical therapy

When prescribing topical therapy several points must be borne in mind.

1 The active ingredient must be prescribed in the appropriate vehicle or base.

2 Adequate, but not excessive quantities must be applied. Once application of cream or ointment for an adult to cover the whole body requires 20 g, one application to hands or face 2–4 g.

3 Instructions must be given to the patient concerning frequency and quantity of application. For some conditions, e.g. scabies in a large family, written instruction sheets will increase the likelihood of successful therapy.

VEHICLES (bases)

A vehicle is defined as the (usually) inert carrier of the active ingredient. Vehicles are made up of liquids, greases, and powders in varying proportions according to the final consistency required. Thus, liquids alone may be used as wet dressings or tinctures, liquids and powders result in a shake *lotion* which is cooling and drying due to evaporation, grease alone is an *ointment*, and a grease and powder mixture results in a *paste*.

Lotions are used in acutely inflamed and moist exudative conditions. A useful preparations is ichthyol 1 per cent in calamine lotion BP. Lotions may be applied directly to the skin or on swabs or dressings which have been soaked in the lotion. In either case, frequent changing of dressings (e.g. every 4 hours) is necessary as otherwise the lotion will crust and cake.

Liniments are lotions with some additional oil which tends to prevent this crusting and it is therefore possible to change dressings less frequently. The advantage of rapid evaporation and cooling is, however, lost.

CREAMS

These are either oil-in-water or water-in-oil emulsions and contain preservatives to prevent bacterial and fungal growth. The commonest preservatives are chlorocresol and parabens. Either may cause sensitization and subsequent allergic contact dermatitis. Oil-in-water emulsions rub into the skin and are easily washed off. They are therefore very suitable for use on the face, but may have a drying effect on the skin. Water-in-oil emulsions are greasier. Less evaporation of water from the skin surface is possible through these preparations and they are therefore useful in conditions characterized by dryness and flaking. Water-in-oil emulsions are based either on petrolatum or on lanolin, which is a potential sensitizing agent.

OINTMENTS

Ointments contain no water but are greases with the permissible addition of up to 40 per cent of powder by weight. A higher concentration of powder would change the consistency of the preparation to such an extent that it would be a paste. The lack of water in ointments renders the use of preservatives unnecessary, but emulsifying agents are frequently added to facilitate spreading. Ointments are useful in any condition characterized by dry skin (e.g. atopic dermatitis, chronic hand dermatitis). They are less easily washed off than creams.

PASTES

These are greases containing more than 40 per cent powder by weight. They are useful for dry surfaces but are very difficult to remove.

Modern dermatopharmacology is a large and important section of the pharmaceutical industry. The current trend is to devise totally synthetic vehicles with a high degree of cosmetic acceptability and many preparations are now available which are neither ointments nor creams, but have some of the advantages (and possibly disadvantages) of both. The tendency to use lanolin less and to avoid preservatives where possible should, in time, lead to a decrease in the incidence of medicament-induced allergic contact dermatitis.

Fatty acid-propylene glycol bases (FAPG) are a newer and generally well-accepted type of vehicle.

For use on the scalp lotions or *gels* are acceptable. Creams, ointments, and pastes all lead to problems with removal. Gels are semi-colloids which liquefy on contact with the skin and are a common base for acne preparations.

Some dermatologists adopt the practice of diluting a commercially available steroid preparation to minimize side effects rather than prescribing an alternative weaker preparation. While this practice is economically sound, the two hazards of dilution are, firstly, inactivation of the active ingredients by use of an inappropriate and incompatible diluent, and, secondly, the risk of bacterial contamination during dilution. For these reasons, the widespread use of diluted steroids is not recommended without a pharmacy that has experience and understanding of this practice.

EMOLLIENTS

Emollients are now available in many different forms, as bath additives, as soap substitutes, and as creams and ointments. They are of great value in the regular care of ageing skin, and of all the dry skin conditions, particularly the ichthyoses and atopic dermatitis. The pruritus which frequently accompanies dry skin conditions can be significantly relieved by emollients and the need for topical steroids can be greatly reduced. This is of particular value in the management of paediatric problems.

Patients differ in their response to emollient preparations and, for this reason, it is good practice to initially offer a range of five or six preparations, so that the patient can select those most effective and acceptable. It is common to find that one preparation is preferred for the body and another for the face.

Useful emollients include:

Soap substitutes: emulsifying ointment B.P., unguentum Merck.

Bath additives: Alpha-keri, Oilatum emollient, Balneum, Emulsiderm.

General purpose preparations: aqueous cream B.P., Oilatum cream, Diprobase.

SUNSCREENS

It is slowly becoming more widely accepted that excessive sun exposure of white skin is the prime cause of cutaneous ageing and also an important factor in skin malignancy. Topical sunscreens are now very effective in preventing immediate sun burning, and have been shown in animal models to reduce the changes associated in man with ageing and carcinogenesis. For dermatological use, a sunscreen with a sun protective factor of 10 or more is required. This S.P.F. measures the factor by which sun exposure can be increased before any reddening of the skin occurs by comparison with non-protected skin. Effective preparations include Spectraban 15 lotion, Roc 10 A + B cream, and Coppertone Supershade 15.

TOPICAL STEROID PREPARATIONS

Topical steroid have already been discussed in the relevant treatment sections, and their undesirable side effects in Chapter 12. At the time of writing, public awareness of possible adverse effects has led to some patients being reluctant to use any steroid preparation. This is a striking contrast to the situation 10 years ago when the more common problem was prolonged and inappropriate overuse of the stronger preparations.

It is likely that 1 per cent hydrocortisone will become available in the U.K. in the near future as an over the counter preparation. Although suitable package inserts have been designed to minimize inappropriate use, it is likely that in the future family doctors will see very few skin diseases unmodified by a trial of topical hydrocortisone. It is worth remembering in this situation that both fungal infections and scabies can be partially masked by topical steroids, but that the underlying aetiological agent is still present.

THE CHOICE OF DRESSING

The need for frequent renewal of topical preparations is reduced by the use of appropriate dressings. For trunk and limbs and expandable stockinette dressings can be made into neatly fitting 'body suits' and worn under normal clothing. Smaller areas can be covered with narrower dressings of similar material. When pastes are used it is often of value to spread the paste on to a dressing with a spatula and then apply the dressing to the area and bandage it in position. Large raw areas should be covered with a dressing such as sterile paraffin gauze which does not stick to the granulating surface.

In chronic dermatitis the use of occlusive tar or ichthyol impregnated bandages may help to break the itch-scratch-itch cycle and allow the skin to heal. These bandages (e.g. Coltapaste, Tarband, Ichthopaste) can be covered with a stockinette dressing and left in position for up to a week.

Occlusive dressings of this type are also extremely useful in the out-patient management of stasis ulcers. A dry gause swab can be used to cover the ulcerated area and an ichthopaste or viscopaste bandage applied from the ankle to below the knee and covered with an elastocrepe bandage. This can be changed by the district nurse at weekly intervals or even less frequently. The Viscopaste bandages have the advantage of being easily unwound from the leg, even after 2–3 weeks in position.

FURTHER READING

Bickers, D. R., Hazen, P. G. and Lynch, W. S.: *Clinical Pharmacology of Skin Disease* Monographs in Clinical Pharmacology, Vol. 7). Churchill Livingstone, New York & Edinburgh (1984).
Seville, R. and Martin, E.: *Dermatological Nursing and Therapy.* Blackwell Scientific Publications, Oxford (1981).
    A useful inexpensive paperback.

Appendix 2

A brief glossary of useful clinical and histological terms

Acantholysis: a rounding up of epidermal cells resulting from a loss of adhesion between these cells. Seen in association with benign blistering disease (pemphigus) and in epidermal malignancy.

Acanthosis: histological term used to describe epidermal thickening due to to an increase in the number of cells in the prickle cell layer.

Atopy: 'strange disease'. The triad of atopic dermatitis, asthma, and allergic rhinitis (hay fever).

Balloon degeneration: gross swelling of keratinocytes in epidermal viral infection. Both the nucleus and cytoplasm are affected.

Basement membrane: a multi-layered structure between epidermis and dermis.

Bowen's carcinoma *in situ* **(Bowen's disease):** a form of intraepidermal carcinoma *in situ* characterized by the presence of atypical giant cells with aberrant mitotic figures.

Cheiropompholyx: an eruption on the sides of the fingers and palms of the hands composed of multiple small blisters.

Civatte bodies (colloid bodies): amorphous pink globules seen at the dermo-epidermal junction in certain diseases characterized by damage to and death of basal cells (e.g. lichen planus).

Comedo (blackhead): a plug of oxidized sebaceous material obstructing the surface opening of a pilosebaceous follicle.

Desmosomes: specialized areas of intraepidermal adhesion between keratinocytes.

Dyskeratosis: premature and atypical keratinization of epidermal cells.

Ecthyma: a pyogenic skin infection characterized by superficial crusting and underlying ulceration.

Ephelis (freckle): a localized area of increased pigment synthesis by melanocytes.

Hirsuties: excessive growth of male-pattern terminal hair.

Hyperkeratosis: excessive formation of normal keratin for the body site in question.

Hypertrichosis: excessive growth of non-androgen dependent hair.

Ichthyosis ('fish skin'): excessively dry and scaly skin.

Inclusion bodies: eosinophilic bodies with a clear surrounding halo. Seen in cutaneous viral infections.

Intertrigo: dermatitis on apposing areas of skin in flexural body sites (groins, axillae).

Kerion: a severe pustular reaction on the scalp in children. Caused by animal ringworm.

Lichenification: thickening (acanthosis) of the epidermis resulting in accentuation of normal skin markings.

Liquefaction degeneration: damage to the epidermal basal layer, seen principally in lichen planus and lupus erythematosus.

Miliaria: vesicular lesions resulting from occlusion of eccrine sweat ducts. Common in hot, humid environments.

Nikolsky's sign: the shearing of epidermis from dermis produced by lateral pressure on the epidermal surface. Positive in pemphigus vulgaris.

Parakeratosis: abnormal or incomplete keratinization resulting in the presenceof *nucleated*, flattened squamous cells in the stratum corneum.

Reticular degeneration (*see also* balloon degeneration): an intraepidermal blister resulting from balloon degeneration of virally infected epidermal cells. Some cell walls are retained and the blister thus has a multiloculated reticular framework.

Rhinophyma: gross hypertrophy of sebaceous gland tissue resulting in increase in volume of nasal soft tissue. A complication of rosacea.

Spongiosis: oedema of the epidermis, mainly intercellular.

Wickham's striae: white linear markings on the surface of the violaceous papules of lichen planus.

Further reading

The two major English-language textbooks currently available are:

Rook, A., Wilkinson, D. S., and Ebling, F. J. G. (eds): *Textbook of dermatology*, 3rd edn (2 vols). Blackwell Scientific Publications, Oxford (1979).

Fitzpatrick, T. B., Eisen, A. Z., Wolff, K., Freedberg, I. M., and Austen, K. F. (eds): *Dermatology in general medicine*, 2nd edn. MacGraw-Hill, New York (1979).

The first of these is a multi-author, mainly British production and the second is a similar style of book from North America. Both will be found to be a valuable source of further information on all the subjects covered in this book and on many rarer skin diseases not covered here. References in these textbooks are reasonably up to date and should be consulted for further reading, as a background to essay writing, etc.

Index

Note: Figures in **bold** refer to main entries.

corns *

* apply Duofilm to corn q d + scrub c̄ pumice stone
q week p̄ soaking or salicylic acid plaster
10% to 40% apply q day

lentigo maligna or Hutchinson's freckle-
(pre)malignant melanoma in situ
Common in older people - may progress
to malignant melanoma